YOSEMITE TRAILS
Camp and pack-train in the Sierra Nevada

BY
J. SMEATON CHASE

Introduction to this edition
and
Updated Plant List by Carl Sharsmith

TIOGA PUBLISHING COMPANY
PALO ALTO, CALIFORNIA

Library of Congress Cataloging-in-Publication Data

Chase, J. Smeaton (Joseph Smeaton), b. 1864.
  Yosemite trails.

  Reprint. Originally published: Boston : Houghton
Mifflin, 1911.
    1. Yosemite Valley (Calif.)—Description and travel.
2. Trails—California—Yosemite Valley. 3. Sierra Nevada
Mountains (Calif. and Nev.)—Description and travel.
4. Chase, J. Smeaton (Joseph Smeaton), b. 1864—
Journeys—California—Yosemite Valley.   I. Title.
F868.Y6C4   1987   917.94'4045   87-40052
ISBN 0-935382-58-5

© 1987 Tioga Publishing Company
  P.O. Box 98
  Palo Alto, California 94302

Distributed by William Kaufmann, Inc.
  Box 50490
  Palo Alto, California 94303-9953

TO

FREDERICK OLIVER POPENOE
OF ALTADENA, CALIFORNIA
AT WHOSE SUGGESTION THE EXPEDITIONS OF WHICH
THIS VOLUME IS THE RESULT WERE UNDER-
TAKEN, THIS ADVENTURE OF A FIRST
BOOK IS BY THE AUTHOR COR-
DIALLY INSCRIBED

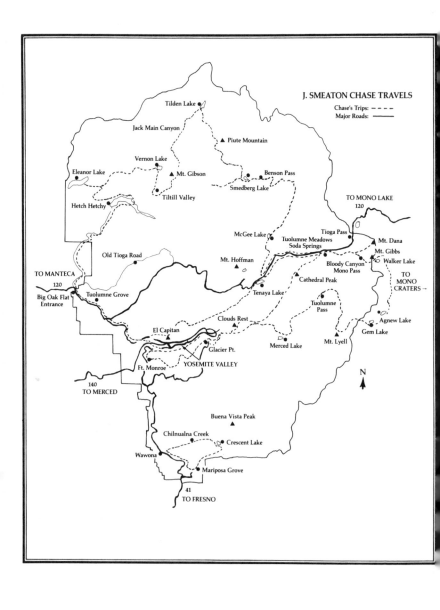

J. SMEATON CHASE TRAVELS

Chase's Trips: - - - - -
Major Roads: ————

Tilden Lake

Jack Main Canyon

▲ Piute Mountain

Vernon Lake

Eleanor Lake

▲ Mt. Gibson

Benson Pass

Smedberg Lake

Tiltill Valley

Hetch Hetchy

TO MONO LAKE
120

McGee Lake

Tioga Pass

Tuolumne Meadows
Soda Springs

Mt. Dana ▲

Mt. Gibbs

Walker Lake

Old Tioga Road

Mt. Hoffman ▲

Bloody Canyon
Mono Pass

TO MANTECA
120

Cathedral Peak

Big Oak Flat
Entrance

Tuolumne Grove

Tenaya Lake

TO
MONO
CRATERS →

Tuolumne
Pass

Clouds Rest ▲

Agnew Lake

El Capitan
▲

Gem Lake

Glacier Pt.

Merced Lake

Mt. Lyell ▲

Ft. Monroe

YOSEMITE VALLEY

N
↑

140
TO MERCED

Buena Vista Peak
▲

Chilnualna Creek

Crescent Lake

Wawona

Mariposa Grove

41
TO FRESNO

PREFACE

THE following pages are the outcome of three journeys, two of them of considerable length, through the Yosemite region of the Sierra Nevada, and of a resulting desire to acquaint the nature-loving public with the attractions more particularly of the less known areas of the locality. The writer has preferred not to limit his work to the specific uses of a guide-book, but has allowed a natural propensity for a loose rein and discursive observation to dictate its range; with the result, he hopes, of a gain in variety and interest both to the general reader and to the prospective and retrospective wayfarer in the region. The volume will be found, however, to have also much of the value of a guide-book for the traveller on the ground, and with this point in view it is furnished with a map.

Especially it has been the design of the writer to direct the attention of mountaineers and lake-lovers to the fact, almost unknown even among devotees of the out-of-doors, that there exists in the Sierra Nevada a lake-land of incomparable richness and peculiar diversity of charm: where lakes are sprinkled like stars, exceeding the possibility of distinguishing them by name. The time is coming when the highlands of this

PREFACE

great Californian range, which it is not too grandiose to call the Alps of our country, with its superb features of mountain, forest, river, glacier, lake, and meadow, and lying under a climate of unequalled regularity and perfection, will be the playground of America. It is largely the purpose of this volume to expedite the day.

Los Angeles, California.

NEW 1987 INTRODUCTION
by
CARL SHARSMITH

I made the acquaintance of this book filled with lovely descriptions of mountain travel and botanical beauty long ago upon the recommendation of Old Jim (my well-read roustabout friend from the lumber camps). Jim, a large man with gnarled hands, had helped rebuild the Old Tioga Road in 1915. These were the days soon after Chase's adventuring trips, and Jim had come to appreciate the mountain perceptions of his contemporary. Back then, I couldn't afford to buy books, so I borrowed Jim's copy and wrote down special passages from Chase's accounts in the high country and committed them to memory. I have recited these words and stories to my students ever since.

YOSEMITE TRAILS is one of those fine old things that certainly should be available today. Chase captured the spirit of a trip to the Sierra Nevada, both in his time and for us today. He had an unusual sensitivity for plants, believing that the virgin forest should be cared for "much as one loves (or should love) one's fellow men, that is to say, both in the aggregate and in the particular." His artistic nature allowed him to see nature as a palette. To his keen eye, granite ledges "gave back quick lights like an opal," and water took on a new dimension "all but intangible."

One of my favorite tales, so different from the rest of the book, is Chase's touching reminiscence of meeting in the hot foothills a Mexican miner who lived with his crippled son, Rafaelito. The canyon's echoing with heavenly strains from the boy's harmonica affected Chase deeply. Perhaps he was so moved by this unusual family because of his previous employment as a social worker for a Los Angeles church. Chase was born in England and came to the United States toward the end of the nineteenth century. His three travel books, which include his long horseback explorations of the California coast and desert, were based on adventures he took in his late forties.

The pages that follow return us to the time when the trails in Yosemite were new, having been built, albeit sketchily in some places, by the U. S. Cavalry. Chase recounts three summer journeys: a circuit of the Yosemite Rim from Fort Monroe (located near Inspiration Point on the Old Wawona Road) to the Big Oak Flat Road; a one-day, 25-mile fishing jaunt around the Wawona backcountry; and a one-month adventure on difficult-to-follow trails from Yosemite to Hetch Hetchy and around to Lake Tenaya and Mono Lake before crossing near Mount Lyell on his way back to the Valley.

One of the things that continues to attract us today is the sense of continuity we gain by realizing that we can retrace these very routes ourselves. On trails used for nearly 100 years, we might glance at the same Noble Firs seen by John Muir and Smeaton Chase. From our armchairs, our minds can flee to the mountains. "The whole prospect was a sea of peaks and ridges, whitened with snow, gloomy with precipices, and sprinkled with lakes of every size and shape. One long trough-like valley led away westward toward the peaks and domes of Yosemite. Over all, the sun shining in a sky of broken clouds sent a thousand shadows flying like flocks of swallows."

I have prepared a brief list of the plants mentioned by Chase with their current names. This information appears on page 347 after the last page of the book.

Dr. Sharsmith is Emeritus Professor of Botany at San Jose State University and has been a legendary ranger at Yosemite National Park since 1931.

CONTENTS

CONTENTS

PART II: THE HIGH SIERRA

New Introduction follows Preface
Updated Plant List precedes Index

PART I

YOSEMITE AND THE SEQUOIAS

" Mother of marvels, mysterious and tender Nature,
why do we not live more in thee? "

YOSEMITE TRAILS

CHAPTER I

A GENERAL SURVEY OF THE YOSEMITE VALLEY

THE YOSEMITE VALLEY is not, properly speaking, a valley. That word conveys the image of a gentle depression with sloping sides, which the patient fingers of Time have smoothed and rounded into quiet, compliant lines. The Yosemite is not in the least of that character. It is a great cleft, or chasm, which one might imagine to have been the work of some exasperated Titan who, standing with feet planted fifty miles apart lengthwise of the Sierra Nevada summit and facing westward, raised his hands palm to palm over his head, and struck upon the earth with such fury as to cleave a gap nearly a mile in depth; then separating his hands he thrust back the sides of the fracture, leaving between them a narrow, precipice-walled plain.

The Act of Congress of 1864 by which the tract was granted to the State of California defined it as "the 'cleft' or 'gorge' in the granite peak of the Sierra Nevada mountain"; and it would have been better if in the early descriptions of the spot it had been referred to as the Yosemite Gorge, which would have more properly described it and also would have been more stimulating to the imagination than the tamer designation which is now, no doubt, securely fixed upon it.

In what may be called its æsthetic sense, however, the word "valley" answers well enough ; for the level enclosed between the walls is a sheltered tract of the richest verdure, mixed of forest and meadow, watered by a wandering and placid river, starred with flowers, and the paradise of birds and friendly, harmless creatures.

It is greatly in this contrast between the grandeur and severity of the encircling walls and the sylvan charm of the protected enclosure that the unique character of Yosemite consists. It is as if Nature had here put herself to show a parable of contrasted excellences, setting the stern heights and solemn silences of the cliffs against the soft demeanor and gentle voices of trees and flowers, streams and heavenly meadows ; and to marry them together she pours the great waterfalls, in whose cloudy graces majesty and loveliness are so mingled that one cannot tell which of the two delights him the more.

The valley — I shall use the term which custom has fixed — may be said to begin, on the west, where the Bridal Veil Fall pours down over the southern cliff, and to end at the conspicuous pillar or buttress of the northern wall that is called the Washington Column ; at which point the cañons of the main Merced River and the Tenaya Creek converge. Within these limits the valley is about six miles long and has an average width of about half a mile. Its general direction is east and west, crosswise to the axis of the mountain chain which it cleaves. The "floor" is remarkably level, and lies at an elevation of almost exactly four thousand feet.

At the point where, in following upwards the course of the Merced River, this altitude is reached, the cañon opens, while at the same time the walls, which along the whole course of the river since leaving the plain of the San Joaquin have been first hilly and then mountainous, become high and precipitous cliffs, destitute of trees or brush except as regards the talus at their feet, the huge blocks and cubes of which give footing to a chaparral of flowering brush interspersed with oaks, maples, and platoons of indomitable pines. The level plain lies between, a long glade through which the quiet river makes its way, winding leisurely from side to side, more like some thoughtful lowland stream than what it is, — the nervous, quick-breathing child of glacier and mountain-chasm. A growth of willows and poplars marks its course, contrasting their summer green or winter lavender against the sombre richness of the evergreens.

Every observant person will be struck at first sight by what he will later find to be the salient geological feature of the whole Yosemite region, — the curved, rind-like forms of the layers of rock of which these mountains are built. A rough image of this can be made by placing the open hands one upon the other, the palms downward and considerably concaved ; or, if the reader will excuse the violence of the illustration, a granite onion of mountain size would well represent the formation. This peculiar structure is clearly seen in the domes of the upper plateau, while on the faces of the cliffs it is exhibited in arch-shaped recesses where masses of the lower strata have become detached and fallen away.

The most noticeable instance of this occurs on the northern face of the wall at a point just to the west of the Washington Column. Immense fractures and displacements of rock have there produced natural arches that are very remarkable in their vast span and deep recession. Another example, and one which I always found very impressive to the imagination, occurs in the southward-facing shoulder of the great rock that commands the entrance to the valley and is called El Capitan. When the afternoon light is reflected from that enormous polished curve, it is easy to imagine it to be the domed roof of some stupendous hall, whose door, like that of another Hall of Eblis, is that terrible half-mile cliff that faces the west.

When the fracture and subsidence which formed the valley took place, the two principal streams that flow into the Merced River at this point, Yosemite Creek from the north and Bridal Veil Creek from the south, became at a stroke the waterfalls which are known by those names. The Yosemite Creek, originating on Mount Hoffman and flowing southwesterly over a high granite plateau, makes in three steps a fall of twenty-five hundred feet, which places it, on the score of height, at the head of the considerable waterfalls of the world. The Bridal Veil Creek runs northwesterly and leaps over a sheer cliff of six hundred and twenty feet at the lowest point of the valley wall, where the upper course of the stream has followed a deep trough which may have been formed when the general subsidence took place. The other two great waterfalls, Vernal, of three hundred and twenty feet, and Nevada, of six hundred feet, occur near together on the course of the Merced River itself, in the narrow cañon which leads up to another and smaller valley known as the Little Yosemite.

These four waterfalls, with their various actions and charms of manner, appear to form the preëminent attraction of the valley to the great majority of people who come to view its scenery. That this should be so is not surprising, for a waterfall is like a hot-house flower of Nature, a kind of rarity for exhibition ; and there is good reason for enthusiasm in the wonderful and changing beauty of the falls. But a great many people are captured by mere novelty, and I venture to think that this trifling feature is a main factor in the judgment which places second, or disregards altogether, the unequalled majesty of the cliffs.

The human palate is, in fact, strangely dead to the majestic ingredient. How often, when I have been passing along a city street while some gorgeous solemnity of cloud-scenery has been offered to the gaze, have I marvelled to see that hardly one out of hun-

dreds or thousands of passers-by has bestowed even
a casual glance upon it, but that their attention has
been given entirely to the store-windows, the pavement, or the hats. There is something rather awful
about this insensibility : what can it mean? No doubt
in the case of many of these oblivious ones it means
that they are engrossed with an invisible companion,
him whom the ceremonious Spaniards name Don Di-
nero. But I am afraid it means also that most people
are bored by anything great, unless it is also novel.
As for the sky, that is an every-day affair, and they
do not account anything that is to be seen there to
be worth attention. These are the people who are
given to stage-drivers for a prey, and who find hap-
piness in tracing those zoölogical resemblances which
that valuable body of men, whose fertility of fancy
would scarcely be inferred from a demeanor often of
singular stolidity, have discovered to exist in the cliff-
scenery of the great valley.

The luxuriant forest that occupies the greater part
of the valley floor, broken here and there by meadows,
also is worth some share of the admiration which
too many people reserve exclusively for the waterfalls. Companies of pines from one hundred to two
hundred feet high, straight, smooth, and taper as ever
tree grew, ought not to be commonplace to most of
us. (Certainly the birds and squirrels do not find them
so, or they themselves could not remain so interesting
and individual, but would tend, like us, to become
dull and uniform. I have known a parrot who has

lived with people, and been "taught," to be dull, even dreadfully dull; but I do not suppose you find them so on the Orinoco.)

If it were only for the perfection of their types, these valley-sheltered trees, which have grown to the completest stature of their kind in this sunny nursery, are full of value and interest. The yellow pine (*Pinus ponderosa*) especially shows here its finest traits, spiring up for the skies with a fervor of tree-desire that is indescribably stimulating, and dressed complete with branches that sweep in loveliness to the very ground. In the shadow of the south wall grows the Douglas spruce (*Pseudotsuga taxifolia*), a Nestor among trees, great, strong, and wise in counsel, plated with dark and rugged bark, and waving plumes of sombre splendor in the cool wind that draws along the face of the cliffs. With him stands here and there the white silver fir (*Abies concolor*), tall, straight, and of admirable symmetry. If the Douglas is Nestor the white fir is Paris.

The cedar (*Libocedrus decurrens*) also reaches here the perfect dignity of its race, and mixing everywhere freely among the pines brightens their dark richness with pyramids of ferny olive. The old trees of this species, fulfilling the characteristics of their type, are nearly always dead in their tops though in full career of life. They rise solemnly amid the forest like many-branched candlesticks, and enforce by their shape the vague idea of a religious association which is suggested by their common name

of "incense cedar," and by the many allusions in the
Book of Psalms to their brethren of the Lebanon forests. It is pleasant to know that the great Israelitish
king was a man of trees as well as of war, and loved
the merry greenwood heartily.

Though the special glory of this forest belt lies in the
conifers, the Yosemite is splendid in oaks also. There
are many magnificent specimens of both evergreen
and deciduous oak in the valley, where the balanced
beauty of their shapes is heightened by contrast with
the straight-pillared pines and cedars. Far up Indian
Cañon, on the north side of the valley, there is growing an oak that I believe would out-oak every oak
that grows on California mountain, foothill, or plain,
if it could be brought to the proof. Very few people
see it, for the cañon is narrow, gloomy, and difficult
to climb. I viewed with amazement the great wall-
like trunk of this solitary monster. A kind of octopus
in shape, his long grey arms go searching up and
down the cañon as though he were feeling for a
way out, and might presently lift his splayed foot
and drag his Cyclopean deformity down to the
plain, to affright the puny sons of men.

In luxuriance of flowers the valley in spring and
summer is notable even beyond the measure of the
plain and foothill regions of the state. Chief in brilliance, and in novelty as regards most people, of the
spring flowers is the snow-plant (*Sarcodes sanguinea*),
which begins to appear on the floor of the valley soon
after the snow has melted, and astonishes the early

visitor with its unexpected blood-red apparition. An unflower-like flower, it is attractive only for its glaring violence of color. Every fibre is red, the red of Burgundy wine. It is a Mephistopheles among plants, a kind of diabolical asparagus.

While the snow-plant still blazes on the brown floor, the forest begins to be lighted up along every watercourse with the six-inch blossoms of the dogwood, gleaming like candle-flames down the dark aisles of the pines, or flickering in the breeze that follows the flowing river. Then the violets enter, white and blue, and the meadows stand thick with purple cyclamens. Next comes on the procession of lilies, that will last all through the summer; and with them arrives the mountain-lilac (*Ceanothus*) in clouds of azure and white that emulate the very sky. Then the azaleas, whose sheathed leaf-buds, like spurts of green flame, have waited impatiently for the flower-buds to join them, break into leaf and blossom together, and every land-path and water-path is bordered with their tropical beauty and rich, exotic perfume. Wild roses mingle with them, delightful beyond all the rest with their rustic associations and wholesome daintiness of air: a very epitome of country delights in every breath of their frank, simple fragrance.

As midsummer comes on, Nature takes up the full burden of her labor of love. Grasses grow knee-high, and, ripening their humble fruitage, roll in russet tides over the meadows and surge against the forest wall. Brakes stand thickly in every opening, their

cathedral richness of tracery matching the cedar-
sprays that fleck them with playful shadows. Oak-
leaves gleam with a dull, healthy polish. The birds
that have been rehearsing all the spring now give
their full concert, and the squirrel rejoices volubly in
the multitude of cones, which he can hardly suffer to
ripen before he must begin to harvest them. Hum-
mingbirds dash and whir about like little thunderbolts of flaming energy, and butterflies drowse on
drooping tassels of goldenrod.

So, in a riot of godetia, columbine, mimulus, pentstemon, lupine, and a score of others, the summer
passes by, and autumn, when it comes, comes in such
a rush and tumult of massed and gorgeous color that
one never thinks to mourn for summer, dead and
gone. Dogwood blooms again, crimson for white;
willows and poplars are all of paly gold; the oaks
burn rusty-red, as befits their iron strength; only the
pines and cedars, of a higher breed than the rest,
stand disdaining change and defying times and seasons. Slow lichens, purple, grey, and "melancholy
gold" (Ruskin's fine expression), creep like the tears
of Time over cold granite of cliff and earthquake-
talus, to find their summer in the yellow autumn sunlight that only reaches them when maple and mountain-lilac have begun to shed their leaves.

Snow rarely falls in the valley before Christmas, although the trails of the upper levels may have been
closed two months before, and the passes of the High
Sierra are often sealed as early as mid-September. In

the deep hollow of the valley a long Indian summer holds the field with an ardor of color that is like a mediæval pageant. A sky of Prussian blue enhances the creamy white of the cliffs and is deeply reflected in the calm river that now saunters and hesitates among shallows of sand. At night the cold leaps down from the upper plateaus, and the meadows are frosted to sallow tones of grey and drab; but by midday the sun burns as if through glass with a sharp, parching fervor. Under it acorns ripen suddenly, falling in showers at every push of wind like raindrops rattling on a roof; and men themselves would cure into a sort of raisins if there were but enough sugar in them. A dry electric energy is in the air, and trees and animals charge themselves to saturation point. As for the squirrels, I believe one might draw sparks from them by applying a knuckle.

At last the weather breaks and the snow falls. In some winters only a few inches of snow may lie on the valley floor; in others, many feet. But it is always the winter of the mountains, vivifying and kindly. The habitants of the valley bring out ski, sleds, and snow-shoes, and the hardy Norse and Saxon strain revives and strikes a blow for freedom. The pines stand as it were with folded arms, resolute and enduring, and rejoice in the Spartan severity. The waterfalls shroud themselves in bewildering phantasmagorias of ice, and act again the glacial age in little. Yosemite builds up a huge white cone five hundred feet in height; a volcano, but of ice instead of fire.

Vernal and Nevada array themselves with giant icicles, and thunder through reverberating caverns of blue and green splendor.

Gradually the balance of power reverses. The sun strengthens and the snows recede. The rush of falling water pulsates through the valley, and the river runs strong and dark. Somewhere the great word is spoken; and the old, strange striving begins once more in herb and bush and tree.

CHAPTER II

WHEN one looks down into the Yosemite from a comprehensive vantage-ground such as Inspiration Point, it is seen that the cross-section shape of the valley is somewhat like the letter U. The walls are in general effect vertical; the floor is smooth, level, and as a whole narrow relatively to the height of the walls, sweeping up at the sides to meet them in a natural curve formed by the débris of the cliffs.

This débris is irregularly disposed, there being in some places vast accumulations and in others surprisingly little of the rock-wastage. Although enormous in total amount it is yet so little in view of the great height of the walls that have contributed it that its scantiness is regarded by geologists as remarkable. An average cross-section drawing of the valley would show the débris-angle as a mere trace, hardly easing the abruptness of the sheer plunge of the cliffs to the level of the floor. The greater part of the wreckage is supposed to have fallen in some momentous earthquake that occurred not less than three hundred years ago, the period being determined by the age of trees at present growing upon the talus-slope. Evidences of the cataclysm are strewn thickly all up and down the cañon of the Merced River, which owes much of its picturesque character to the huge obstructions over and between which the rapid stream pours and pushes its way in mile upon mile of foaming cascades. The additions made during later centuries are so trifling in comparison as to be hardly distinguishable, though the slow, steadfast processes of wind and rain, heat and frost, topple down every year many tons of freshly shattered granite to add to the grey and lichened masses that stretch far out across the valley floor.

At intervals along the face of the walls the time-darkened rock is seen to be scarred to its original color, and has very much the appearance of being whitened by frost. These scars mark the paths of rock-slides of recent years. To witness one such avalanche stimulates the spectator to a vivid impression of the majestic uproar involved in Nature's greater *coups de main*, such as that must have been which, perhaps at one blow, flung almost the whole of this incalculable weight of rock down into the gulf.

Standing one day of late autumn about the middle of the valley, I was startled by a report like a cannon-shot, which filled the whole valley with echoes that roared and boomed, replied and multiplied, in a long-continued, glorious tumult. As the deafening sound died away in sullen mutterings under the vizor of El Capitan, I was able to distinguish the point of attack by the long, clattering descent of a vast quantity of rock. The night had 'been a cold one in the

valley, while on the seven to eight thousand foot
levels of the upper rim the temperature must have
dropped almost to zero. Frost, working quietly with
his Archimedean lever, had just succeeded in shifting
from the shoulder of The Sentinel a trifle of fifty tons
or so of granite. For near a thousand feet the boulder fell sheer, swift and silent; then striking the cliff
it burst like a bomb, shattering into a myriad flying
shards and splinters, and dislodging a smother of
fragments that trickled down to the valley in a stream
that lasted for minutes. Then, from the spot where
the boulder had struck, dust began to rise into the
sunny air, slowly building up and burgeoning like
a summer cloud, and every whit as snowy. It was
the flour of granite, powdered instantaneously by the
terrific shock.

As I gazed, I reflected upon the spectacular features of the catastrophe which we have seen discussed in magazines as a physical possibility, — the
collision of our planet with another stellar body. This
proved soon to be too serious a matter for my un-
scientific mind to contemplate calmly, and it was
a relief to turn to the past, and admire the simple
effectiveness of the device employed by men besieged
in castles and walled cities, who rolled down rocks
and other objects of useful specific gravity upon the
heads of the obstinate persons who were coming
upstairs on scaling-ladders.

The southern wall is noticeably darker in its general color than the northern, probably for the rea-

son that the greater degree of shade encourages a
stronger growth of mosses and lichens, both which
flourish extravagantly in many places. On the great
boulders near the foot of the little Sentinel Fall, thick
sheets of moss hang like mantles, embroidered with
disks of lichen and distilling slow diamonds from
their ragged edges. This side of the walls shows also
more of those avalanche-tracks of which I have
spoken, and more of the rock-flour of recent manu-
facture, which, it occurred to me, might well provide
the bread of that race of earth-giants whom one may
imagine as inhabiting some spacious hall under the
arched roof of El Capitan.

I do not know of any place where the tranquil
beauty of shadow can be so well seen and felt and
studied as in this deep, serene valley. On this unlimited canvas light paints with a mighty brush, in
broad half-miles of cobalt and purple and gold and
grey. There is continual variety in noting the day-
long, quiet changes; continual variety and continual
discovery. One may have studied El Capitan and
The Sentinel and Half-Dome a score of times, and
think that one knows them through and through and
yard by yard; but the next observation will show
some clouding of color or massing of shadow that
quite alters your conception. Even the solid outlines
seem to change, and a slant of sunlight or skein of
mist will upset the most fixed topographical conclu-
sions. Details even of great extent may easily be
overlooked on these huge walls, and such are apt to

be suddenly projected into visibility by some chance arrangement of light and shade. For instance, I thus became aware of a vast concavity in the face of El Capitan which I had never suspected, and which was revealed by a particular obliquity of early morning light in a deep, shell-like bowl of shadow. The Three Brothers, again, seen from the southwest soon after sunrise, show magnificent tone effects, light and shadow being regularly laid in broad, alternate bands of such massiveness and strength as to give a new characteristic to this, as I feel, somewhat formal and uninteresting group.

The Sentinel, that perpendicular elliptical column which stands about midway of the southern wall, is perhaps the least variable in expression of all the notable cliffs of the valley, standing resolutely muffled in shadows until the sun begins to sink to its eclipse behind the high promontory of El Capitan. Then his face glitters with fine Plutonian lines, hard and grim as steel on iron. To me this superb obelisk is, next to the Half-Dome and El Capitan, the dominant point of the valley ; and when I have lain awake at night with that tall grey spectre impending over me and obscuring a tenth of the host of heaven, I have been an Egyptian in Thebes, an Assyrian in Nineveh, a Martian or Saturnian for all I knew, under the spell of his solemn enchantment.

At such times, also, I have tried to imagine what would be the sensations of a person who should be transported unawares to this valley, and set down at night among these dimly seen shapes of rock and water. It would be all the better if it happened to be one of those moonlit but partly cloudy nights, when the light comes and goes here and there in sudden gleams and fadings. Here he would see, or doubt whether he saw, close beside and crowding against him, this perpendicular wall, which his eye would follow up and up, until he wondered where the top might be. Over there would be some incomprehensible shape which must surely be a delusion of his own senses. Yonder where the pale column of Yosemite Fall glimmered in the peering light, he would see what might be the straight ascending camp-fire smoke of the departed Indian genius of the place, or perhaps the reek of some weird sacrifice. The falling waters filling the valley with hollow voices and echoes would confuse instead of enlightening him, and the subtle forest-sounds, intricate and perplexing even by day, would add a thousand small mysteries to his bewilderment.

What El Capitan is to the western end of the valley, Half-Dome is to the eastern. And more, for it is, I think, incomparably the most wonderful, striking, and impressive feature of the region. In strangeness of shape this hemispherical mountain of solid granite is singular among the world's geological marvels, and its sublime height and firm, soaring outline impose it upon the imagination more than would be possible to bulk alone. Professor Whitney in his "Report of the Geological Survey of California," remarks that "it

strikes even the most casual observer as a new revelation in mountain forms ; its existence would be considered an impossibility if it were not there before us
in all its reality ; it is an unique thing in mountain
scenery, and nothing even approaching it can be
found except in the Sierra Nevada itself."

From every part of the upper half of the valley, the
eye is compelled as if by the force of physical attraction to return to this extraordinary mountain, which
one can never tire of contemplating. One looks upon
it almost as one would gaze at some majestic fragment of statuary ; and I sometimes wondered with
what beautiful phantoms these cloudy domes, pearly
cataracts, amethystine gulfs, and sylvan depths of
forest would have been peopled if Yosemite had fallen
to ancient Greece. For even the matter-of-fact mod-
ern mind, surrounded by forms so unusual and
heights so solemn, tends to unwarrantable flights of
imagination ; and one is apt to find one's self pondering why, as much as how, they were brought into
being.

The Half-Dome possesses one feature in particular
that I always found remarkable and charming, —
the strange manner in which it catches and holds
the last light of the day. Often for a full hour after
the valley has sunk into shadow, this high Alp, overlooking by two thousand feet the intervening heights,
receives the western glow, and like a great heliograph
reflects the peaceful messages of the evening over all
the quiet valley.

The most eccentric of all the rock-shapes is the double-pinnacled tower called Cathedral Spires, which forms a part of the southern wall near the western end of the valley, and rises, a sheer monolith, to a height of twenty-six hundred feet above the floor level. It is not often that one meets with any really cogent resemblance between Nature's large, artless architecture and man's self-conscious handiwork, but in this case the coincidence is quite sufficiently striking to warrant the name (although in my opinion the naming of natural objects with regard to such resemblances is always a reprehensible practice). Old inhabitants recall that the rock originally terminated in three pinnacles, but one of them fell decades ago from its high estate, and only a whitish scar close beside the bases of the remaining two marks the spot where it stood. There is, so far as I am aware, no representation extant of the appearance of this third turret, which must have fallen prior to the year 1864, under which date King refers to "the two sharp, slender minarets of granite"; but if it was at all conformable to its companion spires the peculiarity of the circumstance would be greatly enhanced.

In the little oak-shaded cemetery under Yosemite Point, where the fathers of the valley are sleeping, a fragment of this rock marks the grave of James C. Lamon, who died in the year 1875, and whose name still clings to the orchard which he planted near the junction of the Tenaya Creek with the river. His friend John Conway, who, one of the last of the old backwoodsmen of the region, still lives in the Chowchilla country, a few miles to the south, with fine imagination chose this fallen sky-steeple from which to hew the simple monument of "the pioneer settler of Yosemite." Not many of us can hope for a memorial as impressive and dignified.

A notable object of this end of the valley is the great castle-like pile which stands just to the west of the Cathedral Spires and is known as Cathedral Rocks. Here again a particular condition of light is needed to give the mass its true power of outline. I used to find this an unimpressive agglomeration of shapeless humps, offering an almost irritating contrast to the powerful lines of El Capitan on the opposite side of the valley, and only imposing by a certain doggedness of contour. But under a late afternoon sun I have seen the group draw into coherence, and reveal a stateliness and quietude of proportion that I was careful, whenever I passed them afterwards, to remember.

The dome-shaped formation which is the marked geological feature of the region, and which is seen on a vast scale in every view of the upper plateau, is perfectly illustrated at one point along the valley wall, where North Dome stands above the salient angle of the Washington Column. It is a conspicuous object from nearly all positions, facing the Half-Dome across the gulf of the Tenaya Cañon; a polished helmet of granite, rising in a pure curve from a cliff that plunges directly to the valley floor. The south and west inclines of the curve are marked by deep fractures which reveal clearly the concentric laminations of the structure.

Of these laminations, Professor Whitney says that " the curves are arranged strictly with reference to the surface of the masses of rock, showing clearly that they must have been produced by the contraction of the material while cooling or solidifying, and also giving very strongly the impression that, in many places, we see something of the original shape of the surface, as it was when the granitic mass assumed its present position." It is well to bear this in mind, for one is tempted to refer these flowing, convex outlines to glacial action, the traces of which, being so evident throughout the Yosemite region, may easily betray the judgment of the layman. It is natural to the unlearned to conclude that the phenomenon of the domes, accompanied as it is everywhere by striking evidences of glacial denudation, indicates the modelling of the ordinary rugged shapes of mountains by this agency ; especially in view of the fact that no example of the dome appears among the highest peaks, whence the glaciers proceeded, and further, that glacial action is clearly shown on many of the domes up to their very summits.

I have not found in the notes of geologists who have surveyed this region any explanation of the peculiar structure, nor any definite statement as to the depth to which the shell-like formation extends. Mr.

King indeed observes, referring particularly to El Capitan, that the structure appears to be superficial, never descending more than a hundred feet; but in the case of the Royal Arches, where the vaulting is most remarkable, it is seen at a much greater depth; and the insignificant fractures which occur everywhere on the walls but are too small to be noticed except as one passes close to them in climbing the trails to the upper levels, appear to indicate in a multitude of instances the same general construction.

It is one more anomaly of the Half-Dome that the two-thousand-foot vertical precipice of the northern face shows no trace of the concentric stratification beyond the thin, overhanging lip at the brink, although its exterior sculpture strongly illustrates the formation.

The imagination finds a fascinating exercise in trying to reconstruct the appearance of the valley during its glacial period. There is evidence that the glacier which occupied it was at one time not less than a thousand feet in depth. From the three main cañons, the Tenaya, the Merced, and the Illilouette, tributary glaciers converged, crowding with resistless, elemental movement into the box-like enclosure, surging up in medial and lateral ridges, and broken by profound crevasses as the ice-river swept around the compressing angles and buttresses of the walls. It would be a stormy lake of ice, its surface ever rearing up into a new confusion of monstrous shapes; and over the surrounding cliffs ever and anon icy blocks and masses would fall crashing from the brinks, filling the sullen arctic air with solemn uproar.

Traces of the successive terminal moraines of the glacier are still visible to the geologic eye at several points of the valley floor. These moraines probably operated as dams, holding back the water that issued from the retreating glacier and forming the lake which eventually replaced it. This in turn gave place to a meadow formed by the deposit of sediment; and with the arrival of heavier vegetation there ensued at length the present epoch of the valley.

If the future is to continue the revolutions of the past, this loveliest of valleys may still be destined to be the battle-ground of geologic forces; and perhaps it is only our stiffness of imagination that persuades us that the captains will not be as heroic as those of old.

CHAPTER III

SOME OBSERVATIONS ON THE NOMENCLATURE
OF THE VALLEY

I FIND it difficult to proceed further without reliev-
ing myself of some observations upon the names
that have become, I fear, firmly fixed upon many of
the principal features of the valley. I own that I do
not expect to find that my point of view is shared by
a majority of people, but I am sure, nevertheless,
that there must be a large number of persons whose
appreciation and enjoyment of natural beauty are disturbed by the association with it of a name based on
some inopportune feat of humor (or the lack of it), or
on some inept sentimentality.

Particularly irritating examples occur in the names
of two small waterfalls at the lower end of the valley.
At the northwest angle of El Capitan a small creek
pours down in a fall of thirty-three hundred feet. It
is a charming fall, peculiarly airy and childlike; but
the pleasure with which one views it is far from being
enhanced by its fatuous name of The Virgin's Tears.
(Ribbon Fall is now adopted as the official title, but
the other, unanimously backed by the Jehus, easily
holds the field.) On the opposite side of the valley, a
small, inconstant stream known as Meadow Brook

executes a fall which has received the name of The
Widow's Tears. This sickly designation, which bears
all the marks of stage-driver origin even before your
whip delivers himself of the jocose explanation that
the fall only lasts for two or three weeks, has actually received official sanction, and appears upon the
maps of the Geological Survey. This will never do:
is it too much to hope that a dignified Department
of the National Service will refuse to perpetuate this
trumpery appellation, and in future maps employ the
natural title of Meadow Brook Fall?

The name of Inspiration Point is hardly less objectionable. That famous spot gives what is perhaps
the most admirable of all the many great views of
the region. No doubt all of us ought to, and most of
us do, acquire a certain amount of inspiration from
the inexpressible beauty of the landscape that opens
from this renowned station. But I do not think that
it enhances the fine impression, rather I am sure for
my own part that it belittles it, to be notified that you
are expected to feel inspired. The old Adam is a per-
verse rogue, and resents these instructions; and
while it may be to an extent interesting to know that
some worthy gentleman who preceded you experienced here certain creditable emotions, it is irritating to have it conveyed in the very name of the
place that you ought to suffer the same ecstasy. Inspiration, in any case, is a timid bird, which appears
without advertisement, delights not in sign-boards,
and the louder it is whistled for is the more apt to

refuse to come. I have heard the spot spoken of by warm and jocular young gentlemen as Perspiration Point; and although that species of witticism is, generally speaking, distasteful to me, I find that I suffer no pang when it is practised at the expense of this piece of pedantry.

Another instance of this obtrusive suggestion occurs in the name of Artists' Point. I imagine an artist arriving unexpectedly (as an artist should arrive on the scenes of his successes) at this spot, whence he sees with rejoicing a most true and perfect landscape, without fear and without reproach. Eagerly he seizes upon it and marks it for his own; and with hasty fingers he prepares the instruments of his craft, calling upon Winsor and Newton. He sits down and begins those operations which answer to a preliminary survey in engineering. Suddenly he perceives, close by, an object that looks strangely like a sign-post. He reconnoitres it in the manner of the woodpecker in the story: "Looks like a sign-post; ugly enough for a sign-post; blamed if I don't believe it *is* a sign-post." Hurriedly he rises and approaches it: it *is* a sign-post; and it informs him that this is the spot from which, as a matter of course, artists are expected to paint the valley. "Good heavens!" he cries, "am I to be Number Four Hundred and Seventy-three?" and he loathes the stale sweetness like a man who might discover that his bride had been three times divorced.

Bridal Veil Fall suffers, although not so severely,

from the same ill-judged sentimentalism as The Virgin's Tears. Why may we not be left to discover these resemblances, or what others we prefer, for ourselves? Surely what is wanted is a name, and not a descriptive title reflecting the idiosyncrasies of some person who chanced to be early on the scene and hastened to take advantage of the fact. In some instances we know the offender by his own avowal. Dr. Bunnell, in his book of personal reminiscences entitled "The Discovery of the Yosemite," says, —

"The most of the names were selected by myself, and adopted by our command." (He is not here using the idiom of royalty, but by "our command" refers to the Mariposa Battalion, the body of men who under Major Savage in 1851 discovered the valley while pursuing marauding Indians.) "This deference was awarded to my selections because I was actively interested in acquiring the Indian names and significations, and because I was considered the most interested in the scenery."

One can but wish that the names which interested him so much had suited him better.

There can be no great objection to such titles as El Capitan, The Sentinel, and so on; although even there I think pure names would be preferable. Clouds' Rest and Washington Column are harmless, and the naming of the domes, as North, Half, and Sentinel, is well enough. But one may wish that Mr. Watkins had been denied his mountain, and Mr. Murphy his

dome, if it were only for the sake of the poets yet to
be. What will they do with such monsters? I confess
I am thankful that Wordsworth had no such problems
to encounter, but instead such gentle giants as Glara-
mara and Helvellyn. Derwentwater, moreover, is
better than Lake McGee, and Martindale than Jack-
ass Meadows.

When it is a question of trees, flowers, and animals,
it is reasonable enough to designate species by the
names of their discoverers (though Clarke crow is unfortunate in some indefinite way), and the latinized
terminations give a dignified flavor. These things
are more or less intimate and personal. But when it
is a mountain that is to be baptized some adequacy
should be observed, and the names of none but distinguished men bestowed upon them; nor those if for
any reason they are inappropriate.

The obviously best thing would be to keep to the
native names as far as they go, and in adding to them
to eschew local and temporary considerations. The
only valid objection to the use of the Indian names
would be in cases where they were too obstreperous in
pronunciation, which is seldom the fact. The longest
of them all consist of five syllables, and in every case
the sounds are simple and characteristic, and often
also euphonious; as, for instance, Patill'ima, for the
spot which we somewhat inconsequently call Glacier Point; Lo'ya, signifying a camp or signal station,
the name for Sentinel Rock; and Ahwah'nee, meaning a deep valley, which was the name of the valley

itself, Yosemite being the name of the tribe that
inhabited it at the time of its discovery.

I acknowledge that it is a matter of difficulty, at
this day, to secure an exact interpretation, if that
were necessary, or even a reasonably certain pho-
netic spelling, of the early Indian names. In the hope
of getting some light upon a number of disputed
points of this nature, I one evening interviewed at
his camp a friendly Indian (friendly in more than the
official sense) who I had reason to think might speak
with authority. He had been born in the valley, in
the old, peaceful days of "heap deer, heap acorn,
heap big time," and was highly intelligent, willing
to impart his lore, and confident of its accuracy; but
after five minutes of conversation my hopes faded,
and in ten, died.

It was a picturesque scene, at least. With Miguel
was a younger Indian and the latter's squaw, who by
the uncertain light worked silently upon a half-fin-
ished basket of handsome shape and design. We
held our philological powwow by a flickering fire
that burned under an aged cedar. Ten yards away
was a party of women and girls who were seated on
the ground around a larger fire that threw brigand-
ish, ruddy lights upon jetty eyes, ropes and curtains
of dusky hair, glistening teeth, tawny cheeks, and
dirty but shapely feet. Necklaces of beads, blue, red,
and yellow, threw in a vivacious sprinkling of color
that happily relieved the shapeless squalor of "store"
garments of the kind that describe themselves with

innocent precision as "wrappers." Some of the girls were quite pretty, though it required an effort to suppose that any of the older women could ever have been so.

Surly dogs, the intricacies of whose breed would defy the sagacity of Seven Dials, prowled, growled, and occasionally howled in the shadowy purlieus, and the round sleek visage of a pappoose, strapped in its basket-cradle, appeared in a solemn and intermittent manner from behind the bandannaed back of a wrinkled squaw. Something in a pot over the fire sputtered in an interesting manner, and was occasionally stirred with a twig by the woman with the pappoose, upon whom, after every such operation, she economically bestowed the twig with its adhering nourishment.

This party paid no attention to us, but maintained an animated conversation among themselves, accompanied with an *obbligato* of pleasant, low-toned laughter. Finding my Indian at one moment in doubt how to explain to me some fine shade of meaning, I suggested that we might consult the women at the other fire. But this Miguel promptly negatived, dismissing the idea with a contemptuous gesture and, "Pai-utes; no good"; the younger man and the squaw signifying their agreement by sardonic gruntings.

The Pai-utes of the Mono Desert region on the eastern side of the Sierra are in the habit of repairing yearly to the Yosemite for the purpose of sharing in the double harvest, — first of the tourists, later of acorns; and for some reason which I could not discover, their Yosemite neighbors seem to be willing to suffer this encroachment. It may be that the principles of Free Trade, although they have by no means fulfilled among larger communities the generous hopes of the founders of the doctrine by abolishing racial and national jealousies, are succeeding in this small instance, where the exchanges are such humble matters as acorns and piñon-nuts.

My faith in Miguel's ability as an interpreter was badly shaken early in our interview when he averred that many of the Indian words which I propounded to him had no meanings whatever. One after another of them was declared to be "Just name, all same your name; not mean nothing." In vain I labored with him, refusing to believe that it could be as he said, and almost feeling the sincerity of Hiawatha himself to be hanging on the event. Now and then he would verify one of my examples, with an air so frank that I could not suppose him to be deliberately misleading me when, the next moment, he declared some supposed interpretation to be "White man story; no good." When I argued that even white men's names meant something he was vastly interested, but became sceptical when I was at a loss to expound my own at his request. And it was not reassuring to be told, when I put it to him that, after all, the versions I proposed to him had certainly been given by some of his people, "Some time white man fool Indian; some time Indian fool white man maybe." This sounded so alarming at the end of our lengthy debate that I thought it best to retire with what few corroborations I had secured, for fear that a fuller revelation might come; and I did not in the sequel act upon my friend's cordial invitation, "You come 'gain, I tell you some more."

The interview at least left me with a high respect for the Cherokee Sequoyah (after whom the giant trees and redwoods of California have been fittingly named), who early in the last century achieved the feat of reducing the Indian languages to eighty-six syllabic characters. It is unfortunate that his labors did not result in spreading the art of writing among the native populations, which would have availed to define more or less exactly the sound-syllables and their meanings. Any language that is spoken only, not written, must tend to a looseness of pronunciation, extending to the length of neighboring tribes, originally speaking the same language, becoming mutually unintelligible.

A case in point is the word Yosemite itself, which Miguel stoutly affirmed to be no Indian word whatever, declaring that the real word was Er-her'-ma-te (*h* guttural), signifying a bear. The difference is no doubt one merely of local pronunciation; but the difficulty of identifying these elusive sounds is even better illustrated in the word Illilouette. The early geographers of the valley attempted in this case to adhere to the Indian name of the waterfall, but failed to fix the sound in English characters nearer than Illilouette

for Too-loo'-lo-wy-ak, which spelling closely represents the Indian word. Considerable as the diver-
gence is, it is not surprising to one who has contended
with similar problems ; but it seems a gratuitous flourish to furnish a supposed Indian name with the galli-
cized termination " ette "; an anomaly which adver-
tises its own monstrosity.

In the early " Guide-book to the Yosemite " prepared by Professor Whitney, he delved somewhat
deeply into the intricacies of the Indian names of
localities in the region, and gave a comprehensive list
of them. But he was fain to conclude his remarks
upon the subject with the confession, — " The discre-
pancies between the statements of the different inter-
preters it is beyond our power to reconcile." In the
same book he offered a suggestion which I could
wish might have been adopted, — that the general
title of the Cordilleras of North America should be
used to designate the whole system of our Western
mountain ranges. It would be a good appellation
geographically, and an excellent one imaginatively,
wafting the mind back to the day-dream mountains of
boyhood, when we roved with friendly Gauchos over
boundless *llanos* in the shadow of the mighty Andes.

CHAPTER IV

A CIRCUIT OF YOSEMITE RIM: FORT MONROE
TO THE LITTLE YOSEMITE

FOR some time I had wished to make the complete circuit of the upper levels adjacent to the Yosemite Valley when the opportunity at last came to do so, partly in the company of a congenial friend. This was Mr. Carl Eytel, an artist whom the heats of summer had driven from his beloved Colorado Desert, where I had last encountered him among the palms and alkali of that sun-blistered region.

I had frequently, in argument with him, urged the preëminence of the pine over the palm, if only on the ground of the greater amount of drawing in it. But Eytel is a colorist, and when he takes the argument on to that ground there is no following him; for you cannot argue about color, which every man perceives differently according to his spiritual composition.

We left the valley on a fine morning of mid-August, with the two burros who were to carry our necessities for the trip, —Adam, a sedate old grey, and Teddy, a young black with no marked characteristics other than a striking appetite. I always feel that I owe a special debt to nature for providing this humble beast of burden, for in many expeditions into the mountains

I have found him better suited to my needs than either the lordly horse or that durable hybrid which occupies the middle place in the equine scale. My purposes usually require a slow pace and frequent stoppages, and the constitution of the burro is such that he is naturally disposed to conform to my wishes in this regard, and often, indeed, to exceed them.

Our plan was to ascend to the south rim of the valley by way of the Wawona stage-road, and then, taking the Pohono trail which leaves the road at Fort Monroe, to proceed east to Glacier Point. Thence we would follow the so-called Long trail to the head of the Nevada Fall, and instead of descending to the valley and climbing to the north side by the Eagle Peak trail, I (alone from this point) intended to take the Sunrise trail northeasterly to the Tuolumne Meadows, and thence to double back westwards by way of the old Tioga "road." Leaving that relic of adventurous engineering before it turns northerly at Porcupine Flat, I proposed to take the southwesterly trail to the head of the Yosemite Falls, and then to continue westwards, passing Eagle Peak, to the summit of El Capitan. From there I hoped to be able to follow the old trail out to Gentry's Saw-Mill, and so to return to the valley by the Big Oak Flat road, thus making a complete circumambulation.

The road to Fort Monroe was hot and dusty, but mitigated with cool streams and intervals of grateful forest and enlivened by many tracks of deer and bear. The afternoon sunlight was streaming full into the valley as we reached Artists' Point. The narrowness of the gateway as it is seen from this point brings out strongly the gorge-like character of the depression, and in my opinion renders this the most striking of all the comprehensive views of the wonderful valley. When we reached Inspiration Point it lacked only an hour of sunset. The vast shadow of El Capitan lay already far across the valley, and a long purple promontory ran out from the foot of Three Brothers. I was reminded of the line of Virgil, by which, it is said, Millet was always deeply affected, —

" Majoresque cadunt altis de montibus umbræ." [1]

Certainly it harmonizes well with his sombre and sensitive genius.

We camped at Fort Monroe, and ate our supper between exclamations at the sunset color on the pines and cedars on the opposite hillside. The level light illuminated the forest with a radiance that was indescribably royal and august, and the great trees stood thoughtful and reverent, ripening their harvest in the golden air.

From just beyond our camp there opened a wonderful outlook to the west. The land here falls away almost precipitously two thousand feet to the cañon of the Merced, where it forms a sweeping amphitheatre at the point where Tamarack Creek enters from the north. Opposite, the unbroken forest rises to the high ridge that is held by the Merced Grove of Sequoias,

[1] " And the great shadows fall from the high mountains."

and which here forms the watershed between the Merced and Tuolumne systems.

In the gathering dusk the myriad pinnacles of the forest rose into a pale, clear sky, down which the new moon passed musingly to sink behind the western mountains.

I awoke several times during the night, noting the changes of the stars. Toward morning the sky became covered with fleecy clouds, through which now and then a star gleamed for a moment and was quickly obscured. By morning the sky cleared somewhat, and when, after breakfast, we walked back down the road to Inspiration Point, the sun shone intermittently through cloud openings of spiritual grey, and touched the white foot of El Capitan with pale, shifting gleams.

By the middle of the morning we weighed anchor, and leaving the road took the Pohono trail. The animals rebelled a little at the first steep rise, as implying harder times in store, but when we got fairly under way Adam went well in the lead, while Teddy — somewhat strangely, as we remarked — seemed well content with the second place.

The peculiar beauty of the Pohono trail lies in the forest through which it passes. At this western end the timber is mixed of cedar, sugar pine, yellow pine, white fir and Douglas spruce, with a scattering of small oaks; but when at about 7000 feet the main level is reached, the red fir (*Abies magnifica*) takes possession. This superb tree here often attains a height of two hundred feet, and even more. The stem is a fine shaft of dusky purple, and the broad curving fans of dark blue-green foliage, edged as if with an effervescent spray or froth by the silver-grey of the young growth, give the tree a special richness and nobility of color. Imposing as are all the conifers of this forest, to me none other of them quite equals in distinction and stateliness this magnificent fir.

The previous winter had been unusually severe, and the five feet of snow which had lain on the floor of the valley must have been more than trebled on the upper levels. The result was a profusion of cones on all the full-grown trees which was remarkable. Here and there a sugar pine could be seen which flowed gracefully over at the head like the top of a fountain under the weight of its fruitage, and the barrel-like cones of the firs were piled on the upper branches until the last inch of room was taken.

We sauntered easily along, noting these and a thousand other things, until we emerged unexpectedly at the brink. Looking down into the valley from that dizzy precipice, and over to the savage wilderness of grey and wrinkled granite that sweeps round to north and east, we agreed that the prospect surpassed any other that we had seen. The outer semicircle was a billowy expanse of peaks swimming in summer haze, but with dark clouds banked heavily above them. "Terrible, terrible!" said Eytel; and so it was. Three times, at Crocker, Stanford, and Dewey Points, the trail opens upon these amazing landscapes which are enhanced, if that is possible, by the suddenness with which they break upon the obscurity of the forest.

The trail is crossed by many small streams, and varied with oases of verdure. Epilobium was still in flower though it was long past midsummer, and the azalea blossom was only lately dead, and hung in shrivelled clusters of grey among the glossy leaves. Hazels grew plentifully, and we gathered nuts like schoolboys, though as they were hardly ripe the satisfaction lay principally in the sentimental and retrospective aspect of the feast.

Five hours' easy travel brought us to Bridal Veil Creek, and crossing it we went into camp by early evening. The stream was low, and half an hour's fishing resulted only in fingerlings, which were returned to the water to grow into fish of nobler degree.

Tracks of bear and mountain-lion had been fairly plentiful along the trail, and before turning in we picketed our animals securely in anticipation of a scare. But only the humpiness of a badly chosen sleeping-place disturbed our slumbers. We arose at dawn, and before the sun reached us were well on the trail.

The early morning hours are always the cream of time, but most of all is it so in the forest. It is then, even more than at evening, that the profoundest peacefulness that is possible to us on this earth is realized, so long as one is not in a hurry. The nerves, which at evening are settling into rest in a long *de-*

crescendo, in the morning are at zero. We for our part had plenty of time, for we had determined beforehand that we would not attempt to cover more than ten miles or so a day. Our animals stopped every minute to refresh themselves with seductive grasses, while we, far from rebuking them, lounged gently along, listening to the heavenly voices of the birds and delighting ourselves with the flowers. In the meadows hidden rills ran tinkling among delicate carices mixed with purple epilobium, lavender geranium and sultry yellow goldenrod; while at one spot a few blossoms, and even buds, of late wild-rose gave us the sweetest greeting of all.

Squirrels, jays, and woodpeckers were loquacious with table-talk. As the sun rose and the shadows of the great tree-stems fell purple on mats of dwarf ceanothus and manzanita, the leaves of the aspens, which had hung languid and unmoving since the dawn-wind stirred them three hours before, began to swing and dangle lazily, and then as the breeze came up started off as if driven by an engine at full pressure.

Turning north after two or three miles, the trail ran out again to the rim of the valley at The Fissures. The fissures themselves are sufficiently remarkable, — vertical clefts in the west face of a deep side-cañon which opens on the valley opposite Eagle Peak. These clefts, so narrow at the top that boulders of no large size which have fallen into them are caught and held in the jaws of the fracture, are of great depth, apparently reaching almost to the bottom of the cliff. But the great precipice of the abutment of the side-cañon itself is still more impressive. The bench-mark of the Geological Survey gives the height of this point as 7503 feet. The cliff is therefore thirty-five hundred feet in height above the valley floor, three hundred feet higher than Glacier Point, and on a level with Eagle Peak and El Capitan, which it faces. The top, stained with lichens in vivid yellow, Indian red, and purple, overhangs considerably, projecting a magnificent profile against the opposite wall of the valley.

The cañon of the Yosemite Creek presents from this point an interesting appearance. Its whole course lies open to the eye as if drawn on a map, from the thin line of falling water which marks the top of the cataract back to Mount Hoffman and the crest of the southern wall of the Tuolumne Cañon, which bounds the watershed.

There is no mountain in the immediate Yosemite region that surpasses Mount Hoffman in grandeur of outline. Its isolated position on the great plateau of granite which stretches northward from the rim of the valley renders it a commanding object. From this point it rises in imposing bulk in the northeast. Trending up in long slopes from a base of great extent, it sweeps up to a height of nearly 11,000 feet by grades which are nowhere sharp or precipitous, and conveys a remarkable impression of massiveness by the simplicity of its lines.

A short distance further brought us within sight of Sentinel Dome, and soon we emerged upon the stage-road. There is a little emerald meadow hereabouts which I had noticed the previous year, and had made an engagement with myself to camp there when the opportunity offered. I have a liking for making these engagements. They cannot often be kept, and I have always many outstanding; but there is an additional satisfaction in camping where one of them can be fulfilled. Turning off from the road, with its diurnal stages and humiliating tokens of the chewing-gum age, we crossed the plushy oasis enclosed among firs and tamaracks, and camped on the farther side among mint, cyclamens, and lupines, and under a superb red fir whose branches swept almost to the ground.

A tranquil Sunday was ushered in by a pageant at sunrise. A hundred yards to the south the ground rose to a fine view with Half-Dome almost in the foreground, and Hoffman, Clark, and Red Mountain the prominent peaks of the middle distance. The sun rose flashing immediately at the head of the Little Yosemite, and sent long, tremulous beams searching down into the cañon of the Illilouette and up into gulfs of cloud that glowed with volcanic fires above the sullen horizon of the south. As the day went on the sky attained its cloudless California blue, and the distant line of the Sierra shimmered under a powerful sun, while the snow-banks that enamelled the northern slopes glistened with a pearly softness.

On Monday we stayed still in camp, sketching and photographing the trees, tamarack, the two firs, and the Jeffrey variety of yellow pine, all which here offer excellent specimens for observation. Some climbing also had to be done to secure unopened cones of the fir, and when I finally descended after several of these expeditions I was well plastered with pitch and balsam and altogether in a highly inflammable condition.

I do not know of any vegetable object that is more poetic and generous in appearance than the cone of the red fir. The great velvety cylinders take on as they ripen a rich, peach-like bloom, and an almost spirituous perfume exhales from the balsam with which they are saturated. As the cones grow only on the upper branches, and do not fall but dissipate upon the tree, they are by no means as well-known objects as are the cones of the pines and spruces, which everywhere litter the forest floor, and any one is well repaid who climbs into the fragrant world where they grow. He will receive a revelation of the profusion and affluence of nature that will fill him with admiration, and moreover will refresh himself with recollections of the bird's-nesting exploits of youth.

In the afternoon I climbed the southern shoulder of Sentinel Dome, enjoying the march over the clean, wholesome pavement that stretches like an apron around the swell of the dome, and relishing the bite of the good hob-nails into the crumbling granite.

The surface of the rock has weathered into a coarse grit, a kind of granite hail. In the cleavage joints pines have taken root and form a scanty forest. I was amused by the grotesqueness of the shapes of these unconquerable trees, which have undertaken not only to sustain, but to propagate themselves under almost impossible conditions. I came upon aged firs seven or eight feet high, knotted and battered of body and leaning on their elbows, whose shivering branches grimly held up a score or two of cones and seemed to flourish them at the wind in scornful defiance. I could not refrain from crying " Go it ! " to these heroes.

On the precise summit of the round a Jeffrey pine has established itself, the trunk a shapeless, rooty mass and the limbs blown away horizontally to the east. Its branches are like iron, its twigs like whipcord, and its needles like steel. It is a small tree, but I judge its age must be numbered in hundreds of years.

Leaving camp early the next morning we followed the stage-road as far as Glacier Point. Mount Hoffman rose again grandly on our left, and Half-Dome, Clark, and Starr King more easterly. Now and again a white gleam among the trees revealed the position of the Vernal and Nevada Falls, and their distant roar rose continuously to our ears like the incessant beating of surf on the shore. It was even possible to see the great cloud of spray that streams out from the foot of Vernal.

The granite ocean to north and east was veiled in a thin, milky blue (the blue that milk so often is though it should not be). The forest lay in well-defined folds and creases, rising here and there to the sky-line; but the main ridge of the crests stood barren, sharp and clearly cut against a pale cerulean sky. The voices of the birds, plaintively sweet, seemed like a fine embroidery upon the background of silence and space.

Doubling southward at Glacier Point we began the long descent to the bed of the Illilouette Creek. As part of the so-called Long trail this route is travelled every year by thousands of tourists from the valley, under the convoy of realistic guides whose bear-skin "chaps" are artfully designed to thrill the Easterner with a touch of genuine Western life. We stumbled rapidly down this well-worn trail, while the dust rose in clouds and the animals complained loudly as we urged them to persevere.

Near the bottom we emerged at the edge of the cliff over which the Illilouette Creek plunges to join the Merced. The fall is broken a hundred feet or so below the lip by ledges on which the water breaks, and spreads like a film over the face of the cliff. The lower half of the descent is a smooth wall, all but vertical, down which the water spurts, hissing with enormous velocity, gathering at the bottom into a rapid stream, and rushing among huge boulders through a wild and sunless cañon to its junction with the main river. The amount of water flowing was small, but the energy and beauty of the fall surpassed my expectations.

The Illilouette Creek itself in its upper course is of an attractive and stimulating appearance, flowing in a wide bed that shows interesting glacial characteristics. I booked it for exploration at some future time back to its sources among the cluster of peaks known as the Merced group.

After crossing the creek the trail bears northeasterly, climbing to a height of 6700 feet, where it skirts the edge of the cliff which forces the river into the gorge of Vernal Fall. Fine views opened now and again of the upper end of the valley, and I observed, what I had not before been aware of, that at the eastern end of the Royal Arches the rock ends in an impressive vertical fracture, falling to a deeply curved recess. Basket Dome I found to be cut away on its eastern face in the same manner; both fractures possibly having occurred at the same time that Half-Dome suffered his frightful amputation.

As the trail begins to round the extreme eastern end of the valley the eye takes in at a glance the majestic nature of the Yosemite sculpture. To the left rises for three thousand feet the huge rock which forms the abutment between the valley proper and the Illilouette Cañon. Opposite, the profile of Mount Broderick sweeps up steeply to a hardly less height; and between lies the green and level valley, the product of the enormous grinding energy of the ice-river.

A steep descent through heavy timber brought us

to the open plateau at the head of the Nevada Fall. The river here flows smooth and silent to the edge of the cliff over which it goes thundering down in a broad torrent of snowy foam.

No other of the Yosemite waterfalls conveys so sublime an expression of dynamic power and irresistible energy as does Nevada. Seen from below, the water seems to be hurled in masses over the polished brink, to burst wildly on the ledges and fly out in whirling water-smoke, like storm-waves crashing upon a rocky coast. In the berserk fury of its rush it might embody some stalwart young god of Norse mythology, and its voice might be the death-song of a Jötun.

Crossing by the bridge just above the fall, we turned eastward toward the Little Yosemite, following the stream while we sought an eligible campsite. This we found about half a mile up, and went into camp on the bank of the river among white firs and the ubiquitous tamaracks. The sun had set for us although it was only four o'clock. After supper I fished for half an hour with indifferent success, and closed the day by fighting a merry bout in the twilight with a handsome fish, losing him honorably in a tight place of sunken snags and boulders.

We were not to move camp the next day, and I lay an extra hour in bed, watching the eastern grey turn to lilac, and conjuring to myself with the cryptic word "values" as if I understood it, while I noted the relative tones of trunk, branch, and foliage against the brightening sky. A squirrel in the fir overhead barked quarrelsomely at me, insisting that I get up and leave the valley immediately, as if the whole place were the possessions of the house of Douglas. Not so loud, my peppery young friend; I admit your prior claim, but all the same " J'y suis, j'y reste."

I suppose we all in our turn come into the debt of the inventor of bacon. For myself, when I am in the city I never touch the thing ; but here twice a day I eat it with relish, and find even the etymology of the word interesting. I never knew that Bacon was an Irish name ; yet I understand that Ireland has given this valuable product to the world.

There are two small lakes (so marked on the map), that lie just at the base of the " helmet " curve of the Half-Dome, and about a mile from where we were camped. We walked over to see them, and found them to be excellent examples of the evolution of the mountain meadow. By the gradual filling up of the lake-beds by detritus from the mountain at whose base they lie, they had already become marshes rather than lakes. Trunks of fallen trees lay rotting in the swampy soil, and a rank vegetation had grown up that all but obliterated them. The transformation was nearly complete, and a few years, I imagine, will suffice to give them the full meadow character. The place was exuberantly flowery with the blossoms of a tall weedy plant, and, enclosed within a ring of forest, was windless and silent as a vision.

While we stood enjoying the perfect stillness, and ourselves silent, I saw not forty yards away the wagging ears of a fawn that stood in the shade on the edge of the meadow, persecuted by flies. He was submerged, all but his ears, in the green and white sea, but now and then lifted his head and showed his delicate muzzle and spiritual, innocent eyes. He had not seen us, but soon there was a warning whistle from an older deer behind the thicket, and the fawn turned and walked quietly out of sight. Coming by a détour to the place where he had stood, we came upon a handsome buck, the same, no doubt, that had whistled. We were within twenty feet of him before he saw us, but then in a few great curving leaps he reached the opposite side of the meadow, and the congenial forest instantly absorbed him.

The designation of "Little Yosemite" well enough describes this valley to any one who knows the larger original. It lies at approximately two thousand feet greater elevation, but in general features it is simply a narrower and smaller Yosemite. Its walls, though not so high nor so precipitous, are imposing enough in boldness of outline and severity of polished granite. It has the same level meadows, and the river, though in places rapid and broken, flows generally with a valley quietness. Even the timber and underbrush are the same, except for a larger admixture of firs and tamaracks among the prevailing yellow pines and cedars; and though it lacks the waterfalls that grace the lower valley, there is a noticeably fine cascade at the upper end, where the river debouches from its narrow cañon. The water is broken at the head of the cascade into coarse grains, like the heavy spray that is stripped by the wind from the crests of ocean waves in a storm, and races in a broad band at frightful velocity over an ice-planed slide into a rocking pool of emerald.

Eytel was to return to the valley from this point, and I was to make the remainder of my circuit of the Yosemite rim alone. We sat long that night by a noble fire. The moon shone down on us between black shafts of fir and pine, like — as Eytel, the artist lost for the moment in the "camper," remarked — "like the lid of a lard-pail." The river rushed and murmured, now loud, now quiet, and gleamed white where the moonlight fell on the hurrying water. The soliloquy of the fire drew us inevitably into reminiscence. Vague recollections were warmed up into full remembrance; details and trifles came to mind in manner and number that astonished ourselves. From reminiscences we came to plans; old enthusiasms awakened. By George, what things we would do! New York, London, and Paris should marvel at our pictures and eagerly discuss our books. Buy them, too. And if they would n't, who cared? All the world could not prevent our painting and writing them, and how fine that was! Careless heroes, we defied fate. Art was long, we knew, but "the thoughts of youth" — we still say we are young —"are long, long thoughts." In our enthusiasm we forgot that we had an audience and commentator. The solemn, unchanging forest stood quietly around ; the sparks flew up like dancing stars and came down in feathers of ash that powdered us over like grey snow ; and moth after moth came flitting from the outer gloom into the firelight, circled twice or thrice around the fire, and plunged madly into it like Empedocles on Etna or gilded youths at Monte Carlo.

Walking a short distance up the valley in the moonlight, I was charmed by a new appearance of Half-Dome. The sky was partly overcast, and as the moon passed from behind a cloud and shone full upon the great southern round of the mountain, it was as if a vast hall, dim, grey, and unsubstantial, had come suddenly into being by enchantment. It hung glimmering, high and close above me, in the northern sky, spectral, weird, visionary, its half-mile height multiplied into an incomprehensible vastness in which terms of size had no meaning. De Quincey might have dreamed it. It completed my mental subjugation by this strange mountain, and I half feared that I might be visited by a nightmare recurrence of it in my sleep.

CHAPTER V

A CIRCUIT OF YOSEMITE RIM: THE LITTLE
YOSEMITE TO THE TUOLUMNE MEADOWS

MY sleep that night was certainly broken, but from a different cause. I had noticed what appeared to be a sleeping-place of particular excellence some little distance from camp, where a big Jeffrey pine had laid down a carpet of dead needles, and I had removed my blankets to the spot. I had no sooner lain down than numbers of large black ants, appreciating the increase of caloric, and recognizing me as the author of the friendly warmth, began to swarm upon me. They did not bite, but simply explored, travelling slowly and with evident pleasure over my face and neck, and penetrating in frightened rushes under the clothing when I tried to sweep them off. I lay in misery until past midnight, when I arose, rolled up my blankets, and marched a hundred yards back to camp, where I slept magnificently until six o'clock.

Bidding farewell to Eytel, whom I was to rejoin in the valley, I took the Clouds' Rest trail with the animals who were to be my sole companions for the remainder of the trip. As we moved quietly along I was free to notice the thousand and one things that make up the silent conversation of the trail, — the sweet tangle of bush and herbage, the wavings of branch and fern-frond, the small, child-like voices of the birds, the changes of the mountain walls from white to purple and from purple again to white as the clouds passed over, even the crackling of twigs underfoot, and the quiet weaving of the shadow tracery across the trail. How superbly silent and uncontaminated the world is, after all!

Coming after a mile or two to the point where the Clouds' Rest trail turns northward, I took the little travelled track which passes easterly over Sunrise Mountain. The animals were in good trim and humor after their rest, marching steadily along the levels, and taking the steep rises in fine, determined bursts of twenty yards or so at a time.

I note that the centre of intelligence in the burro appears to lie about the middle tract of the back; at least, the first movement of response arises there. A slight, almost imperceptible, elevation of that region is followed by a downward jerk of the head; the ears wag responsively; last of all the legs receive the percussion, and the tough cylinder of the trunk lurches forward. With Adam, a single word or a pebble is sufficient to initiate the operation. In the case of Teddy it requires three sharp words, *crescendo*, or a like number of admonitions by the rod. The first creates no impression whatever; the second is acknowledged by a slight tremor of the frame, which, however, subsides almost on the moment; at the third the back rises, the head drops, and we all move forward together.

Deer are plentiful in this locality, and I found that they were objects of interest to the burros almost as much as to myself. I was sometimes amused by their intelligent behavior when we came upon these creatures. On one occasion we encountered a doe and a fawn standing together in an opening of the forest. I did not at first see them, and my attention was directed to them by Adam, who was in the lead, stopping abruptly and looking curiously round at me, with as plain an air of asking " Do you see that?" as though he had spoken the words. The deer and we regarded one another respectfully for some ten or fifteen seconds; then, as I tugged to release my camera from an over-tight case, they turned and leaped lightly back into the forest. May no worse harm befall them than would have come from my peaceful gun.

Clarence King truly says that "from every commanding eminence around the Yosemite no distant object rises with more inspiring greatness than the Obelisk of Mount Clark." From any point of view this is a splendid mountain, but especially from this side, where the bold upward swing of the crest is seen in profile. The heavy belt of forest at its base wavers off into tenuous lines and patches, and ends in scattered dots before the final spring of the grey, razorlike summit begins. As I passed in the early afternoon a shell of delicious shadow was still lying in the great western curve from which the mountain spires up to its apex, "jutting two thousand feet from a rough-hewn pedestal of rocks and snow-fields."

To the north Clouds' Rest still kept me company, showing a much more abrupt peak than any one who has seen the mountain only from the familiar valley side would expect.

At the second crossing of the creek I found a small triangle of meadow, and stopped to lunch. The animals plunged with ardor into the riot of herbage, eating ravenously until they suddenly sighed and ceased for very weariness.

The trail here follows a long ridge bearing steadily northeast. Throughout the Sierra it is always interesting to note how regularly the changes of altitude are registered in the character of the forest. In the Little Yosemite I had left a mixed growth of cedar, yellow pine of two varieties, tamarack, sugar pine, and white fir. The cedars had been the first to disappear, then the common yellow pine (*P. ponderosa*), then the sugar pine, and last the white fir, while the red fir, first appearing as a straggler, had come into the principal place and was now joined by the mountain pine. This species (*P. monticola*), like all the other conifers that year, bore an extravagant crop of cones, and the ground under the trees was thickly littered with the fallen burs. The cones are curved and slender, about six inches long by one in diameter before they open, and are borne singly or in clusters at the tips of the upper branches, where they hang like bunches of commas. From bright green they turn to deep purple, and ripen at last to a lively fawn-brown. The foliage is rather short, set in tufts in the manner of the tamarack, but having the fine feathery grace of the sugar pine. It is altogether a handsome tree, robust but airy in habit, and expressing more of lightness and playfulness than any other conifer of the region.

The tamarack is something of a free lance in the matter of habitat, scattering through the forest promiscuously at all altitudes except the actual extremes. The trail-blazer has a natural preference for this tree, on whose thin, smooth bark a good blaze is more easily made than on the rougher stems of the other species of pine, or the firs or spruces. Moreover, the tree when cut quickly exudes a great amount of bright yellow resin, which fills the blaze and marks it as plainly as if it were painted. The tamarack is a brave, hardy tree, more handy than handsome, the useful plebeian of the conifers.

The trail here was particularly attractive. For a considerable distance it followed a high ridge whose easy northern slope carried a forest of unusual variety and perfection, while to the south it fell away steeply to the cañon of the Merced. Beyond rose again the wilderness of mountains, swelling up from darkly forested bases to desolate barrens and heights of uncompromising granite.

As we entered Hopkins Meadow, Adam halted at sight of the good green pasturage and turned upon me an interrogative and appealing eye. It had been

my intention to camp a few miles farther on, at the
lower end of Long Meadow; but the place was un-
deniably desirable, and I waived the point and made
camp on the edge of the willow-bordered creek
under a hospitable looking tamarack of unusual size.
At this point a trail takes out southeasterly to Merced Lake, the same by which I had reached this
meadow on my return from the High Sierra the previous summer. I had some debate with myself before
I could make up my mind to forego revisiting the
lake; but I reflected that if I once surrendered to this
kind of temptation I should find myself every day
confronted with similar appeals of ever-increasing
urgency, and might ultimately be dragged to Mount
Lyell, or even to Mono Lake, while I should almost
certainly be landed in difficulties for provisions.

Mosquitoes were intractable for an hour or two,
but the evening chill of 9000 feet of altitude quieted
them early. The moon rose with a frosty brightness,
accompanied by a court of little silvery clouds, delightfully tender and airy, that drifted dreamily along
like sky-fairies. Dead pines stood around the
meadow, as smooth and white as the masts of ships.
The tamarack more than any other pine appears to
seek the neighborhood of swamps and hollows, and
yet, strangely, oftenest suffers early decay from the
excess of moisture.

I awoke several times during the night and sighed
for one more blanket. But at any rate, cold was better than ants. Nature we can stand; we are her chil-

dren and know her rules. I arose at five o'clock,
really too cold to get breakfast, and took a run
through the meadow to verify Harvey's great discovery. The burros were standing as if frozen, and
viewed my athletics unsympathetically.

It is in these mountain meadows that the birds
congregate whose comparative scarcity in the Sierra forests is remarked upon by casual travellers.
From willow-thickets and matted tangles of dwarf
ceanothus they emerge in troops as the sun rises,
like English sparrows from an ivy-bush. Then begins
the morning concert, the jay, you may be sure, taking the part of first violin. As I ate breakfast the
din grew till I was quite bewildered. Chee-ings and
whee-ings and trillings and chucklings resounded on
all sides. Then the woodpeckers brought their power-
drills into action, and the woods rang again. Now
and then sounded, far away, a haunting, plaintive
cry, — surely the voice of the beloved "organ-bird"
of my last year's earlier summer memories. Sweet
bird, thou wilt never be forgot.

As I stood quietly beside a big fir, a hawk came
flying low among the trees straight toward me. He
did not observe me until I suddenly moved, when he
almost collapsed with fright. With a tremendous
flapping and scurrying he starboarded his helm
and bore away on another tack. "Thus conscience
does make cowards": I have never seen other and
weaker birds, with cleaner records, behave so.

I packed leisurely and carefully in view of the steep

climb which I knew lay ahead, and it was eleven o'clock before I started. Few works of man consume so much time in proportion to apparent result as the operation of loading a pack-animal; but precaution pays many times over, for equally few things are more discomposing than to have packs loosen or slip when one is on some steep grade or other awkward place; and it is of course just where the trail, and consequently the jolting, is worst that trouble is most likely to occur.

Clouds' Rest now lay to the west, extending northerly in a barren crest that rose in places to odd little nodules formed of weathered slabs of granite, such as occur at the main peak of the mountain. To the direct north was Sunrise Mountain, over which my trail ran. It was a long, trying climb, palliated with expansive glimpses of the fine, open country to the south. At 9700 feet I crossed the divide and descended into a meadow lying between bouldered slopes, with an impressive sweep of snowy mountains on the north.

At this altitude the firs had disappeared, but the tamaracks still held out, and with some *monticola* made up the bulk of the forest. Here also came in the mountain hemlock (*Tsuga mertensiana*). This tree is strikingly distinctive. In delicate, feminine habit of growth it greatly resembles that favorite of the nurserymen, the Himalayan deodar. The foliage is of the same silvery daintiness, and the branches and the topmost sprays of young trees take the same graceful, drooping curve. The cones are quaint and small, of long oval shape, like olives, and take on also as they ripen the purple color of that fruit. In old trees the smoke-colored bark turns to reddish, the close-growing branches dress the tall shaft with rich but scanty plumes, and the general appearance is much like that of the red fir.

Here appeared also the outposts of the dwarf pine (*P. albicaulis*). This is the hero that carries forward the flag of the tree kingdoms to timber-line, and I saluted him with respect. The low, straggling growth and grey bark, and the foliage, of a peculiarly clean light green, render this pine easily recognizable when it has once been identified. The staminate blossoms are of the shade of pink which is known in dry-goods circles, I believe, as " crushed strawberry," and the egg-shaped cone, consisting of a comparatively small number of thick, blunt scales, is unlike that of any other tree of the region. But the seeds happen to be particularly grateful to the palate of the Clarke crow, and he arranges that very few of the ripe cones fall to the ground to attract the observation of the traveller.

One encounters little game in these higher altitudes, but grouse are not uncommon. One of these birds, getting up as is their wont almost from under our feet, startled Teddy into a highly creditable jump, pack and all. There was a sound of tinware in commotion, and for a moment I trembled for my pack ; but with a snort which I fancy was partly invented to cover his confusion, he hastened on to overtake his comrade, who was better employed with the bunch-grass.

A slight descent through rocky country opened a magnificent view of the Cathedral, Echo, and Unicorn Peaks. The evening light threw the multitudinous pinnacles of this remarkable group into the strongest relief. It is evident that the glacial action which partly produced the typical rounded outlines of the Yosemite topography was diverted from this small region, where splintered crests and toppling crags remain to illustrate the Titanic shatter of the original upheaval. To-morrow I hoped would find me threading my way among them.

It was nearly sundown when we emerged into Long Meadow. I had covered only four or five miles, having spent a good deal of time in climbing trees and in other small excursions. Passing a mile or two up the meadow I camped at its upper end, where a thin trickle of water ran among the boulders of a rocky creek bed. A chilly wind blew strongly down the valley, and I chose my camping-place with care.

The altitude was 9500 feet. I stretched one of my canvases between two trees to form a wind-break, built a fire that might have alarmed a Swiss canton, and sat listening to the weird outcries of killdeer plovers (*Oxyechus vociferus* well named), far down the meadow, and noting with not unmixed admiration the frosty twinkling of the stars.

Before I turned in it was intensely cold, and but for my wind-break I should have passed a miserable night. Once or twice when I awoke and sat up for a moment the wind cut like a whip, and I could see the frosted meadow shining like snow in the moonlight. There was no temptation to stay in bed after daybreak, and I sat hugging the fire while I sipped boiling coffee and watched the solemn beauty of the coming of the day.

Straight down the meadow rose Clark and his surrounding mountains, sheeted on this their north side with snow. Slowly the phantasmagoria changed from spectral grey to the first flush of warmth, passed through rose to orange, and so to glistening white painted with broad washes of purple shadow. The thin splinter of granite that is called Columbia Finger shot up a thousand feet into the air to the northeast, while close to camp, for convenient geological contrast, a small isolated dome rose from the very edge of the meadow.

I was again amazed at the abundance of small life that sprang into existence as soon as the sun rose. It was quite a case of boys and girls coming out to play. Birds in troops came flitting about, hopping among the tussocky grass, and pursuing one another in and out among the trees with playful ardor. Marmots frisked about the fallen logs or sat upright eating the grass seeds, holding them neatly to the mouth like "corn-on-the-cob," but without a trace of the humiliating expression which most of us are conscious of when we venture upon that trying vegetable.

It was the middle of the morning when I started up

the valley. The trail at first bore easterly, heading straight toward the spike of granite ; then, skirting its southern base, it entered Cathedral Pass at an elevation of 10,000 feet. Reaching the summit of the pass a wild prospect, purely Alpine, spread before me, and involuntarily I stopped, almost staggered at the grandeur and savageness of the scene. Half a mile to the east rose a steep, keen slope on which a few dwarfed pines struggled, almost consciously as it seemed, to maintain a footing. From where they ceased, inaccessible cliffs and *aiguilles* sprang up sharp and white against the intense blue. In the powerful light every scar and seam was marked with glittering distinctness. The long curving swing of the ridge expressed a terrible strength and austerity, and the grim line of the crest seemed almost to impend ominously. On the other hand, the white obelisk stood close beside me glistening with a vitreous hardness, and in the north again rose spires, turrets, and scarps of granite. It was a maelstrom of mountains, whose crests broke on all sides into the wildest shapes of leaping water.

I felt again there, as I have often before, how deeply the sense of solitude is enhanced by the presence of wind. It is a difficult emotion to analyze, but I suppose that the monotonous sound and pressure may revive in the subconscious mind some memory of early experiences of our race during its migrations. I am often curiously aware at these moments of a background of Russian steppes and Asian plateaus to my sensations, and the apparent incongruity is not, for some reason, disconcerting.

Even at this elevation the trail was varied with patches of meadow in which grew alpine willows and many flowers. Along the runnels of water bryanthus grew thickly, and I found a few sprays on which the rosy blossoms were still unwithered. The plant, which is, in fact, of the Erica family, is delightfully heathery in character, the stems tough and wiry and the foliage brittle and stiff. The blossoms as they fade take on a heatherish purple, and it is altogether a fine, rough, Scotch-looking highlander.

I never saw the sky of so fervent a blue as it was that morning. I have always hoped to observe in it that appearance of violet darkness which has been remarked by many travellers as occurring at no greater altitudes than some that I have reached ; but so far the experience has been denied me. Here, however, the color was so deep as to be very remarkable. It was a pure ultramarine, and I was encouraged to hope that I might yet observe from these mountains the coveted phenomenon.

Crossing another divide among ledges of granite that were thickly studded with protruding crystals of feldspar, the trail passed over a small snow-bank and then descended to a meadow which encircled a little lake with rocky shores and islets. From the eastern margin of the meadow Cathedral Peak towered directly up a thousand feet into the glowing blue. The mountain shows here a very symmetrical double peak, and the white, precipitous face bears a look of unutterable age. The topmost turrets are as fragile and delicate as finely carved masonry that is crumbling to decay, and I could almost fancy that I saw the richly crocketed pinnacles and spires of the abbeys and minsters of my native land. As I passed along the west shoulder of the mountain the two points of the summit merged into a single perfect needle, and from a little farther again, the crest showed a series of even, sharply cleft notches, from which it sloped off to a ridge that terminated in an abrupt cliff.

Half a mile to the west I could see Cathedral Lake, half hidden in deep forest. It was too early to think of camping, or I would willingly have stayed to observe the appearance of this remarkable mountain by moonlight, when its peculiar shape and pallor must produce a night picture equally impressive and ghostly.

Again I entered the forest. In a strip of meadow through which flowed a lively stream a late lily was upholding still a score of ruby chalices. Could anything be prettier, more child-like and innocent, than these green lawns, sown with tall lavender daisies, and with the quiet forest shadows falling athwart them? I trow not, unless it be in heaven, or England. (Forgive, gentle American reader, the Englishman's fond exception.)

It was verging towards evening, and the birds were busy with their small housekeepings, convers-

ing abstractedly as they foraged. At the root of a
giant hemlock a spring of water issued, as cold as if
the earth's interior were of ice instead of fire. At a
turn of the trail I came upon what appeared to be
a camp. A considerable volume of smoke was rising
from a little clearing which exhibited the usual ugly
litter of cans and other rubbish. Some party had
camped there and had neglected to extinguish their
fire when they left. I was just in time to prevent a
serious conflagration. A fallen log was burning in
two places, and at every draw of wind blazed up
fiercely, while the ground for a considerable distance
around was smouldering threateningly. The animals,
whom I had allowed to get some distance ahead,
fortunately had decided that this was to be our camping-place, and were waiting for me. I hastily tied
them, cut through the log with my axe, and hauled
the burning end to the creek, into which I tumbled
it. Then, stamping out the fire where it was eating
its way through the thick matting of pine-needles, I
cleared the ground around the smouldering portion,
leaving a ring within which the fire, if it should revive, could burn itself out.

No penalty that could be exacted would be too
severe for the offence against the public good which
is committed by persons who, merely to avoid a few
minutes' work, will expose a tract of forest to the
danger of destruction. Carelessness so selfish and so
colossal rises to the dimension of crime.

It was by now past sundown, and I hurried the animals down the long descent. I really believe that, as burros go, my good Adam came as near perfection as could well be. He had but one fault, and even that I am willing to believe arose from a physical ailment, — his nose appeared to be afflicted with a chronic itch. Fifty times a day he must stop to rub the sensitive organ upon some convenient object (often myself), and his countenance when thus employed expressed a degree of enjoyment which was highly irritating when I desired to make quick progress ; though, after all, that occurred but seldom. I recall that David Copperfield's Aunt was marked by the same peculiarity, but with her the action seems to have been involuntary, and a symptom of perplexity of mind, while Adam made his infirmity an excuse for securing a pleasurable titillation.

When the timber at last thinned I saw before and below me the wide plain of the Tuolumne Meadows, with the river winding along in peaceful convolutions. In a few minutes the trail ran out on the level, and, a creek converging at the same point, I went into camp, escorted by hordes of the mosquitoes for which, almost as much as for its scenery, this locality is celebrated.

I walked some way down the meadow before turning in, and noticed that the massive clouds which with some apprehension I had seen piling up in the north during the afternoon, had entirely vanished, leaving again that clear and starry firmament which renders the California night, no less than its day, a continual miracle to our visitors. An opening of the forest to the south gave a glimpse of Cathedral Peak rising superbly against an indigo sky, with a snow-field high up on the eastern shoulder shining in the light of the rising moon like a floating cloud.

I had tethered the animals on the farther side of the creek, where the pasturage was better. Some capacity for the feeling of loneliness by which these companions of man have become infected manifested itself as they observed my preparations for the night, and they hailed me with weird sounds, incipient brayings, which died unregretted upon the frosty air.

CHAPTER VI

A CIRCUIT OF YOSEMITE RIM: THE TUOLUMNE MEADOWS TO YOSEMITE FALLS

THE -fine enthusiasm of Mr. Muir never burns more brightly than when he writes of the gentian meadows of the Sierra. During a month of wanderings in the high country the previous summer I had been on the *qui vive* for a sight of the flower, for I was infected with his spirit, — as who is not that reads him? — but I could never catch a glimpse of his cerulean darling. This year, also, I had thus far searched for it in vain; but at last, here in the Tuolumne Meadows, I came upon it. I knew it at once though I had never seen it before; this deep chalice of glowing blue must be the long-sought blossom; and so it was. But delightful as the flower is, it can never supplant with me that most charming flower of the Sierra, the lavender daisy. With no fervors of color, the latter embodies the sweetest of floral (as of human) virtues, simplicity, and stands face open to the sky, well-bred, slender, and quietly gay.

It was with reluctance that I now turned westward. A few miles to the east were Mounts Dana and Gibbs, with the fine territory lying beyond and to the south of them; and in the north, unseen but not unfelt, lay the Matterhorn country, in whose long cañons and by whose solitary lakes I had wandered the previous year. But I had reached here the extreme easterly point necessary to my purpose, and from here could make my way back to the north wall of the valley, keeping all the time on the high levels.

The Tioga road, which I should follow for some fifteen miles, is a rough track built in historic days by the owners of the once famous Tioga mine, which, long since abandoned, lies near the crest of the Sierra about twelve miles northeast of the meadows. For purposes of technical "control," a wagon is still driven over it once a year by an adventurous teamster ; and deserted cabins mark here and there the sites of "stations" such as Porcupine Flat, Dark Hole, White Wolf, and Aspen Valley.

Turning westward along this ancient highway, I came at once among the familiar Yosemite formations. Slopes of glabrous rock swept down into the level green of the meadows. Fairview Dome, a perfectly turned cupola of granite, towered twelve hundred feet above the road, and facing it stood another monstrous hummock, carved in peculiarly massive plates and ledges, from the crevices of which battered hemlocks and junipers peered down like stumpy dwarfs.

The road led through open forest, at first of tamarack alone, then mixed with hemlocks and mountain-pines. The clouds of yesterday had returned ; by noon the sun was obscured, and I looked forward with enjoyment to a rain. The forest wore its finest aspect of gloom; every tree stood observant and waiting. There was no wind; no branch moved, nor leaf whispered. The birds too were mute, flitting quietly among the pine-aisles as if lost in a dim church. Grey sky, grey mountains, grey stems of innumerable trees, — all was grey, calm, expectant.

There is a melancholy amount of dead timber throughout this region. Long stretches of tamarack forest have perished, as if at a stroke. Close examination shows that they have been destroyed by fire, although the polished skeletons would seem to indicate almost any other agency. The thin bark of this species burns like paper, and when it falls off leaves the trees complete from trunk to twig, apparently blasted rather than burned, the mockery of a forest. But among the dead trees there are numbers of prosperous young saplings from one to ten feet high. One can only hope that the new generation is not doomed to the fate of the old, and that the late-awakened zeal for forest preservation will avail to save other tracts from destruction.

Dome succeeded dome, the road descending gradually and bearing southwest. Passing close under the treeless easterly slope of Murphy's Dome, I came early in the afternoon in view of Tenaya Lake. On the left rose another mountain, hardly less barren, but with a few whitened junipers high up on the ledges standing backed against the precipices in fine fighting attitudes. A good meadow lies at the upper end of the lake, and into this I turned to look out a place for my camp, for the rain was now imminent.

When looking for a camp-site I usually go ahead of the animals, leading Adam by the halter-rope. This is the signal for Teddy to fall behind and hunt out titbits undisturbed, but he has a youthful horror of being left behind and lost, and generally keeps a sharp lookout to hold us in view. On this occasion he was betrayed by some agreeable morsel into allowing us to get out of his sight, and while I was tying Adam preparatory to unloading, I heard a weird, multitudinous kind of sound, and beheld Teddy racing along toward us at a swinging canter, his packs jouncing rhythmically as he came. His ears were rigid, and his excited eyes gleamed wildly about with an expression of ludicrous anxiety. The sound I heard was compounded of rattling cans, creaking harness, and the attrition of the heterogeneous articles comprised in his pack; among them, I reflected, certain liquids and semi-liquids that were not arranged for such rapid transportation. He had made half the circuit of the meadow, careening over at a fine, cutting angle as he bowled along, before he espied us, when he bore down upon us, still at a canter, came to anchor handsomely, and in a moment was chousing his consort out of the best of the pasturage.

I had hardly unpacked before it began to rain briskly. Throwing a line between two trees, I fastened the pack-canvases together and made of them a rough shelter, sufficient for my purpose. Then, with

my blankets safely under cover, I sat botanizing in
my humble, popular way, and rejoicing over the rain
and my gentians.

With the rain came a strong wind that drove it
in heavy swirls against my shelter, and made the dead
pines rock and strain like the masts of ships at anchor
in a squall. The wavelets drove crisply up on the
beach with a joyful sound of chattering water, and two
sandpipers ran up and down the wet edges of the sand,
happy and excited, or flew out over the lake, skim-
ming over the crests with sharp, curving wings, and
uttering little wailing cries of pleasure in sympathy
with the storm.

The rain lasted for two or three hours, and then
cleared suddenly away to a spectacular sunset. The
wet rock of the mountain sides wore a more sombre
majesty of color, and a patch of snow that lay in a
niche five hundred feet above me flushed almost to
damask in the last red rays of the sun.

I had staked the burros a little way back from the
lake, and when about dark I went over to picket them
on fresh pasturage for the night, I was surprised to
see the smoke of a camp-fire rising at the upper end
of the meadow. Lake Tenaya is a favorite camping-
place for travellers to and from the High Sierra or
the Mono country, and it was not the fact of a camp,
but the place chosen for it that struck me as strange.
After attending to the animals I walked over to satisfy my curiosity.

I found that my neighbors were a party of Indians;

two men, one of middle age, the other younger, a young woman whom I guessed to be the squaw of the younger man, and two little girls of six or eight years. They showed no surprise at my appearance, hardly looking up as I approached, and I had no doubt that with Indian quickness and secrecy they had watched my arrival at midday, and could have given me as exact a statement of my proceedings since that time as I myself could have furnished. My formal salutation was acknowledged by a glance and an inarticulate monosyllable from the men, and by the slow retreat of the two children until they backed against a tree, where they stood and gazed at me with serious unconcern. The woman had not even looked up. She was crouching on hands and knees over a smouldering fire, which she was endeavoring by blowing upon it to cultivate into a blaze.

In the half-darkness the swarthy face with its hanging ropes of hair, and the tense, muscular arms, glowed with ruddy gleams as she blew on the embers. The silence of the spectators and the intent attitude of the single actor in the group conferred upon the operation almost the quality of a rite.

It was difficult to read hospitality into the general situation, and I allowed a minute or two to elapse while I absorbed the pictorial elements of the scene. But I was too well aware of the native taciturnity of the Indians to feel it as a rebuff, and, moreover, I have a genuine liking for them, based, I confess, more upon indirect than upon first-hand knowledge.

The offer of tobacco is to-day as ever the friendliest advance one can make to an Indian. For that matter, it is understood in the same light by Mexicans and whites also ; and I have often been thankful that nature has provided this universal medium of friendly exchanges. It now supplied me with the means of an introduction, and walking forward I tendered my pouch to the older man with a friendly gesture and a word of appreciation of the fire, which was now burning brightly. It was at once accepted, and when at my invitation the younger man and the woman also shared my long-cut, the way was open for a friendly powwow, and in a minute or two we were all seated and smoking sociably. As I used a pipe I was able to abandon the pouch to them, and as cigarette followed cigarette it passed from hand to hand with a rapidity that would have defied the intelligence of a detective.

A fragmentary conversation brought out that they were Mono Indians returning from the Yosemite to their valley on the eastern side of the mountains. The fact that I had been there the previous summer, and that we had some mutual acquaintances among the Indians of the valley, opened the way still further ; and when I had lured the children into partial amity with a bait of ornamental brass buttons which I chanced to have in my coat-pocket, and which they promptly transferred to their mouths, we got on swimmingly.

The woman and the younger man took no part in the conversation, entering into it only to the extent of emphatic nods and other symbols of acquiescence in the sentiments expressed with regard to the persons who came under inquisition. The discussion, if it could be called such, took, in fact, a range not much beyond the discovery of common acquaintances, and was conducted in some such manner as this : —

"You sabe Indian Simon?"

"Him live Mono?"

"No, him live Yosemite ; stay Yosemite all time."

"Oh, ya-a-a, sabe Simon."

"Simon my friend, good man, yes?"

"'*Stá 'ueno.*"

A pause, the adults smoking determinedly while the children kept me carefully skewered. Then, —

"Manuel, you sabe?"

"Manuel live Mono? Yosemite?"

"Yosemite, rancheria."

"Oh, ya-a-a, sabe Manuel."

"Him good man, too."

"Ya-a-a, him good man, Manuel good man, sure."

Another pause.

"You see me when I come to-day, afternoon?"

"Oh, ya-a-a, see you come. Bringum two burro, Adams, Teddee."

"How you sabe my burros?"

"Oh, ya-a-a, sabe burro allright. Burro not belong you."

"No, not belong me. How you sabe?"

"Oh, ya-a-a, sabe oleman Dickson, Hite Cove. Him haveum burro for pack, I see. You buyum, how much?"

" No, I not buyum ; rentum."

(I found myself, with half-conscious amusement, adopting the pidgin-English of my friends.)

" *'Stá 'ueno:* I sabe you rentum."

" How you sabe ? "

But to this I could get no answer. They grunted in energetic chorus, but left me in ignorance and admiration ; and I am in doubt to-day whether he really knew my business as thoroughly as he seemed to do, or whether among the other interesting traits of the Indian is to be reckoned that of being a superlative and unnecessary bluffer.

With such innocent exercises we passed an hour of true Indian sociability, smoking industriously and speaking about once every three minutes. The children had retired, that is to say, they had burrowed under a heap of nondescript bedding and odoriferous saddle-blankets which lay, sufficiently near, at a few yards' distance. When I arose to go, my pouch, a nickel-plated, horseshoe-topped affair, had not returned to my custody. It was an old friend, and I was loath to lose it ; but when a casual glance around failed to reveal it I gave it up, rather than institute a search which, if unsuccessful, might seem to reflect upon the honesty of my hosts. So, saying nothing about the pouch, I bade them good-bye and groped my way in the pitchy darkness back to my camp, twice narrowly escaping a plunge into the creek, which stole with a canal quietness between deeply cut banks.

When I reached camp my lower half was well chilled by contact with the rain-laden bushes. I made a genial blaze by which to dry myself, and as I sat by it I pondered upon the mysterious nature of that law by virtue of which the smoke of a camp-fire blows always, without regard to the direction of the wind, into the face of the bystander. Large spiders, of the kind whose pin's-head of body is suspended upon long legs of miraculous thinness, ambled over me, exploring the creases of my costume; and I wondered whether there is not suggested in the anatomy of these creatures a mechanical principle which an architect might turn to remarkable account.

Sunday was to be a day of rest and mending, and when I awoke next morning I was determined not to forsake my blankets until I could emerge upon a comfortable temperature. When at length I arose I looked in vain for the smoke of the Indians' fire. Evidently they had already broken camp and departed. I thought I would walk over after breakfast to their camp, and make a search for the pouch in case I had overlooked it in the semi-darkness the night before, but I confess I thought it likely that it was in their company and well on the way to Mono.

While I sat at breakfast I saw the older Indian loping down the meadow toward me on his pony. As he came up and we exchanged "*Buenos dias!*" he held out the pouch to me, explaining that the "*muchach'*" had taken it because it was bright. He was sorry, and he had "beatum good." I thanked him for returning it and asked him to keep it for his trouble, but I could not persuade him to accept it. While we fraternized over the coffee-pot I learned that they had started at sunrise and he had actually ridden back several miles to restore my property. I had known that these Indians bore a high reputation for trustworthiness, but I own I was astonished at this scrupulous honesty, and was heartily ashamed of my suspicions. With some difficulty I got him to accept a small canister of tobacco, and he rode off to overtake his party, under pledge not to "beatum *muchach*'" any further on my account.

My animals gazed at me with surprise and gratitude when, instead of bringing them in for packing, I presented them with a breakfast relish of onions. Some repairs were necessary on my clothing, and as I (to use the ingenious expression of a plainsman friend) "staked out" my buttons with copper wire, I was struck by the degree of polish of which khaki is susceptible which has been well treated with pine-gum.

In the afternoon clouds again came up from the north and a heavy thunder-storm broke over the lake. Mount Hoffman in the west grew leaden and veiled, and looking down the lake I could see skeins of rain falling from the edges of the clouds that overhung the valley. The wind blew strongly enough to raise waves of respectable size, and I again retreated to my shelter. The thunder became continuous and made a noble jubilation among the mountains. There is an amphitheatre of cliffs far up on the east shoulder of Tenaya Peak which seemed to focus each peal, wrap it together, and hurl it down in explosive bursts upon the lake. It was a superb Sunday concert.

The rain was heavy and lasted for several hours. At the foot of the tamaracks among which I was camped solid masses of resin had collected. I kicked off lumps from these with my boot-heel, and with them kept up a handsome fire, independent of my rain-soaked supply of firewood. By sundown again the clouds had vanished, and the day closed in an idyll, with the evening star beaming in a thoughtful sky and drawn in quiet, tremulous lines on the tranquil surface of the lake.

The stillness of the night was broken by the sound of newly formed cascades that poured in many places over the bare rock of the mountain sides. Thoreau relates that people used sometimes to remark upon the loneliness of his life in the Concord woods, and rejoins in his quaint fashion, " Why should I feel lonely? is not our planet in the Milky Way?" I confess I am not built on that sublime scale; but with trees about me I find that I seldom suffer for lack of company. And besides the trees themselves there are their populations of birds and squirrels, all friends and comrades alike.

My lash-ropes, which had been thoroughly soaked in the rain, were frozen during the night as stiff as wire cables, and it was impossible to pack with them next morning until I had got them thawed out. As I wrestled with the ice-bound knots and hitches I realized faintly the melancholy nature of the seafaring life, and marvelled that any one should voluntarily "follow the sea" as a profession.

By mid-morning I had packed as well as I could and we again took to the road, which follows the north shore of the lake almost to its lower end. Clouds' Rest came again into view to the south, and Mount Hoffman closer to northwest. The rocks showed here a remarkable degree of glacial action and shone with the dull lustre of polished marble.

At the foot of the lake, where an ancient rail-fence lies submerged and decaying among the grass of a small meadow, the road turned to the north, and climbing a steep grade opened a lovely landscape of which the lake, at a distance of a mile or two, was the centre. Directly from the water's edge on its farther side Tenaya Peak rose for two thousand feet, with Cathedral Peak showing over its shoulder remarkably like an English parish church. The foreground was a slope of glistening rock strewn with an incredible litter of boulders.

A sun of spring-like freshness shone over the landscape, and under its warmth the wet ground poured out its spiciest odors. The dead cones that lay in myriads on the forest floor had closed their scales like umbrellas, and resumed for a brief time their living shapes. One is apt, unless he is acquainted with the appearance of the growing cones, to be deluded by this behavior into supposing that he is meeting some species of pines that are new to him. The cones of the tamarack and hemlock in particular are not easily recognized under their temporary transformation.

The road trended northward almost to the foot of Mount Hoffman before it turned again westerly and began a gradual descent in company with a versatile little creek. An opening of the forest to the south gave a glimpse of Half-Dome under yet another aspect, seen at right angles to the well-known semi-profile that commands the valley. Far to the west the blue of timbered mountains closed the view, running together fold on fold, their myriad tree-tops scratching the sky-line like needle points.

Vivid ovals of meadow broke the forest, starred with daisies that were more engaging than ever in their rain-washed freshness. Rounding the base of Mount Hoffman I discovered the expected southwesterly trail, and striking into it headed directly for the valley rim. The timber here again was strikingly fine, the firs especially statuesque and dignified ; and the afternoon sunlight flooded the forest with a grave and solemn splendor.

I had prepared myself for trouble when I packed in the morning, and now it overtook me. The lash-ropes, stretching as they dried, had gradually loosened until at a steep descent the packs of both animals slipped bodily forward on to their necks. A few excited gymnastics completed the ruin, and nothing remained but to unload and repack. The operation is a harassing one when the ground is a steep and brushy side-hill, and a good deal of time was consumed by it.

After crossing the creek which flows down Indian Cañon to the valley, the trail rose to a low divide, then again descended, now in full view of the great precipice which rises at the west of the Yosemite Creek. This was already deep in shadow, a sombre and imposing object, and enhanced by contrast the sunset color that pulsated on the summit of Sentinel Dome, directly to the south. The forest became more open, Jeffrey pines and junipers growing sparsely on the pavement-like expanse of disintegrating granite. A final abrupt descent brought me to Yosemite Creek, and crossing by the bridge just above the head of the fall I turned along the west side of the stream and camped where a scanty growth of herbage offered the only provender for the animals that I was likely to find in the neighborhood.

I had arranged with my friend Eytel that I would signal my arrival at this point to him in the valley below. By the last of the daylight I climbed to the highest point of the cliff on the east of the fall, and lighted my signal-fire. The floor of the valley three thousand feet below twinkled with electric lights, and I anticipated without enthusiasm the time when a captive balloon will be anchored in the middle of the valley, and airships moored at favorable spots for doing the sunsets and sunrises.

Early next morning I climbed down to the lip of the fall. It is a wild enough place, and the tremendous escarpment of Yosemite Point, projected in strong profile against the morning haze, was powerfully impressive. The upper end of the valley was filling with misty sunlight, but below the village everything was still in obscurity, except where the salient points of the southern wall caught dull, purplish gleams. In middle distance loomed the colossus of Half-Dome, and beyond, Mounts Clark and Starr King stood forward like the advancing waves of the sea of Sierra peaks.

At this time of year, the end of summer, the fall had lost much of its beauty and grandeur, but even now from where I stood at the verge of the first sheer drop of sixteen hundred feet it presented a fascinating sight. The creek, after passing through two or three deep, cauldron-like pools, falls in cascades for a hundred feet. Then leaping another hundred it strikes a ledge and is broken into dust, which drifts idly away upon the wind and is lost to view.

From observation of the walls of the gorge above the fall I could partly realize the stupendous energy with which the stream when in flood hurls its waters far out beyond the lip of the fall, and was able to imagine the magnificence of the spectacle at this point on such occasions. I could also faintly conceive what King's fine geological sense suggested to him at the same spot, — "how immeasurably grander must it have been when the great, living, moving glacier, with slow, invisible motion, crowded its huge body over the brink, and launched blue ice-blocks down through the foam of the cataract into that gulf of wild rocks and eddying mist."

I had often noted from the valley the splinter or flake of rock which stands separated from the main wall near Yosemite Point. Climbing along the edge of the cliff I found that this remarkable monolith, standing perhaps a hundred feet clear of the summit of the precipice, is so tall, straight, and slender that I was nowhere able to observe where its base joins the parent rock.

From the Point another enormous prospect opened. Here again, as everywhere in the neighborhood of the valley, Half-Dome was the overpowering ingredient in the view. The light was still misty and uncertain, and the great disk of the northern face hung like a blue curtain from the edge of the mighty fracture. From this elevation of 7200 feet the convexity of the dome is depressed to a low, swelling curve, and the laminations of its concentric structure show like fine toolings on a ball of ivory. Directly to the east North Dome showed as a mere hillock, only five hundred feet above me. A broad splash of sunlight shone dully on the apron of granite over which an arm of the ancient glacier had flowed.

In the foreground the forest swept down at a keen angle, halting only at the very edge of the precipice which plunges sheer to the valley floor. Opposite, across the gulf, frowned the dark escarpment of Glacier Point. The broad foot of solid rock which sinks into the forest below this great cliff is to me one of the arresting features of the valley. The most casual mind is struck by the massive slope of burnished granite, and comprehends something of the majestic movement of the glacier which, pouring down the cañon of the Illilouette, encountered here the converging mass of the Tenaya glacier, and, deflected westwards, was crowded against the impeding buttress.

Turning to the south, Sentinel Dome marked the head of the magnificent panorama of the valley wall, the shadows of the highest points projected blue-black across the park-like level. In the west Eagle Peak and the abrupt faces of the Three Brothers shone in clear morning light, and below lay the deeply cut trough where the river gleamed palely among obscuring masses of timber.

It seemed somewhat of a pity that since the authorities had placed, or permitted some one to place, a flag-pole at this much-visited point, there could not have been found a worthier emblem to fly from it than the scrap of sacking which, to judge from internal evidence, had then long disgraced it.

Reluctantly I left this fine coign of observation. A marmot, which when I arrived I had noticed lying on a projecting rock apparently waiting for the sun, was still, after perhaps half an hour, watching me with frank curiosity. He was not more than five yards distant, and I felt flattered by his confidence and spoke appreciatively to him as I turned away. In acknowledgment he politely changed his position so as to keep me in view until I disappeared below his horizon.

It was already nearly midday, and I made my way directly back to camp, striking obliquely across a steep slope of ledges and house-like boulders. Gnarled pines gripped the crevices and thick beds of buck-brush filled the sheltered hollows. The junipers were here in unusually fine foliage, spreading in firm rounded outlines like full-leaved oaks. The disinte-grating rock gave good footing to my nailed boots, and I found it exhilarating to stride rapidly down over shelves of sparkling granite that often tilted under my weight. I crossed the creek almost dry-shod between two of the "pot-holes" with which its bed is honeycombed, and climbing up a brush-choked gully, emerged, almost as much to my own surprise as theirs, exactly where my animals were tethered. Their pasturage had been scanty, and with cheap generosity I eked out their commons from such of my supplies as promised to show a surplus.

CHAPTER VII

A CIRCUIT OF YOSEMITE RIM: YOSEMITE FALLS TO THE BIG OAK FLAT ROAD

IT was well after noon when I broke camp and started out on the Eagle Peak trail. Almost immediately I met once more that magnificent zone of firs which I can never enter without a feeling that approaches the religious. There is something in the demeanor of these trees that ministers to an instinct for gravity which receives little satisfaction in these days, and I could not refrain from occasionally halting the cavalcade while I indulged the sentiment to the full. The conservation policy is perhaps more politic than it knows, conserving not only the nation's resources, but, in a manner, its men.

The trail, after bearing northward and rounding the high cliff that rises to the west of the creek, turned again to the south, passing along the edge of a meadow full of cheerful daisies, and then rose steeply to Eagle Peak. This point, the highest of the Three Brothers, is several hundred feet higher than any other accessible summit along the walls, and gives the finest of all the views of the upper end of the valley. The scene was that day enhanced by broken masses of cloud that hovered over the High

Sierra, through which a pale sun threw sensitive, shifting lights over the ranks of distant peaks. But for the interference of the hemisphere of Half-Dome, the sweep of the prospect was unbroken. Again I admired the scimitar curve of Mount Clark, and again felt the Alpine fascination of that noble cluster of mountains of which Lyell is the nucleus. The nearer distance was filled by a sea of granite, shaded in severe black and white; and almost in the foreground but thirteen hundred feet below, I could see the delicate scarf of the Yosemite Fall, drifting airily down the great cliff on which I had stood at early morning.

To the south I looked directly down upon a long gable that is cut vertically away on its eastern face to a precipice, and runs on the west in a steep plane to meet the flank of El Capitan.

The summit of Eagle Peak itself is a satisfactory pile of huge leaves and boulders of weathered granite, loosely thrown together. As I sat intent upon the wistful play of light and shade over the distant mountains and the pageant of the sky-scenery, I was startled by a rattling whistle of wings overhead. Before I could get up from the cleft into which, for protection from the keen wind, I had wedged myself, the bird was gone from view, leaving me in uncertainty as to its kind, but willing to believe that I had shared that fine solitude with an eagle.

From Eagle Peak a southwesterly trail of not over two miles leads to the summit of El Capitan. It is seldom travelled, and in many places is obliterated by chaparral. A mountain-trained burro will ordinarily pick out a bad trail better than the generality of mankind, but here Adam was at fault and wandered aimlessly about, or stood helplessly gazing back at me for instructions. Fastening Teddy's halter-rope to the back horn of Adam's pack-saddle, I took the lead and they immediately followed, ripping through scrub-oak, buck-brush, and manzanita with what seemed ostentatious disregard of their packs.

We feasted as we went on thimble-berries, I on the ripe fruit, they impartially on the whole plant, which they alternated with fern, bunch-grass, young oak-leaves, and herbs of sundry kinds. Now and then a mouthful of pennyroyal or spearmint odorized the atmosphere agreeably. For some unexplained reason none of Nature's children seem to consider the wild gooseberry a desirable fruit. The bushes here hung full of tempting-looking berries, prickly, but of good flavor. No doubt the bear, an absolute omnivore, appreciates them, but the bears of the region have mostly repaired to the valley, where banquets of piquant refuse from the camps are freely spread for all.

The trail crossed several small creeks, but all of them were dry. I was somewhat disconcerted at this, for I particularly desired to camp on the summit of El Capitan, and I knew that I should find no water there. I had watered the animals at the meadow, but where was my evening tea and morning coffee to come from? As we threaded an unpromising tract of brush I heard a sound as of the subterranean trickling of water, and traced it to a small hole just big enough to admit my hand. By lying face downward I could with difficulty reach my arm down to the tiny stream, and I devoted ten minutes to filling my canteen with a compound of gravel, dead leaves, ants, and water.

A few handsome sugar pines appeared as the forest thinned out. This fine tree, which is here at about the upper limit of its growth, is conspicuous even among such monarchs as the firs. The lithe branches express a steel-like temper, and take a spirited sweep that is wholly different from the reserved manner and statuesque symmetry of its companions; and when the tree is hung with full-grown cones there is an opulence in its aspect that marks it as the head of its family.

The timber ceased suddenly at a shelving expanse of rock and sand, and I recognized the contour of the vast headland which marks the gateway of the valley. Not a blade of grass grows on this barren tract, and I followed the western edge of the cliff, looking for pasturage, until I came to the Ribbon Fall Creek. At the head of the 3300-foot fall (which is the highest of all the Yosemite waterfalls, but also the most ephemeral), I found a little swale of verdure and there made camp, staking out the animals among grass literally up to their heads and mosquitoes not a few. I made a hasty supper and fled, leaving them to enjoy their riches and bear their trials alone.

As for me I was determined to sleep on the very crest of El Capitan. A certain nausea has crept into my feeling for this famous mountain since eager advertisers have claimed it for their own, and publish its lineaments on soap-wrappers and beer bottles. But up here on this austere and lonely brow, all that could be forgotten, and taking my blankets and materials for a partial breakfast, I marched back half a mile to the summit of the elephantine forehead of the mountain.

I had heard of a monster juniper, *juniperus juniperorum*, surpassing all the junipers of Yosemite, that grew hereabout, and by the last of the daylight I searched for him, hoping to pass my El Capitan night beneath or at least beside him. My knowledge of the habit of the species ought to have guided me to the wind-swept western edge, where next morning I found the tree; but I had to content myself with a gallant hulk of Jeffrey pine whose topmast had been blown over in some winter's gale and now hung by a few tough shreds creaking somewhat dismally in the wind. Here I made a royal fire and sat in great content, watching the red light fade in the west and congratulating myself on the fulfilment of a long-cherished desire, — that I might see my camp-fire smoke ascending from the "skyish head" of the Captain of Yosemite.

Before I turned in I walked a short distance farther out on the promontory. It was a strange and somewhat unearthly situation. In the dim starlight I seemed to stand on a grey plain that sloped gradually but perceptibly away on all sides. A few gaunt trees, uncertainly seen, showed stark against the night sky, and seemed to peer and listen. I walked over to the eastern slope and looked down into the valley. It was a misty void, in which the gaze sank, and sank, as in a bottomless gulf. One dark shape loomed in the obscurity, the great arc of mountain which soars up to Glacier Point. Beside that there was nothing but the pallid glimmer of the rock on which I stood, and the stars shining in the indigo vault with a faint, high radiance that enhanced the solemnity of their immeasurable distances. The wind, which had blown strongly from the east, had almost died away, and passed me with a low and dreary sound. I might have been the last survivor on an asteroid.

At five o'clock next morning I was astir and drinking my coffee. The sky was yellowing in the east, and the irregular line of the Sierras was cut upon it in opaque, lifeless blue. Overhead the long needles of my pine hummed in the dawn wind, a dull, resonant tone like the reluctant *smorzando* of a bass-viol. The great cañon to the west was deep in sleeping mist, and above it a few stars shone greyly in a firmament that was still dark, as if the night had retreated there. The air was like poetry, and the "one touch of nature" was supplied when a small yellow bird arrived, fluffed himself out with an easy appearance of taking a chair, and fraternized sociably while he awaited my crumbs.

Then I went down to the brink of the precipice.

There is a long, rounded slope to the south, at first gentle, then steeply shelving. The ground is a coarse granite sand through which the friable rock pushes in shelves and ledges. I climbed carefully down among huge slabs, and crept out along the edge of a flake which leans out over the cliff. A monument of piled rocks stands on the verge, and hard by it I found the bench-mark of the Geological Survey, recording 7042 feet of altitude. I was at first tempted to lie down and secure an absolutely vertical *coup d'œil;* but I had no difficulty in refraining when I heard the warning tone that the loose rock returned when I stamped upon it to test its stability, and I contented myself with toppling a block of granite over the edge as my proxy. No sound of its striking came back from the abyss.

From a niche among the rocks I looked down upon the valley, slowly growing into distinctness as the light strengthened. El Capitan Meadows lay directly below, a carpet of quiet half-tones, grey-green, russet, and umber. The river shone like a ribbon of steel, bordered here with white shallows of sand, there with deep green of pine and cedar, and again with clumps of poplar whose lighter foliage showed the first touch of autumn gold. At the foot of the cliffs, sharp lines of talus stood boldly out like capes into the meadow, ashy grey, or darkly forested with pines. The southern wall ran in mile on mile of sombre precipice, alternately rifted with purple shadows and scarred with white avalanche scorings.

The sun rose at length, gilding the bald crest of Sentinel Dome and sending shafts of misty amethyst streaming between the outstanding buttresses of the walls. The picture was still magnificent, but the deeper enchantment passed away as the light increased. I made my way to the west cliff and there found my juniper: a sort of arborescent Atlas, twenty-three feet in circumference at four feet above the ground. Its height does not exceed its girth, and the farthest reaching limbs are of about the same length and some five feet around near the trunk. The stem rises in thick coils, like a twisted column; every branch and twig is furred with the yellow moss of age, and the whitened twigs and branchlets stream out wildly, like grey hair. Yet the tree is in full vigor, the foliage dense and brushy, the arms well balanced, and the whole appearance expressive of enormous age allied with unfailing strength and hardiness.

As I returned to camp I noticed, attached to a small tree, the fluttering remains of a sack which bore the advertisement of some brand of flour, of course "the best." The fitness of things is apparently of small account to most of us, after all our generations of culture and decades of magazines. I willingly halted and climbed the tree in order to detach the rag, and had the pleasure of incinerating it before I left the mountain.

My animals received me with incoherent sounds of welcome, and hastened toward me to the limit of their ropes. They were standing amid the wreckage of their feast, surrounded by a cloud of mosquitoes, like spendthrifts among the ruins of their fortunes, beset by creditors. I made a second breakfast, packed, and about noon started to make my way if I could by the ancient trail to Gentry's, on the Big Oak Flat road. By returning to the valley over that road I should make my circuit exact and complete, and fulfil my purpose in the letter as well as in the spirit.

Half a mile brought me to a small stream, the main Ribbon Fall Creek, crossing which I came upon a little hunched-up cabin, doorless, and leaning half-a-dozen ways. An old pack-saddle lay near by, and a disabled Dutch oven reclined in a Dying-Gladiator attitude on a talus of empty cans that descended to the stream. On a sleeping-bunk within the house lay an object which in the gloom I took to be the form of the owner of the dwelling, but which proved to be only a wood-rat's nest of imposing dimensions. Sundry articles of household use lay about with that waiting expression which such objects in a deserted habitation seem to contract.

On leaving this house of dejection my troubles began. For a quarter of a mile the trail could be kept, with difficulty, though for all evidence to the contrary it might have been years since anybody had travelled over it. But it became more and more obscure, and I frequently had to tie up the animals while I made wide casts before I could recover it some distance ahead. At last it ran out on to a meadow (Blue-jay Meadow, as I afterwards found it

is called), and there vanished finally. The most diligent
search failed to reveal any token of it coming out on
the farther side. After wasting much time I decided
to cut loose and make across country as best I could,
bearing west and somewhat south, knowing that if I
could but keep going in that direction I must sooner
or later strike the road.

My brave little burros stepped out gamely, and we
plunged into the forest. It was not long before we
were entangled in difficulties. Windfallen timber
blocked us in, whichever way we turned, and we
spent exciting hours in climbing up and jumping
down among stockades, moats, and circumvallations
such as civilian quadrupeds are not often required to
encounter. They would scramble, packs and all, over
logs of such corpulence that when their forefeet had
made the passage their bellies rested on the round.
A convulsive spasm would bring the hind-legs over,
and they would stand for a moment gazing eagerly
at me with an air of asking "What now?"

I looked anxiously for blazes, scanning each old
scar with my glasses in the hope of finding it to be
of human origin; but always without avail. It was
near sundown, and I was beginning to think of working down hill to the nearest cañon where I might
find forage and water before the light failed me,
when at last I came upon the trail and we cheerfully
marched straight ahead. The only obstructions now
were occasional newly fallen trees, and these we
could generally circumnavigate by breaking through

patches of stubborn buck-brush or affectionate manzanita.

In the twilight we tramped industriously along for
two or three miles, the trail descending rapidly and
leaving the fir-belt for an open forest of sugar pines,
yellow pines, and at last cedars. About dark we entered an old clearing beyond which ran the good
grey road. I identified the place as being our goal,
the site of Gentry's Saw-Mill. The mill itself has long
vanished, but the name and a few ancient planks remain to remind an oblivious world that it has been.

A quarter of a mile down the road we found water,
and I camped among sugar pines and dogwood, the
blossoms of the latter hardly yet withered at this
altitude of 6000 feet.

The feed for the animals was scanty and undesirable, but some equine magnifico who had lately
dined hard by had left a considerable quantity of
prime oat hay by the roadside, and this, with a few
handfuls of onions and potatoes which I contributed
from my own supplies, provided them with a supper
of unusual attractiveness.

All that remained for the next day was a commonplace tramp of five dusty miles down the road to the
point where, at the foot of El Capitan, it converges
with the other two roads into Yosemite, — that from
El Portal by which travellers over the railway now
enter the valley, and the old stage-road from Raymond
and Wawona by which they used to arrive (often
in hysterics) in days of more leisure and less luxury.

Lunching at noon by El Capitan bridge, a friendly soul who was resting for the midday hour from his work on the road, the terrifying dust of which is being at last suppressed by a just if procrastinate government, and of whom I asked the news of the ten days during which I had been out of range of news and newspapers, inquired whether I had heard about the North Pole. In some alarm I asked him, "What?" and then learned that while I had been on my puny travels tidings had come that the greatest of geographical feats had been accomplished, and that the North Pole, the desire, the defier, and the death of many dauntless men, had been at last conquered, and, in a manner of speaking, was no more.

CHAPTER VIII

THE FORESTS OF THE YOSEMITE REGION

THE coniferous forests of the Yosemite Park, and of the Sierra in general, surpass all others of their kind in America, or indeed in the world, not only in the size and beauty of the trees, but in the number of species assembled together, and the grandeur of the mountains they are growing on." So says Mr. Muir; and among those who have travelled through the sublime woodlands of which he speaks there will be no dissenting voice from that high praise.

In the valley itself the timber, fine as it is, is an incidental adornment, a feature subordinate to cliffs and waterfalls. When one is sight-seeing the mind naturally focuses upon the principal objects, and takes no account of accessories, beyond observing, perhaps, that they obstruct the view. But a forest is not a sight, and the forest frame of mind is not a wide-eyed-wondering frame of mind, but is made up of innumerable small and quiet sensations, incidents, and reminiscences. Its glades and glooms, its trees and flowers, its stealing airs and rivulets, even its sounds, are the ingredients of a calm and peaceful mood; and whenever I find myself leaving the great valley, with its varied wonders and beauties, and entering the un-mixed forest, I experience a feeling of comforting ease, and relax like a man returning home at evening to walk in his garden. I know all these things and like them; and I feel that they know and like me too.

I suppose this sensation, which no doubt many people experience, might be traced to a scientific psy-chological source. Unless I am mistaken, learned men tell us that the branch of our race which peo-pled Northern Europe migrated thither from Central Asia, consuming in their interrupted journeys a long period of time. I imagine the region through which they moved like a slowly spreading wave to have been at that time a region, generally speaking, of forests; and it seems reasonable to think that in the course of their long wanderings the *wildeslust* as well as the *wanderlust* would enter deeply into the spirits of our sires, to break out in us in what we call spring fever, and treat blindly with sarsaparilla or more wisely with camping-trips. Be that as it may, every good man loves the woodland, and even if our con-cerns keep us all our lives out of our heritage, we hope to lie down at last under the quiet benediction of slow-moving branches.

The stately beauty and perfection of the trees that compose this forest are very impressive to the trav-eller; and when one sees from every summit and open-ing its illimitable rise and fall, mountain beyond mountain, range beyond range, fading into the wistful blue distance, then one recognizes the literal truth of Mr. Muir's statement quoted at the beginning of this chapter.

The regularity with which the various species of conifer appear at certain altitudes is a matter of unfailing interest to the tree-lover. Species succeeds species in orderly procession, each of them marked by special beauties, and all merging harmoniously like the colors of the spectrum. At the lower limit of the pine-belt comes the Digger pine (*Pinus sabiniana*), also called bull-pine and piñon- or nut-pine. (The usual mild anarchy that exists among the popular names of natural objects has full play in the case of the coniferæ, and in common speech the names " bull," " pitch," "silver," "red," "yellow," and so forth, are generally applied in an indiscriminate and misleading manner.)

This outpost of the pines begins to occur, in the Yosemite latitude, at about six hundred feet of elevation, and is noticed by travellers on the railway to El Portal almost as soon as the foothills are reached after leaving the San Joaquin Valley at Merced. It is always to me a somewhat uncomfortable and unpine-like tree, more suggestive of the arid Australian flora than of our lusty occidental types. In shape it is loose and spindling, and the foliage, though long and well-tempered, is so sparse as to give the tree almost a dying appearance. The straggling branches have a thin-blooded look, and cast a grey, anæmic shade that scarcely mitigates the stroke of the California sun.

In comparison with the sturdy vigor of the family it is just what one might expect to find on the torrid foot-hill slopes which it mainly inhabits, where vitality is drained away by a sun of semi-desert power, and the rainfall is barely sufficient to support tree-life.

Yet it has a pallid grace of its own, and the languid, transparent shapes impart an individual character to the landscape, somewhat akin to that which the yucca palm gives to the Mojave region. The handsome oval cones are only exceeded in size by those of *Pinus coulteri* and *Pinus lambertiana*, and contain edible nuts that provide the Indians of the locality with a relief from the overworked acorn. In the aggressive tusks which guard them we seem to see the beginning of the quarrelsome traits that mark the purely desert growths.

Next in order appears the pine which preponderates on the floor of the Yosemite Valley, the yellow pine, or pitch pine (*Pinus ponderosa*). It begins to mingle with the *sabiniana* at about two thousand feet of elevation, and continues in its common form up to about five thousand feet. This type exhibits the pine characteristics of symmetry and shapeliness at their best. No other tree is so perfect in its slender tapering form, and it keeps this perfection remarkably even in old age. The bark, of a dull buffy color, is arranged in large irregular plates like alligator skin; the foliage is long and of a brilliant dark green, growing in fine star-like bursts that well indicate the vigor of the species. In the midst of these tassels of foliage the bright brown staminate blossoms make a lively contrast in early summer, and later the cones are set, usually in twos, but sometimes as many as six in a generous cluster. The lower main branches of old trees are particularly picturesque, reaching outward and downward in lines that are at once graceful and elastic, and full of fine Japanese drawing.

In the sheltered valley this tree grows in perfection, and succeeds in fulfilling Ruskin's somewhat arbitrary statement regarding the pine in general, — "Thrust a rod from its last shoot down the stem — it shall point to the centre of the earth as long as the tree lives." The largest specimen I have found is growing about the middle of the valley, close to the Ford road, and measures twenty-three and a half feet in circumference at five feet above the ground. The industrious Yosemite woodpeckers find the thick plates of bark well adapted to their housekeeping methods, and the grey squirrels levy ample toll upon the plentiful cones. The ground under the trees is littered with the cores in amazing numbers, and one would think that every grove must support a tenement-house population of invisible squirrels.

Overlapping the common yellow pine in some places but not everywhere, comes what may be called a mountain type of the same species, known as the Jeffrey variety. It is usually of less height but greater spread of limbs, with redder and more broken bark and much larger cones. This versatile and adventurous pine inhabits a wide range of altitude, and has a way of turning up in all manner of unlikely places. Wherever conditions of life are hardest, there it sees its opportunity, and like Mark Tapley "comes out strong" under discouragement. On wind-swept granite pavements, which the trees proper to the altitude decline with thanks, there the Jeffrey appears, takes a wrestler's grip, and holds on like a bull-dog. One of these trees has rooted itself on the topmost round of the Sentinel Dome, and there romps joyously about in the terrific wind that rushes continually over that exposed spot, its branches and foliage streaming out horizontally like a stormy oriflamme of war. Whenever I see it I think of

> " Einar Tamberskelver, bare
> To the winds his golden hair," —

and a magnificent Saga of the Pine it is that he sings.

On the long promontories that stretch out into the Mono plains on the eastern side of the Sierra, this brave pine marches out green and sturdy among the bleached and wizened desert growths. Wherever you find it, it is always heartening and cheerful in bearing, an entire contrast to the misanthropical juniper that often grows with it. The one chooses the starkest places because they suit its own dour temper; the other out of pure *joie de vivre* and love of fighting.

The Douglas spruce (*Pseudotsuga taxifolia*) is the most limited in vertical range of all the Sierra conifers. It dislikes extremes of heat and cold, and shows everywhere the preference for shade and moisture which makes it the preëminent tree of the Oregon and Washington forests. It begins to appear at about thirty-five hundred feet, growing freely on the talus-piles of the southern side of the valley under the shadow of the wall. Its upper limit of growth in this latitude is about fifty-five hundred feet, and the handsomest specimens are usually found at the higher elevations. In youth it is a poetic tree, child-like and dainty, and in full growth I find it peculiarly attractive by the contrast of the dark, rugged stem with the flowing grace of the sprays of foliage that play in sunny zephyrs or droop in the surging mists of waterfalls. When the young leaves first open they are of a vivid yellow-green that gives the tree a particularly lively look, like a Christmas tree dressed with lighted candles. The cones are small but numerous, growing often in clusters that are as graceful and fragrant as hops.

When one looks down upon a Douglas spruce from some cliff under which it is growing, the distinctiveness of its structure is beautifully displayed. The foliage flows down in hair-like tresses from the branchlets, which stand out in fine lines as clearly as if drawn on a plan. I have often found it a fascinating sight to watch from above the play of branch and leaf-spray in a gentle wind, when the whip-like branches shine like veins of silver on the ground-work of waving, weaving foliage.

The unquestioned king of the pines, as apart from the firs and spruces, is the sugar pine (*Pinus lambertiana*). There are very few trees of this species in the Yosemite Valley, where it is at its lowest limit, about four thousand feet. From this altitude it continues upwards to almost seven thousand feet, royally conspicuous even among the splendid forest of yellow pine, Douglas spruce, silver fir and cedar which mixes with it. The shaft is a fine example of tree architecture, round, true, and taper, and over two hundred feet in height when full grown. The color under oblique or level sunlight is a true imperial purple, the finely netted bark reflecting the light with a dull, healthy polish like buck-horn. At midday it has become a shaded spire of smoke-tones, and I have seen it by red sunset light kindle into an intensity of color that was glorious almost to the point of solemnity.

The foliage of the sugar pine gives a particular impression of grace and lightness. It is short, arranged five leaves in a fascicle, and clothes the tree with starry sprays which form a lovely foil to the vigorous stem and the lean, far-reaching branches. As for the cones, they are amazing revelations of Nature's opulence, and of her love for her favorite tree-family. Generally about sixteen inches in length, sometimes as much as twenty or even more, they express a royal generosity, whether pendent like ornaments from the tips of the branches or tossed in careless profusion on the forest floor. As they hang ripening in the brilliant sunshine of midsummer they drip with crystal gum and glance with prismatic colors.

When I have found one of these green cones fallen prematurely through some mischance from its high place, I have been thankful that the Sierra squirrels do not "take after" those questionable monkeys whose alleged practice of pelting explorers with cocoanuts made a deep impression on my young imagination. The pleasure of camping and travelling in these forests would be seriously disturbed if one needed to be on the watch for aerial torpedoes of three or four pounds' weight which might be quietly launched from a height of one or two hundred feet.

When one lies awake at early dawn beneath these trees, while the lithe arms are traced in sooty blackness against the brightening sky, they seem to express a wonderful power and nobility. The mast-like stem shoots up with magnificent stateliness; and often some tall and aged tree, barren almost to its top, will there produce a crown of branches that stream out with every gesture of freedom, compliance, hopefulness, or severity; and I will confess that I have even found my breath quicken as I drank in the vigor and beauty of their lines.

Scattered throughout the belt which contains the sugar pine, yellow pine, and Douglas spruce is the cedar (*Libocedrus decurrens*), commonly called the incense cedar. In color and foliage it is a noble tree. The bark is a warm, lustrous brown of fine texture, which one may strip off in silky ribbons. It detaches easily from the tree in plank-like shards, and furnished the Indians of the region with the material for the picturesque huts (o'chums) which they used to inhabit before a too generous civilization enriched them with its packing-cases and coal-oil cans. The foliage is particularly handsome, richly carved and fronded, and of a deep glossy olive color.

In perfection of symmetry the young cedar is remarkable even among so shapely a race as the coniferæ. It forms a pure geometrical cone with a height of about twice its base-diameter, and is so thickly clad with foliage as to appear almost solid. As it approaches full development, it opens robustly to the sun and shows the marked feature of the species, the larger limbs growing squarely out and then straight up in vigorous attitudes, like the bent arms of an athlete. In late summer the tree is thickly powdered over with the small vase-like seed-vessels, which as they ripen add an autumn tinge to the ferny olive of the foliage, and enable the trees to lighten the sombre forest with tones of cheerful color.

At about the altitude of the Yosemite Valley the white silver fir (*Abies concolor*) appears, and soon after, the red silver fir (*Abies magnifica*). A few of the former may be found in the valley, growing along the southern side ; but the true fir-zone lies at from six thousand to nine thousand feet,. and it is only there that the most splendid features of the two great firs are revealed. There they form often an unbroken belt, expressing the very noblest of tree beauty, and not inferior, in my estimation, even to the Sequoias. In fact, if I were called upon to choose the one among the conifers that I would live and die by, I should choose the red silver fir, with no fear of ever wearying of its sublime companionship.

Both trees are perfect parables of order. In youth, especially, they surpass every other tree in charm and regularity of construction, both as regards their outline and the marvellous perfection of branch and foliage. The fine smooth arms, set in regular formation, divide and re-divide again and again, *ad infinitum*, weaving at last into a maze of exquisitely symmetrical twigs and branchlets. To look up at the young tree from any point of the circumference is to behold a bewildering succession of these intricate and delicate branchings, dwindling away less and less, and shimmering with finely broken sunlight until the tree seems to perform that feat which Hamlet vainly desired to achieve, and literally to "melt, thaw and resolve itself into a dew."

Both the firs attain a majestic growth, and often reach a height of over two hundred feet with a girth of from twenty to twenty-five or even thirty feet. The bark of the mature white fir is a dark ashy grey, and of the red, a dusky purple; both alike rugged and deeply furrowed. The two species, though hardly distinguishable from each other in general appearance, are easily known by their foliage, that of the white being set in flat, lateral rows, while the shorter

and thicker leaves of the red stand up on end like fur,
or a magnificent sort of plush. A branch of red fir is
truly a superb object both in color and line. It sweeps
out with a joyful vigor that carries one's very heart
with it ; the branchlets spread and sub-divide with intricate precision, fanning out at the extremity of the
branch into a rounded curve that is like the spreading of a wave on a gentle beach. The foliage, darkly,
healthily green, stands up in the manner of grass,
tray above tray, and every fan is edged with a silvery
froth or effervescence by the fresh young growth.
One branch of it would furnish a room with beauty.

The cone of the red fir is worthy of such a tree, —
a generous cylinder with a color and surface of
peachy richness, distilling rare balsam and exhaling
an almost spirituous fragrance. It is from six to eight
inches high and half as wide, built up of a large
number of flaky scales that are stained at their bases
with crimson and purple. The white fir cone is exactly similar, but about one half the dimensions of
the other.

I shall not easily forget one summer afternoon in
the Wawona forest when I sat down to rest by a little spring, hidden among flowery brush and musky-
smelling fern. Alders and white-flowered dogwood
grew along the gully which the spring supplied with
a little thread of water that crept quietly away
through thickets of ceanothus and azalea. Spiring a
hundred feet above the lesser trees there rose close
beside me a young silver fir. It might have been fifty

or sixty years old, and was at the very crisis of its youthful beauty. It seemed as if it could not yesterday have been so transcendent, nor could such perfection last until to-morrow, but that I had chanced upon it at the culminating moment of its life, as at the blossoming of some glorious orchid. Like a young goddess at her bridal, it stood divinely beautiful, shimmering in a mist of transparent silver just tinged with ethereal green. I watched it with delight; and as the sun declined, his serene rays enveloped the tree in a baptism of light, revealing new mazes and mysteries of loveliness. I felt almost as though I had violated a sanctuary, and fancied that the Angel of the Trees was incorporated and made manifest for the moment in a revelation of immortal glory.

The delightful essayist, Mr. A. C. Benson, refers somewhere to the feeling we are apt to experience in entering suddenly a place of trees or flowers, of some silent action having been in progress which we have interrupted, and which is suspended while we remain. I felt it that day. Once before, years ago, in a high and lonely spot near the southern end of the Sierra, I came upon a great company of white, gleaming lilies. There were hundreds, perhaps thousands, of them, and every one of the shining host, as it seemed, was endowed with the same unearthly perfectness as my silver fir. I remember that I stopped and half drew back, with the same abashed feeling of having unwittingly strayed into a place where some heavenly work or play had been performing but had ceased at my entrance. There was not a movement, nor a sound; it seemed as if the pure creatures waited for my withdrawal. Even the sunshine seemed to pause on the multitude of white flower-faces that were turned towards me. When I think of it now I can feel again the listening silence and the trance-like stillness of the scene.

Contrasting clearly with the firs and mingling here and there among them grows the sturdy mountain pine (*Pinus monticola*). It, too, is a giant, but of a different humor, powerful more than graceful, and expressive of a rugged, mountainous strength. It begins to appear at about eighty-five hundred feet of altitude, and continues up to nearly the limit of tree-growth: a noticeable tree, widely branching for a pine, with bark of a fine rust-red color that seems well suited to its hardy strength. The foliage is airy and sensitive and resembles that of the sugar pine; which is true also of the dainty tapering cone, though it is not one fourth the size of that king of cones. Taken in conjunction with the stalwart appearance of the body of the tree, the foliage and cone of this species exhibit a grace and lightness that are very welcome and beautiful in the high regions which it inhabits, where one expects only stubborn attributes.

There is a fine tract of mountain pine growing almost unmixed with other trees on the southeasterly flank of Clouds' Rest. Standing as they do there on a wide and even slope, they display their robust character to the best effect. But handsome as the tree is, I have never quite felt for it the love which other pines inspire in me. I seem to feel something of discord and unfriendliness in it. I do not remember, however, that I have ever made camp among them, and I think that when I do I shall come to understand them better.

The fir-belt is also the territory of the tamarack or lodge-pole-pine (*Pinus contorta*, var. *murrayana*),[1] although the species ranges far below and above it. This is the least distinguished in appearance of all the pine family, and much the most common, forming vast homogeneous tracts of forest on the rugged plateaus of granite that form a great part of the western slope of the Sierra. It is a wiry, grey-coated little pine, quite unimposing, rarely growing to more than seventy-five feet of height and three or four of thickness, but full of friendly virtues and good-comradeship. The foliage is short and stiff, with a tufty, foxtail style of growth, the branchlets all curving upward in a cheerful manner. The cone is small and ordinary, hardly distinguishable while green on the tree; but when it ripens the fertile scales open widely while the base remains closed, giving it the appearance of a brown rosette. In summer the tree is quite showy with the numerous Indian-red blossoms, which burn like points of flame at the heart of every tuft of foliage; and at night, when their color

[1] Some botanists distinguish the *murrayana* variety as a separate species, under the name of *Pinus murrayana*.

is enhanced by red camp-fire light, the tree makes a strangely brilliant appearance.

Although the tamarack is not a striking tree in the single specimen, it impresses one strongly in the vast forests where the species multiplies upon itself unbroken, and one sees everywhere the same type reproduced to infinity. The commonplace grey stems rising closely on all sides become as momentous as an army; and standing at some opening surrounded by the illimitable sweep of the forest, one receives a deep impression of the power and conquering majesty of the tree-kingdoms.

Every species has its own well-marked character. For sheer loveliness the hemlock spruce, or mountain hemlock (*Tsuga mertensiana*), bears away the palm. Appearing on northward-facing slopes at a little above eight thousand feet, it comes to perfection at from one to two thousand feet higher, where it meets the dwarf pine, the dweller on the threshold. The pure grace of the tree would render it remarkable anywhere; in these high and lonely altitudes it is doubly delightful. The young trees are especially beautiful, quite fountain-like in their flow of line, and exquisitely feminine and yielding. The foliage is of a dark, earnest green, redeemed from sombreness by the silver of the young growth. Trailing branches sweep to the ground, and all the outer branchlets, and even the spiry tips of the trees, droop with a fragile grace. The small, dainty cones are borne in great profusion on the downward-hanging sprays, enhancing the richness of the tree with their clusters of dark purple.

As it comes to full growth, which may be over a hundred feet of height and five of diameter, it takes on the ruggedness of bearing that belongs to age and stormy experiences. Under the scouring of a thousand tempests the bark tans to red and the lower limbs disappear, leaving perhaps thirty feet of clean, bright stem bare of branches. In general appearance the tree then much resembles the red fir, but on a near approach the two species are easily distinguishable by the foliage, girlishly graceful in the spruce, firmly masculine in the fir.

The juniper (*Juniperus occidentalis*) is a kind of churlish relative of the conifers, entirely unlike them and opposed in every line and instinct to their aspiring characteristics. For purposes of contrast, nothing could be better than this squat, Japanese-wrestler looking tree, which one encounters growing in the most difficult and uncomfortable places at all elevations from six thousand to ten thousand feet. Wherever storms career most wildly, and on glacial pavements and ledges of the most uncompromising granite where nothing else beside lichens and mosses cares to grow, there this embittered tree exists, — it cannot be said to flourish, — and hugs itself into a morose longevity, like a miser living to a hundred on crusts. High up on wind-swept angles of mountain you may see them peering and leering down at you, their stumpy trunks twisted into alarming contortions.

The bark of the juniper is of a cinnamon-red color, similar to that of the cedar, and frays out, like it, into silky, fibrous ribbons. The stem has often the appearance of being formed of three or four thick coils that have become welded together, and sometimes a grey knee or elbow, in appearance like disintegrating bone, pushes through the red skin in a grisly, skeleton-like manner.

Even the foliage is of a sour, sage-green hue, with a harsh look and an acrimonious odor ; and the fruit, a grey misanthropical berry of violent flavor, is just what one would expect, and seems well suited to be the food of the Clarke crow, whose imprecations most often resound from this inhospitable tree. Still, one must respect the juniper for its hardiness and self-reliance. And there is even humor in the tree, of an ugly, surreptitious kind: as there is, too, in the Clarke crow, who is himself a sort of Mephistopheles. The element of humor is otherwise not much in evidence in this high region, where Nature still has rough work to do, and handles her severest tools.

Junipers may often be found whose trunks are no higher than their circumference at base ; and this is not always, though it is sometimes, due to the tree having been broken off, or having died, at the top. The trunks of perfectly grown trees sometimes taper so rapidly that the height may not be more than three times the diameter. This is due to the unusual size of the branches, the lowest of which are often one fourth the thickness of the stem, and push out only two or three feet above the ground; so that the shape of the tree, so far as any shape can be assigned to a growth so unconventional and irregular, is that of a heavy, flattened bush, much wider than it is high.

Last of all and least of all, yet in a way finest of all the Sierra tree-clans, comes the dwarf pine (*Pinus albicaulis*). It begins to mix among the hemlocks, mountain pines, and tamaracks at about ten thousand feet, and, leaving them all behind, struggles on alone up to the limit of tree-life, which in this latitude is about twelve thousand feet. This is never a handsome tree, but grows always in a straggling, shapeless fashion, branching out in poles that lean at all angles, more like a brush growth than a tree. The branchlets are usually thick and not dividing, curving up in somewhat unpleasing lines, clothed with tufty foliage. The leaves are of an attractive, clean, light green, and in late summer provide a strong contrast of color for the almost black cones which protrude from the tasselled ends of the twigs. With its pale grey bark this tree is particularly suggestive of the hard white sunlight and the shrouding snow between which its life is about equally divided.

On the high plateaus about timber-line this pine, never much over twenty feet in height, suffers dwarfing to a remarkable degree. In exposed places such as the Tuolumne Pass, I have found it spreading horizontally only a foot or two above the ground, crushed flat by the weight of the snow that lies on it through fully half the year. The foliage becomes felted into a springy mattress on which I have lain in the greatest luxury of ease that is possible to conceive. Sometimes these shrubby masses are found as smooth as a table, the surface being kept planed down by the bitter winds that sweep continually over them. In places where they are less constantly exposed to wind, they struggle hard to assert something of the tree shape to which they are entitled, but they achieve at best a doubtful compromise. I have a weird little tree of this species, not quite seven inches high, which has all the airs of a veteran of centuries. The trunk is four inches high and half an inch through, thickening at the head into a ganglion of knotty branches, all gnarls, scars, and elbows, on which grows a towzled thatch of foliage. It was in Cathedral Pass that I came upon this fierce little kobold, and I liked the mettlesome look of him so much that I pulled him up, root and all, and brought him away in my pocket.

Under one form or other this indomitable pine edges its way up to the uttermost limit that Nature will allow, twisting and dodging about, shielding its devoted head as best it may, only bent upon carrying forward the standard. When I think of the glorious winters they experience, the low, crouching skies, the whirling storms, the deadly frosts, the hurricanes of spring and autumn, and the thrashing rains and tearing lightnings of summer, I love and admire and envy them beyond all the others, fine as they all are. I think that when next I am among them I must

make a point of removing one of them carefully to
the very top of the mountain that it is so set upon
climbing, and planting it there, live or die, as a re-
ward.

On the eastern face of the Sierra, which is much
steeper than the western, the species are naturally
somewhat more mingled, though they preserve of
course the same relative positions. Two other species occur on this side. High up near timber-line
comes the limber pine (*Pinus flexilis*). It may easily
be mistaken at first sight for the tamarack, with
which it is often associated. It is remarkable that this
pine has never spread to the western slope, where
the conditions of tree-growth are in general more
favorable than on the eastern. No doubt some shade
of distinction in the quality of climate or soil, that is
too fine for us but not for this hardy pine to observe,
rules the point.

The level plains and the foothills of the Mono
Lake region are the home of the nut-pine or piñon-
pine (*Pinus monophylla*). This is a quite different
tree from the nut-pine of the western slope, although,
like it, it occupies the lowest range of elevation. It
is a bushy, uninteresting-looking tree, from fifteen to
thirty feet high, and about one foot in average thickness of trunk. The leaves, which are short and spiny,
are set singly on the stiff twigs, whereas the foliage
of all the other Sierra species is arranged in fascicles
of two, three, or five leaves. It is the small, egg-
shaped cone of this tree that supplies the piñon-nut,

a thing of small importance to most of us, but a true staff of life to the Indians of the region.

The trees which I have briefly described, *plus* the great Sequoia, spoken of in the succeeding chapter, are all the species of coniferæ that the visitor to the Yosemite region of the Sierra Nevada is likely to encounter, though a few other kinds occur in distant parts of the range, and still others occupy the Coast Range and the seaboard. There is one, the knob-cone pine (*Pinus attenuata*), which grows at low elevations on the western slope, but does not come under the observation of travellers by any of the ordinary roads into the Yosemite. The nearest point to the valley where I am aware of this species growing is Texas Hill, some twelve miles west of El Portal, on the North Fork of the Merced River. Its foliage is long, and set in loose, airy tassels, and the tree has the peculiarity of keeping its cones unopened year after year, so that the seeds are released only when the tree falls. I have cones of this species that were gathered years ago, and remain to-day as closely sealed, and as solid and heavy, as on the day they were gathered.

There is a small tree which is found growing in a few places in the Yosemite region, particularly on the stage-road from El Portal to the valley, against which the traveller who may be interested in the coniferous trees should be put on his guard. In its general appearance, and particularly in its foliage, it bears a very close resemblance to the coniferæ, but it does not belong to the family. It is the California nutmeg-tree (*Tumion californica*), — a slender, spiry tree with grey bark, and leaves much like those of the white fir, but stronger, and prickly to an offensive degree. It bears a smooth egg-shaped fruit, about an inch and a half long, which contains a nut that is considered edible in Japan, where also the tree is indigenous. Both fruit and foliage are charged with an acrid, astringent juice. The wood is exceedingly tough, and would be useful if the tree were more common.

The Sierra forest of all but the highest altitudes is the home of a goodly array of brush plants. Of them all, none is more charming than the chamœbatia, a shrubby, foot-high plant, with a pretty, ferny leaf and a white flower like that of the strawberry. It grows freely in the Wawona locality, at an elevation of five or six thousand feet, covering the ground with a continuous carpet that is easily mistaken at a distance for grass. The stems, matted and wiry, offer a pleasant resistance to the foot, and often as I brushed through them, I could have fancied myself again among the heather had it not been for the pungent scent, like that of witch-hazel, which the plant exhales profusely. Washing up everywhere around the bases of the great trees it gives an ideal completeness to the forest landscape, and all my recollections of the splendid timber-belt which it inhabits are pervaded with the healthful odor of this friendly mountaineer.

CHAPTER IX

THE GREAT SEQUOIAS

To the lover of trees it is something of an epoch when he enters for the first time the vast virgin forest of the Sierra Nevada, and his eye roves, with that perfect satisfaction of which delight is only the froth and lightest part, so deep and pure is it, through and over the countless, countless, countless myriads of the stateliest members of the noblest family of trees (for so I rank the conifers). From every rise and opening he sees with exultation still, and only, the unbroken forest: mountains, yes, leagues and ranges of mountains, as far as sight will carry, dimming away into blue infinity, still clad with the illimitable forest.

For one loves the forest much as one loves (or should love) one's fellow men ; that is to say, both in the aggregate and in particular. The tree-lover, surveying a great expanse of forest, is transported in fancy over among the objects of his love. He walks in spirit among them, and responds to every individual of all the beloved host. He perceives by a mysterious sense their distinguishing beauties : the noble sweep of this one's broad and level boughs ; how that one is braided and shagged with moss ; and where that other is rubbed and polished by the horns of deer. He sees and hears, a day's march away, the tinkling monologue of the tiny forest rivulet, creeping and stealing about the mossy roots of his friends; yes, and lights his "little friendship fire" by it, pulls out and eats his bread and cheese and reads his pocket Thoreau by it. So that the quality of a forest, like that of mercy, may be said to be "twice blest."

If then to the tree-lover it be a privilege to enter the great Sierra forest, he will feel almost as if he engaged in a rite when he stands for the first time in a grove of the great Sequoias. If among the innumerable hosts of the pines and firs he finds true companionship and feels joy and thankfulness, among the great Sequoias he will receive a more solemn message and return a deeper response. In them we have what seems to be the last survival of the Heroic Age of the earth, that misty dawn of time when all things, man perhaps included, reached the gigantic in stature and age. They are an anachronism, an unaccountable oversight, a kind of arboreal Rip Van Winkles; and it is a high distinction of California that it is her exhilarating air and her sun-drenched soil that have tempted these patriarchs to remain with us in our feebler times, instead of joining their old companions "the monsters of the Prime" upon some lustier and more youthful planet.

The spectator experiences among the Sequoias something, I imagine, of the awe of an Egyptian who should be introduced into one of those vast temple-halls where he would see ranged on all sides the colossal figures of the king-gods of his race ; the awe of unutterable age, irresistible power, and infinite repose. It might be called, in fact, an Egyptian impression that is made by these mighty trees upon the beholder. They are Egyptian in their size and ponderous immobility ; in their color, which is Egyptian red in the stems of mature trees, while the great limbs far overhead are of a strange flesh-bronze hue, round, smooth, and gleaming, like Cleopatra's arm ; and I cannot conceive of a more magnificently Egyptian portal to some vast hall or temple than would be formed by using two of these huge trunks for pillars with another laid crosswise for lintel.

In some other regards the impressiveness of the Sequoias is of an architectural kind. This is due partly to the incomparable shaft of the tree, which seems to stand column-like upon the earth rather than to be rooted in it. No limbs break the perfect roundness for half the tree's height, only there may be thrown out at one or two points a branchlet, hardly more than a twig, of delicate foliage, bursting through the covering of bark like a spurt of green smoke in token of the energy within. These sprays of lace-like foliage are a noticeable characteristic, and add an unexpected grace and playfulness to the dignity of the tree. Even very old trees will break out in these flights of fancy, like youthful old gentlemen who are fond of sporting loud neckties.

The massiveness of the trunk is relieved also by a fluting of the bark which is often so regular as to be remarkable, and which adds to the architectural suggestion. This fluting is often broken up near the base of the tree into a network of tracery, the bark running into a maze of niches and foliations that is richly Gothic and beautiful. As one stands in the dream-like silence of these groves of ancient trees, the solemnity of their enormous age and size, together with the grace and fancifulness of this carved and fretted ornamentation, combine to produce a cathedral mood of quietude and receptiveness.

The two species of Sequoia, the *S. gigantea* of the Sierra Nevada and the *S. sempervirens* of the Coast Range, seem to be the last survivors of a genus which was once widely distributed, and which can be traced by its fossil remains throughout Europe and Asia, as well as North America. It is remarkable and fortunate, in view of that fact, that there is no indication of decline in the surviving members of the family : rather the contrary, for on all hands the sons of the giants are arising in stalwart thousands to carry on the royal line.

Impressive as it is to gaze upon these trees that have kept note, as it were, of human history from its beginnings, it is at least equally so to imagine the course of time with which a sequoia that is now beginning its career may run parallel. On a moderate comparison the Sequoia may look to live fifty years for every year of human life. What a kaleidoscope of fantastic pictures rises in one's mind when one thinks of the possible conditions of life and society

five hundred or a thousand years hence! Yet the
Sequoias that are now foot-high seedlings will then
be only in what answers with us to youth or boyhood.
He would be a desperately bold American or Briton
who should calmly forecast the world-position of his
fatherland ten centuries hence, when these infant
trees will hardly be approaching maturity; while if
one attempts to look forward through the mists of
the slow-passing centuries during which they will be
standing in unchanging strength, the phantasmagoria becomes too wild for the mind even to wish to
dwell upon. It is solemn enough, standing here, to
conjure up the long drama of the past which these
great trees have seen enacted; but it is almost heart-
shaking to reflect how unimaginably strange will be
the course of history of which the tree that grows
from the papery seed which I shake out of last year's
cone may be the impassive spectator.

The young Sequoias for the first few years of their
life show no mark of their royal nature, but crook and
twist about in a particularly ambitionless manner.
Their branchlets sprawl out in a short-sleeved, lanky
fashion, and their heads, as if they were young
anthropophagi, "do grow beneath their shoulders."
Standing generally in tangled clumps and thickets,
they have an awkward, schoolboyish air, very different from that of the pines and firs, which even while
crowded in their nurseries show their lineage in an
aristocratic trimness.

But after a few decades blood begins to tell. The

Sequoia becomes conscious of his destiny, and, answering the inward urge, makes for the skies in a climbing, high-hearted fashion that is fine to behold. Still the family likeness does not shine out clearly as they stand mixed in the general forest of the conifers, all of high birth. They keep yet the thin whip-like branchlets that grow irregularly from foot to crown, by now bare of foliage, but furred instead with yellow moss. By the time he reaches his first century of age, however, being then perhaps eighty feet high, the young tree sloughs his skin and begins to take on the noble color and habit that mark him at a glance as a sequoia, of the old nobility of the tree-creation. He "mews his mighty youth," and casting off with it the undistinguished features of childhood, the trunk, clean, bright, and tapering, which is to bear aloft his massive head through the long procession of the centuries, stands revealed.

By five hundred years the full color is taken, the taper has widened to a slight curve at the foot, and the pointed reticulation of the bark is noticeable. The characteristic shape is now fully marked, — the head a sugar-loaf cone, remarkable in its regularity of outline, and the trunk a steadfast column of shining red. Thenceforward they go from strength to strength, ever more glorious and excellent. Their deep-rifted bark clothes them with dignity and age; the great limbs, mossed and lichened, stand out oak-like above and athwart the pines and firs whose dainty tops spire a hundred feet into the air; and still higher, their sumptuous tops are built up in dense bosses of corded foliage. In those high places they bear their multitudinous cones, pendent singly or in twos or threes on stout, bracted stems ; till in due time the sun ripens them and coaxes them to open their tight-locked caskets, and the wind, careful old forester, winnows out the flaky seeds and sows them in generous broadcast over the warm forest floor.

When the first millennium is reached the general shape is unchanged, only that the curve at the base is wider, and the lowest limbs are becoming weary and trend downward from the weight of the snows of uncounted winters. Another age passes, and Atlas has planted his feet still wider as he bears up the enormous weight. The symmetry is broken : he has now entered upon middle age, and his individual features are stamped upon him. You may tell Achilles from Agamemnon, and Ajax from Menelaus. Here a thunder-bolt has ploughed a heavy furrow, and that fearful scar marks the place where a tree-like arm was torn away.

A second millennium passes, with thirty more generations of the sons of men, and the Sequoia shows no change but that he has settled at his base into a convex curve, which may be reversed as it enters the ground ; — a very beautiful form, exhibiting the perfect combination of strength with grace which marks this noblest of trees. From then onward Time has no dominion over him, and the passage of centuries does but mark his inexhaustible fertility and power.

A thunder-storm in this forest is a memorable experience, and one which even enhances the awe of the great Sequoias. I was roaming one day about the lower Mariposa Grove, commiserating the tourists who were driven swiftly past on schedule, when I became aware of that quickening of the senses which one feels before a heavy storm. I had noticed an unusual quietness of the population of the brush, the birds going about their concerns with a serious air that was quaint and amusing. The robins in particular foraged silently through the silent woods, passing and repassing one another alternately with that comical appearance of being pushed in jerks from behind, like perambulators. The snow-bird's soliloquies were carried on under his breath : even the jay, impudent and voluble in general beyond the wont of birds, refrained himself and pursued his persecutions almost politely.

Suddenly a heavy wind roared overhead, from which the firs and pines recoiled ; but I noticed that the Sequoias stood stately and unmoving, only their foliage was roughly tossed. Then came a wild slither of lightning, then a crash of thunder, and then the rain came tearing down. For ten minutes the elements were in a paroxysm ; lightning thrust and parried, thunder roared incoherent applause, and the rain fell savagely as if it were flung by an angry hand. Then with another burst of wind, that filled the air with sodden tassels of foliage, the storm passed on, and the only sound was that of a hundred rills trilling tiny carillons. When one considers how many times the thunderbolts must have hurtled about these ancient trees it is astonishing that one of them is left standing.

The roots of the Sequoia are noticeably short, astonishingly so for the enormous growth of the tree. The base, as one sees by trees that have fallen, consists of a number of short, stout tentacles, and there is no taproot. It seems a miracle that the tree can stand, and still more that it can grow. It must draw directly from the air almost all its sustenance; but then, what air it is! I suppose there flows in the Sequoia's mighty veins not the common earth-drawn sap of trees, but some celestial ichor, such, in fact, as would account for their almost immortality. For the Sequoia is all but imperishable, even when overthrown, and trees that can be proved to have lain for two or three hundred years show no trace of decay. Only two things can destroy them: Fire, the rapacious element, and Man, the rapacious pygmy. Even fire the Sequoias can almost defy, wrapped in their panoply of bark of two feet thickness; but man, — there is something pathetic in the fact that nothing can stand against him. He is put, as it were, on his honor, and a weak defence it has proved when weighed against gold. It is a shocking thing to see any tree cut down, — a sycamore, an oak, an elm: that living green tower, with all its halls and chambers and galleries of whispering delight, which Nature with her great patience has laboriously built up to perfectness, — to see it so briefly, so trivially, all undone. But the Sequoias, one wonders that any one could bring himself to put axe or saw to them. However, although the individual man is not to be trusted when he smells gold, he yet, in the aggregate, has sensibilities under his pachydermatous rind, and can be prevailed upon not to murder his grandfather: so that practically all the great trees are now protected, and have been enclosed in national parks.

Since my first acquaintance with the Sequoias I had cherished a desire to sleep with them. Many times I had enjoyed the hospitality of the friendly guardian of the Mariposa Grove, and had slept beside the generous fires that cheer his lonely cabin. But I had a particular wish to camp for a night under that tree of trees, the Grizzly Giant; and one clear summer night I shouldered my blankets, and with a frugal half-breakfast in my pocket marched off to keep my tryst.

The forest through which I tramped was dimly lighted by a half moon. The stars burned with a still, high radiance. Straight, silent, and vast the Sequoias stood up into the night, while the moonlight crept quietly over the open spaces of the forest and flecked with ghostly silver the deep-channelled stems of the immemorial trees. It was very quiet; only now and then a bird twittered, or there was a sudden rush in the undergrowth, or the distant hooting of an owl. The dead firs and pines, white and barkless, gleamed pale in the moonlight, and the innumerable pinnacles of the conifers rose on all sides into a sky of clear darkness. A cool breeze met and passed me, and the foliage played for a moment like the restless fingers of a dreaming child, then was again intensely still.

I wandered on and on in a mood of vagrant reverie, often stopping to listen to the flawless silence and to delight in the ageless virginity of the earth. Suddenly I came upon the giant, a vast black shape, rising unexpectedly close before me. The moon chanced to be shining just behind him, and made a soft and wistful glory among the forest of branchlets, twigs, and foliage of his head. The mighty shadow was projected toward me, the arms traced in grotesque shapes, intensely black, upon the open glade that surrounds this king of trees. (How many times, I wondered, had that shadow passed, with the solemn imperceptibility of Time itself, over that silver earth-dial?) Huge as its bulk is by day, it was multiplied tenfold in the peering light of night, when details were obscured and only size and shape were left to possess the imagination.

To me that night it was an awful tree. I felt much as one might who, walking among the grey ruins of Babylon or Thebes, should come upon some primeval man, ancient as the very earth, who, overlooked by death, had lived on from age to age, and might now live to the last day of Time. Its great arms were uplifted as if in serene adoration, and all around, the lesser forest stood aloof, like the worshippers in an outer temple - court, while this, their high - priest, communed alone. And when I reflected that on the night before the Crucifixion when Christ stood in Pilate's hall, this tree was standing much as it stood now, lifting its arms, ancient even then, to the hushed sky, it seemed to take on in truth the character of an unconscious intercessor, a representative of the awe-stricken mute creation.

In the presence of this monument of Time, one's thoughts take the same solemn and peaceful tone that comes upon them under a wide, starry sky; a solemnity so deep that it rises into joy; a peace so absolute that it touches the infinite goodness. It is a place in which to go over one's favorite poems; for instance, Milton's "Ode on Time." The great lines incorporate themselves, and stand about one like the vast columns of the trees, forming a temple in which the mind ranges more freely than is its wont, with a clearer vision and a deeper understanding.

I rolled myself in my blankets and tried to sleep, intending to be up at daybreak to enjoy the hour before sunrise. But it was long before I became unconscious. Lying at the foot of the giant I gazed up, and felt more than saw the great bole sweep up majestically into the night. The moon, now setting, touched with soft brightness the limbs that stood out far above me. The silence was profound, and the owl's hooting echoed around the forest as if it were an empty room. All the old solemnity of night was upon the world, and the riddle of the Sphinx was

still unanswered. This old tree should know something of it, but the wisdom of perhaps threescore centuries is locked in its iron heart.

At last I fell asleep, but soon was awake again.
The moon was down, and the velvet blackness was
pierced by innumerable stars. The Great Bear glinted
between the bossy plumes of the firs and pines whose
spires outlined the mat of open sky. Two sharp re-
ports broke the stillness; it was the sound of the
breaking and fall of a great limb from some lord of
the forest. I slept and awoke, and slept and awoke,
again and again. A faint silvery blueness grew in the
east, a pure, dark light. The stars receded, lingered,
glimmered, and died. The cold dawn-wind blew (that
unearthly wind, eternally as fresh as on the first
morning of creation), and the hearse-like plumes
tossed for a moment, then again were still. The first
bird awoke and twittered faintly; another answered,
and another, and then many, with rustlings in the
low brush close to where I lay. A squirrel barked.
It was a quarter to four.

I rose and wandered through the forest, eating my
unprodigal breakfast with zest and sober exhilaration,
and drinking a draught of icy water at the spring.
The owl hooted once, reporting his night-watch
ended. Soon the sun touched hesitatingly the topmost arm of the great tree; then, in a moment, the
whole head kindled and blazed like a beacon above
the lower forest.

As I take my way slowly back, the day is spreading and flowing, mile on mile, mountain on mountain, lifting the shadows as the sun lifts vapor. The trail of the old grey coyote is fresh on my own last night's tracks. Slinking and grinning and slanting he goes, lean and wary, to his rock-pile den. Glancing back I wave farewell to the giant, whose sunlit face glows cheerfully down at me in reply. The greatest arm, turned to the south, carries a magnificent suggestion of prowess and adventure, the long tapering shaft at its end standing out and up like the bowsprit of a tall Indiaman. What, old hero, is thy heart still so young? Adios! adios!

And here let me say that I for one hope that when the great clock that tells the centuries marks the last of the Grizzly Giant's innumerable days, nothing will be done to avert his fall. It would be a sort of impiety, an indecency almost; as if one should prop and bolster up a dead king on his throne to be gazed at. He is too illustrious a thing for us to meddle with; and surely he will have earned his rest.

No conception whatever of the majesty of the great Sequoias is possible to be conveyed by statements of their size. What idea of Charlemagne would you get from his tailor's measurements? I myself always feel that, as illustrating the wonders or beauties of Nature, processions and columns of figures (like the well-meant but desolating chatter of cathedral-guides) detract from instead of adding to one's vital impression. Speaking in terms of phrenology, I imagine that the "bump" — excuse the inept word — of veneration, for instance, would be found retreated into the farthest possible corner of the cranium from the one that revels in mathematics. When they told me that the Washington tree was a hundred and one feet in circumference and two hundred and forty-five feet high, I only found that I suffered a painful relapse, for I had just been seeing it infinitely greater. One needs to see such things with the spirit: the mind sees them about one tenth of their size. Lying down at the foot of the pedestal of Grizzly Giant for an hour of enchantment, seeing and hearing invisible and inaudible things, a plague on the gowk who blunders into my dream with "Half a million feet of lumber in that tree, sir!" Is that all there is in that tree? I assure you, my friend, I can see vastly more in it if you will but leave me alone.

But then, I am driven to suppose that I am singular in my feeling for the great Sequoias as objects of dignity and glory. I cannot understand how, otherwise, the childish, unsightly, and paltry practice could have arisen, and could continue apparently without objection, of labelling them with the names of cities, states, and persons. I confess I am amazed at the general obliviousness to the disgrace of the thing, even among cultivated persons, and am compelled to believe that the people who come to view them have no real appreciation of their grandeur, but look upon them merely with a Barnum eye as curiosities and "big things." Their admiration for the Sequoias seems to be of a commonplace and commercial kind, for there is no recognition of the anomaly involved in disfiguring objects of such nobility and beauty with hideous tin labels. I am sure that to every thoughtful person the charm and impressiveness of these groves of ageless trees are greatly spoiled by this fatuous and trivial proceeding ; and I can but hope that some day the authorities will cease to consider the Sequoia forests as freak museums, but with a better appreciation of their value and splendor will order the removal of these ignoble defacements.

A feature of the Sequoias which always interested me is the strange manner in which they receive and hold the earliest and last light of the day. Often I have watched some great tree at sunset, as it stood facing the altar-fire of the west. Slowly the red light left its base, passed up the columnar trunk, and burned in a lingering glow on the many - branched head ; then reluctantly, imperceptibly, faded and died. But for an hour still, and long after the lesser forest had sunk into darkness, the Sequoia's high smooth bole held the light, and shone as if by its own preëminent glory and strength.

Often, too, when I have been camped beneath them, waking when the dawn had hardly begun to brighten the eastern sky I have seen their tops begin to flush and glow above the sleeping pines and firs : like prophets who caught and rejoiced in the vision before the rest. And when a sunset or sunrise redder than usual has lighted them, I have seen their color deepen to a hue that was almost ominous, and they have burned with a volcanic intensity, the violence of which, in conjunction with the majesty of their demeanor, affects one in much the same manner as the reading of a great drama.

The Sequoias grow always upon hill-sides, and thus their beauty of proportion may be fully observed. There is nothing to obscure them unless it be the growth of intervening conifers, for no other families of trees inhabit the Sequoia zone: only bushes and low-growing shrubs share these choice places with gardens of flowers and meadowlets of greenest grass. Little trickles of water steal and tinkle almost unseen in their narrow channels, and spread here and there into small pools that charmingly mirror sky, and foliage, and fluted bole.

Around these basins the bird-life of the forest loves to centre, peopling the hazels, currants, and chinquapins with multitudinous voices. Hither come the deer to drink, and mixed with their dainty tracks you may often find the big round pads of the mountain-lion and the coyote's smaller footprints. The summer air swarms with floating and darting insects, playing out their day-lives with tragic unconcern amid the monumental trees. As I sat ruminating at the foot of one of these oldest-born of Time, I could not be unconscious of the irony of man's small moralizings: but then, length of mortal days is a vain criterion, for, after all, with a bit of iron one could soon undo the growth of a hundred generations of his own measure of time.

It is not surprising that one should experience a

certain soberness of feeling in bidding farewell to the great Sequoias. Shall I (I asked myself) look down from some immortal sphere upon these trees a millennium hence, and will they still be standing as I see them now, changelessly watching the unchanging sky? It may well be; I deeply hope it will be. As I pondered the question, and looked with love and reverence upon them, the massy tasselled plumes, moving softly in the sunny air, seemed to say, "Yes, we shall meet again." And with a long, backward gaze I answered, "Yes, yes; surely, surely; farewell, farewell."

CHAPTER X

THE WAWONA COUNTRY

W AWONA lies sequestered at the bottom of a bowl of forested mountains. The South Fork of the Merced River emerges here from its narrow cañon into a gentle expanse of meadow, through which it dreams a short course before it is again caught and imprisoned by its rough gaoler.

All forest places are places of rest, and meadows and valleys are even more so in their nature. Wawona combines them all, and indeed I do not know a more idyllic spot. Seclusion is in the very air, and its beauty is of that gentle and perfect quality that does not so much command one's admiration as it quietly captivates one's heart. Even its wonders, the great Sequoias, are friendly wonders, living and personal ; and I for one always feel that if Yosemite has the greater glory, Wawona has the deeper charm.

Wawona, moreover, is classic ground. Fifty years ago, when California was very young indeed, Clark's Station, as the place was then called, was the centre of the life of the Sierra backwoods. The lower creeks and reaches of the Merced as much as anywhere were the scene of the boisterous epic which Bret Harte has immortalized. The names on the map of the region are themselves a directory of picturesque episodes; and along every creek are relics of the Golden Age, — old shafts, and uncouth mounds of dirt; some of them tokens of "prospects" only, to which such a name as "Nary Red" might have appertained; others which you look at with respect as your driver, pointing with his whip up some cheerless cañon, remarks that "a half a million was took out of that there gully. Who by? Old man Dougan, him as they call Hard Luck Sime, down to Mariposa. Where's the hard luck come in? Well, you see it was this-a-way: —" and there follows a chapter from life, a wild but fully credible story, beginning in toil and hardy bouts with Fortune, traversing a spectacular region of glitter and riot, and ending in poverty and crime.

Here and there you may come upon an abandoned *arrastra*, the ponderous water-wheel warped and sagging under a long alternation of dry and wet seasons. In one such spot which I encountered the ghosts of the Fifties came crowding thickly around me. There lay the great stones still beside the pit, the rotting cables still holding by a rough mortising of lead. The rough-hewn timbers were pulling apart, and shed out, when one tapped them, a yellow, lifeless dust from a thousand worm-holes. Skeletons of chairs, scraps of looking-glass, and such débris lay about. Mixed with mouldy rags and sacking were shreds of a woman's finery, frills and ruffles; and nailed to one of the empty window-frames, half hidden by giant lupines, was a little bird-cage made of slips of cedar, from which the mocking-bird or meadow-lark that once made it his unwilling home had long been emancipated. Adjoining the house was an enclosure of half-an-acre or so. The fence lay on the ground, and in the long grass two rose-bushes and a lilac were slowly strangling to death. The place seemed to hold the memory of some very human action; and I was fain to hope that the cage and roses might mark it as an innocent drama of love and children's laughter.

A few miles east of Wawona stands a sightly peak, Mount Raymond, which carries its snow well into midsummer, although it rises only forty-five hundred feet above the warm and sheltered valley. One sunny day of early summer, leaving my camp in the upper Mariposa Grove of Sequoias, I started leisurely on the easy ascent. Making due east and keeping to the ridge which here forms the watershed between the Merced and San Joaquin river systems, I entered the forest, which here is principally of the red and white firs. The delightful company of these my favorite trees constantly drew me into side explorations, and delayed me into a saunter. Now and then faint traces of a blazed trail appeared, but they were so doubtful and elusive that it was fortunate that there was no difficulty in keeping my direction without their help. The trail, moreover, was often blocked by fallen trees that made ramparts of a man's height, and offered the choice of climbing convex walls or making circuits which were often prolonged by unexpected entanglements. On the north side of the ridge the mountain ran steeply down in an unbroken slope of thirty-five hundred feet to the river ; on the south the slope was not so sharp and was somewhat more broken.

The timber thinned out to a scantier growth as I left the fir-belt. The brush grew sparse and stunted, and patches of snow lay in the hollows. Then rather suddenly I passed out on to bare rock, and straight ahead rose the peak, glistening white and cold. Here it became necessary to keep to the southern slope, for the snow on the other was treacherously soft and shot down at an uncomfortable angle, unbroken but for a few black bolts of rock or decapitated stumps of pine.

Heavy blue clouds were massing in the south and east, and the wind suddenly blew from the same quarter in heavy gusts and with a bitter rawness. I began to have a suspicion that a storm was brewing, but was unprepared for the abruptness with which it came. It was late in the season for snow to fall, so that I was surprised to see the first warning flakes. It was not a comfortable spot in which to stand even a short siege. The storm was coming from the south, and I was consequently exposed to its full force, as I had no desire to bivouac on the steep, soft snowfield of the northern slope, especially in the strong wind that was now blowing. I was well above the main forest belt, and the few isolated Jeffrey pines within reach were too small to afford any shelter. Under the circumstances I judged it best to hurry forward and try to reach some favorable spot before the height of the storm was upon me. I was not far from the summit, and after twenty minutes of pretty violent exertion I arrived there, and found partial shelter under the topmost point of the mountain.

Almost on the moment the storm reached me, and I was enveloped in a swirl of snow that charged at me horizontally with dizzying velocity. I flattened myself against the friendly rock that bore the brunt of the onset, and debated what was best to do. I had no fear that the storm would last longer than an hour or two at most, but I was heated with the exertion of the climb, and in the icy temperature, and without opportunity of exercise, I began to chill at an alarming rate. Fortunately, after the first blinding gusts had spent themselves the snow lightened somewhat, and I seized the moment to make a sortie in search of dry brushwood for a fire, if I could succeed in kindling one. Fifty yards down the mountain side I found what I wanted, and gathering an armful, I scurried back to shelter. In a few minutes, by manœuvring with coat and sombrero I had cherished a few twigs into burning, but then had much ado to keep them together in the furious wind. No sooner would I get them fairly ablaze than they would be contemptuously swept off by the wind into the snow-filled air. Again and again I tried, with numbing fingers, while my little stock of matches decreased until I began to lose hope. But at last I got a good blaze, and then, after another sally for larger fuel, I sat down in great exhilaration.

If I had set my mind to imagine the best possible experience for the day I could not have succeeded half so well. Here I was, on the summit of my first Sierra peak thus far, snugly sheltered in the middle of a snowstorm which could not, I felt sure, last long enough to become dangerous ; with a noble fire roaring defiance to the screaming wind, lion against panther ; only midday, with time and daylight to spare ; lunch in pocket, with pipe and tobacco to follow. It was huge luck. I even found in my pocket a small quantity of tea. Quickly I filled my tin cup with snow, and in a few minutes had a cup of boiling amber fragrance ready to accompany my bread and cheese. Then I sat down, back to my stout rock and feet to the fire, and rejoiced in the hurly-burly, while my pipe-bowl glowed almost to the point of incandescence with the intense combustion.

All the time the storm came whirling past, the flakes shooting by level in the heavy gusts as if they had been fired from a gun, and I sat and watched them stream away into the void. My bivouac was on the very edge of the snow-slope, so that the fire gradually ate out a semicircle of the snow-cliff opposite me. It was an inspiriting experience. I was in a little world alone with the lusty elements, sometimes unable to see for ten feet around me : above and all about was nothing but the whirling white void, from which and into which the crowding snowflakes hurried, seeming to push upon one another in their silent haste to be gone.

Suddenly it brightened, and the leaden dullness changed to a silvery glow like that we used to see on the faces of angels in our childhood's dreams. In another minute, while I wondered at the quickness of the change, a thin sunlight washed past me, and I looked up to see the last flakes pelting like black specks across the glistening haze of the sky. Two minutes more, and the storm was over; I could see its rearguard, blue and misty, crossing the gorge to the north. Then through the snowy veil the eastern peaks began to glimmer, whitely glorious under a broken sky. Looking over the sharp northern edge of the mountain, Wawona Meadows glinted greenly in the sun, and all around on west, north, and east, the wide slopes, blue and dark with timber, were flecked with rapid cloud-shadows.

Opposite gleamed the stony forehead of Wawona Dome, and midway between, but far below, the river ran palely. I fancied I could hear its hoarse cry. Turning to the south I saw a high, summery sky in which floated bands of little fleecy clouds, and along the horizon lay the faint fawn-color stretches of the valley of the San Joaquin. Nearer, in middle distance, the forest rose higher and higher, running in wavy undulations; and nearer yet it was broken by patches of gleaming snow. From a hollow not five miles away smoke was rising: alas, it marked a lumber-camp.

Though the storm was over the icy wind still blew, and more clouds were massing. By the middle of the afternoon I began the return, keeping closer to the spine of the mountain than in the ascent. The exhilaration of the wild day and place gave every sense its widest range, and I noted a hundred new things with quickened sympathy and perception, — the quaint, inch-high blossoms that trembled in the wind in such myriads that I almost believed I could catch the sound of their vibrations; the angry cry of a hawk fighting his way up wind and compelled to veer and temporize, against his haughty nature; the snow-bird that, blown almost into my face, chirped a humorous apology as he swung over the ridge; the Douglas squirrel who disputed my passing under his tree so viciously that he nearly barked himself off from it and was fain to scramble up again ignominiously; the dwarf oaks just in bud as though it were February, that splayed over the rocky ground; the dwarf currants that seemed grotesquely trying to clamber away out of sight in an awkward, high-legged fashion, like spiders; and the young ten and twelve foot firs still lying full length and half buried under last winter's snow, that sprang up and threw handfuls of frozen snow in my face when I gave them a lift to free them from their covering. And so back again to my camp among the great Sequoias, standing dark and stately against the fire-strewn sky of a still stormy sunset.

On another expedition I made in the Wawona region, I had the company of a lanky Stanford undergraduate who was recuperating at the hotel from the stress of examinations. He was an ardent fisherman, and kindled at my mention of a chain of lakes, of high repute among the craft, that lie up on the high plateau over which the Chilnualna Creek flows to its leap into the chasm that opens beside Wawona Dome. It was early in the summer, and the trail beyond the head of the fall had not been travelled that season ; but that was all the better. So one morning Longshanks and I marched out upon our quest.

For a mile or two our way led through the valley forest, where now, at the end of May, every sunny opening was enamelled with fresh grass and flashed blue with lupines, lilac with cyclamens, and white with the large nemophila of the Sierra. Half an hour brought us to the foot of the falls of the Chilnualna. These falls have been so much eclipsed in fame by the great waterfalls of the Yosemite that they are not as much celebrated as their fantastic beauty deserves. Without depreciating the glories of the mighty cataracts of the valley, I acknowledge that I for one find these less renowned falls equally beautiful and more romantic. The lower part of the descent is an alternation of boisterous cascades and most seductive pools. The wayward water every moment changes its mood, now plunging in bursts of hissing spray, now circling in pools where you wonder whether some slender naiad has not slipped under the rocking water at your approach, and fancy that it is the lifting and spreading of her hair that makes that misty gloom in the emerald depths. The rocks are of a formation which breaks vertically, and the water shoulders its

way among the obstructing cubes and pillars in a
thousand bolts of white thunder.

From the foot of the fall the trail starts away on a
wide détour, tacking in legs and reaches that seem
to take a most unreasonable circuit. Fresh tracks of
deer accompanied us, and presently we came upon a
group of three quietly feeding seventy or eighty
yards ahead. For a few moments they did not see us;
then as our scent reached them their heads went up
all on the same instant, as if by clockwork, and they
stood gazing with nervous curiosity, but with no sign
of fear. After a long pause two of them went on grazing, while the other from time to time scratched his
ear with a quaint expression, apparently wondering
how much longer we meant to stand staring at nothing. When at last we started toward them they
allowed us to approach within forty yards, before
with two or three great bounds they vanished into
the friendly chaparral.

A hundred varieties of blossoming plants called for
notice and admiration: delicate iris, that embodiment
of French elegance, pushed up through the foot-high
thicket of chamœbatia; the manzanita was still in
bloom at this elevation, though by now its "little
apples" were ripening in the valley below; and many
varieties of compositæ shone up with friendly re-
minders of English meadows dappled with daisies
and dandelions. Moreover, there was continual interest in noting the exits and the entrances of the
various conifers as we climbed, species after species

appearing, waxing to its prime, waning, and disappearing.

The traveller in these mountains is generally in the company of three kinds of coniferous trees,—the one through whose proper belt he happens to be passing, the one next below, and the one next above it. One comes after a time to feel the changes subjectively, as it were, becoming aware of the tree-company one is in, almost without noticing it, by a kind of intuitive knowledge. Without consciously observing the transition I find myself in a yellow pine mood, or a red fir mood, or a tamarack mood, my senses automatically taking their key from the nature of the prevailing forest. When I enter the tamaracks, for instance, the background of my mind shifts into a sense of the illimitable, weird, and dreary: the yellow pines affect me with laziness and easy views of life: among the Sequoias my consciousness takes on an Egyptian tinge: I am somehow aware of crocodiles and ibises. Every species has its own atmosphere, and I fancy that if I were led blindfolded through the Sierra forests, I should know at any time in what companionship of trees I was by recognition of their familiar spirit. Only the Jeffrey variety of *P. ponderosa* is somewhat of an uncertain quantity, the wanderer of the family, making erratic appearances, sometimes high up on the upper margin of the firs, and again picketed out among the sun-bleached brush of the Mono plains.

Coming after a climb of twenty-five hundred feet

to the head of the fall, we stopped to view the leap of the water. The stream comes down from the rough plateau of its upper course in a series of steps, runs for two hundred yards through a chain of pools and reaches, and then is drawn smoothly over a rounded lip into the dark and well-like gorge. Fifty feet down it breaks upon a ledge and rises in a great arc or wheel of water. As the still early sun shone obliquely upon it, the wild wind that ascended from the tumult of that black chasm stripped off every moment the edge of the whirling rim of water in vaporous rainbow-flames of red, and blue, and orange. It was a solemn and beautiful sight, such a vision as might have found a place in the sublime narrative of a Hebrew prophet. I have never seen elsewhere anything of the kind, and the recollection of the hurrying flames playing upon the wheel of racing water comes over me now with a sense of having witnessed some deep parable, of which, though I saw the outward glory, I had been too gross to understand the meaning.

While I still stood fascinated, I noticed a white butterfly come drifting over the gulf. It hung fluttering for a moment, then with a curious leisureliness circled down, following the falling water, until it passed out of my sight. In a few moments the little insect reappeared, sailing up out of the tumult with a superb carelessness of flight. I watched the frail emblem of the soul with a feeling which I did not trouble to analyze, recognizing unconsciously, perhaps, some allegory of innocence and victory.

Our trail lay now over a rough plateau thinly timbered with pines whose foliage was of a black and serious cast. These wind-swept table-lands, open to every weather, have often a peculiarly stark and forbidding appearance; the blazing sun and withering winds seem to have bleached the very granite to a shivering complexion, and the shallow draws and contours, marked with dark timber, are drawn in lines like the creases in an aged face. At about seven thousand feet we began to enter snow, which as we climbed soon became continuous and left us only scanty blazes by which to follow the trail. Now our mild troubles began. The snow, though fairly deep, was well softened, and every few minutes one or other of us would go through, often up to the knees. Uphill travelling of this kind is very slow and tiring work, every step up and forward being discounted by several inches of slipping down and backward, and the strain is severe and continuous. However, the exertion put us in good state to withstand our constantly increasing wetness as we plunged more and more frequently through the thin crust which had frozen during the night and was now every moment softening under the sun.

One thing that we had not taken into account was the likelihood of having to ford the stream; and as usual, the unexpected happened. The Chilnualna Creek is but a trifling affair as rivers go, and in later summer no doubt one could easily jump it. But as we stood on the snowy bank and cogitated our problem, we faced a swirling stream of icy water, varying from knee-deep to waist-deep, and of considerable strength of current. A cast up and down the bank for some distance convinced us that the trail had made no mistake as to the best place to ford the creek. As my companion put it with scholastic precision, the problem was simplified by the elimination of the factor of place, leaving only the points of time and method to be solved.

Here Longshanks had the advantage of me. His bodily configuration was arranged upon the useful principle of a pair of compasses, and, moreover, he was fresh from the Olympic "stunts" with which college students temper the academic severities. On the other side of the stream a large rounded boulder offered the chance of escaping a ducking to an athlete who might expect to reach it by vaulting. Longshanks provided himself with a pine branch, straight and long, and pluckily made the essay. Sound muscle and judgment stood him in good stead. He sailed through the air; his pole struck in a friendly crevice, and he landed neatly on the boulder and jumped down, exhorting me to follow without delay. I felt morally sure that I could not make the leap with the best vaulting-pole that ever grew; but the stream had to be crossed somehow, so I plucked up heart, found a likely looking pole, and vaulted my best. My pole, through some concealed defect, broke in halves as my weight came on it, and I fell in midstream in four feet of water. Luckily I came down

on my feet and was able by a strong effort to brace
myself against the current, and so splashed ashore.

After all, I was not much worse off, for I had been
wet to the knees for an hour already. It was almost
a satisfaction to be so completely soaked: I could
now go ahead, careless of snow and water alike.
When in the course of a mile or two we had to cross
again, I simply marched through and squelched on
my way, Longshanks enviously searching for narrower places while I assured him that the wide cross-
ings were much the best, for the water had only
reached to my equator.

Mile after mile we ploughed along, perspiring
heartily and occasionally glissading down snow-slopes.
The blazes grew more and more casual, until we
began to think we might have passed our lakes,
hidden in some fold of the snowy landscape. Suddenly we came upon the first of them,— Grouse Lake,
a dark steel mirror of water, intensely still, almost an
exact circle in shape, and ringed with banks of pure
unsullied snow. From the further side came the sharp
bark of a fox, and a troop of snow-birds flitted silently
across and away. It was delightfully Arctic and solitary, and we gazed with admiration and with something of the elation of discoverers. At least it was
certain that the identical beauty that lay under our
eyes had not been seen by any other, for we were the
first to travel the trail since the winter snows (which
usually fall on the Sierra at this altitude by mid-
October) had shut the lonely lakelet up to its eight
months' solitude.

It was well past midday, and eight hours since we had had breakfast, so here we decided to eat our meal. Longshanks ate his in a fisherman's hurry, for he was itching to cast his flies on that untried water. My own first necessity was to forage for firewood and to pray that my block of matches, which I had stuck in my hat-band to dry, might fulfil their office. As one after another of them gave up the ghost with only a fizz and an evil smell, though I tried every variety of friction, from the drawling scratch of the experienced cowboy to the vicious jerk of the tenderfoot, my opinion of the inventor of that curious survival, the California block-match, sank very low.

At last a fortunate twist brought success, and I soon had a royal fire blazing. Then, peeling, I hung my sodden clothes on the brush within range of the generous heat, and proceeded with my own lunch, wondering the while how many centuries might have elapsed since last a gentleman had dined there "in the buff," and surrounded by snow. My clothes steamed away industriously, but I had time to smoke a pipe before they were reasonably dry. I could see Longshanks working his way round the lake, casting assiduously but apparently without success; and by the time I was dressed he rejoined me, fishless indeed, but excited with the vision of an incomparable trout that he had seen swim out from under a submerged log, leaving, so he declared, a wake like a Mississippi steamer.

We knew that two other lakes lay a short distance

to the west, and struck across country to find them, over snow that was deeper and firmer. A mile brought us to Crescent Lake, which we found to be a larger sheet of water, of irregular shape, still partly covered with melting ice. At the northern end of the lake we came upon a forlorn little cabin, half buried in a snow-drift. Entering, we stood upon a floor of clear ice : the melting of the snow had flooded the house, and the hard packed earth floor had held the water, which had frozen solid. Bones of deer and of other game were littered about the room, one end of which was cumbered with the wreck of a huge chimney of rock. I had heard of the place : it was once the summer home of Jim Duncan, a man whose fame as a hunter still lingers in the memory of old Sierra back-woodsmen.

The exploits of Jim Duncan, if they ever come to be written, will make a stirring tale. It is known that he kept a diary of his hunting-trips, but I learned from his sister that when questioned about it during his last illness, he denied its existence, and it is supposed that he had destroyed it. Mr. Galen Clark,[1] now of Yosemite but anciently of Clark's Station (the present Wawona), who was intimate with him, tells me that Duncan at one time intended publishing this

[1] Since this was written Mr. Clark has passed away, high in the regard of all who knew him, and close upon the completion of his ninety-sixth year. His body lies in the little Yosemite cemetery, and in the Sequoia-shaded grave which, after the tranquil fashion of those Biblical patriarchs whom in simplicity of spirit he resembled, he had prepared for himself years ago.

diary, and with that view put it into the hands of
some acquaintance of his to edit and put in form for
the publisher. For some reason, which can hardly
have been that the subject-matter proved to be not
of sufficient interest, the editor-elect failed to fulfil his
office, and Mr. Clark supposes that Duncan, under
the influence of his disappointment, may have destroyed his manuscript.

The few facts regarding him which I have been
able to gather from his old companions in these
mountains are to the following effect: About the
year 1857 Duncan came up into the Sierra from
Visalia. It is likely that he was one of the many unsuccessful gold-hunters who about that time were
left stranded by the retiring wave of the gold excitement all up and down the foothill creeks and cañons
of the Sierra Nevada. His native state of Michi-
gan contributed her full quota of these defeated Ar-
gonauts. Duncan, for his part, forsaking the quest
of gold had declined upon pork, and in the year
named was roaming with a band of hogs among the
virgin pastures of the lower Sierra, after the manner
of those *Newtys of Pike* whom Clarence King has
immortalized in his delightful pages.

The course of his wanderings brought him to the
green meadows of Wawona (as now called), and here
his career as a bear-hunter began with a chance
encounter. Walking up one day from the meadows,
where he was camped, in the direction of the grove
of Sequoias (which had that same year been dis-

covered by Mr. Clark), Duncan met his first bear. He was carrying a combined rifle and shotgun, but he had at that time such a high estimation of the California grizzly that he forbore to fire. A few days later he had another encounter, this time at close range. Hurriedly firing a heavy charge of buckshot at the redoubtable foe he turned and ran for dear life without waiting to ascertain the result of his shot. On the third occasion he killed his game; and as time went on, and he and Bruin had frequent misunderstandings regarding pork, he began to match himself against his enemy with more confidence.

Those were the golden days of hunting in the Far West, and bears were incredibly plentiful. In one day of his early career Duncan killed five bears, a father, mother, and three well-grown cubs; and from that time he lost all fear, and settled into his stride as a hunter with a special mission for bear. As years passed, and notches multiplied on the stock of his old muzzle-loader, he set himself the task of an even hundred, or century, of bears. But it was not to be: he died some ten years ago without completing his task, but with an authentic record of between eighty and ninety bears to his credit. It may be that chagrin at his failure to reach the goal he had set himself was the cause of his destroying the diary to which I have referred.

Mild tourists to the Yosemite, where now a degenerate race of bears dwell under the protection of the incomprehensible laws which have banished their mutton, may denounce the killing of nearly a hundred bears by one man as slaughter. But in Duncan's time the boot was on the other leg; and as Longshanks and I stood and looked at his little cabin in this desolate and lonely spot, we paid sincere homage to the spirit of the departed pioneer.

As it was impossible to cast a line beyond the ring of half-submerged ice that encircled the lake, Longshanks gave up all idea of fishing; and the afternoon being well advanced we were fain also to abandon our intention of seeing Johnson Lake, and take the trail homeward. I was by this time comfortably warm and dry, and the thought of having to wade the stream again on our way back was highly provoking. In the hope that we might evade it we left the trail and made a wide cast to the north, which we figured should bring us in somewhere near the head of the fall. Without a compass or knowledge of the ground such calculations are open to a host of mischances. For one thing, it is not easy to estimate the arc of a circle in covering rough country, and for another, unexpected obstacles may make it impossible to keep even reasonably near to the proposed line of travel.

Progress was slow, for the snow was softer than it had been in the morning; but we floundered along, mile on mile, up and down, tobogganing helter-skelter down every practicable slope. In the exhilarating air even the uphill work was a sort of play. Whenever we heard the roar of the river sounding near us we took another cast, and flattered ourselves that we were outflanking the enemy. But as the hours and the miles passed it began to be a question how long this was to go on. Nature is hard to beat at the game of patience. Then we found ourselves facing the river once more. It was getting dusk and we decided to cross, neck or nothing; so it looked as if I, at any rate, was in for another bath of snow-water. Prospecting up and down the bank for the best place to tackle the annoying job, we espied a dead tree that had fallen at a steep slant partly across the stream, the further end overhanging a broken stump that leaned from the other side. Blessing our luck we swarmed up, and with a ten-foot drop landed on the stump and slid down on the other side.

The rest was plain sailing, for we were headed in the right direction and began to leave the snow behind as we came to lower levels. The way lay then over a wide expanse of granite, almost treeless, and curving in overlapping layers into seams and folds, along which ran arrowy brooks of water from the snows we had left. The sun had set behind rifted clouds, but on our left the high ridge of Buena Vista Peak suddenly flushed to almost crimson, culminating and sinking to ashy gray in a breath, as with a sigh of ineffable beauty.

We reached the head of the falls as the light was almost gone, and after a few minutes' rest plunged down the well-marked trail, swinging along at five miles an hour, sore of foot but with spirits unflagged. By nine o'clock we made the Wawona road, and half an hour later were at headquarters. We had been out fifteen hours, and had covered about twenty-five miles of pretty rough country, mainly over soft snow, and with a rise of forty-five hundred feet in altitude. Longshanks successfully dodged the enquiries of rival fishermen, and we turned in after an impressive supper, desperately tired but satisfied exceedingly.

Wawona Meadows themselves might be called the Sleepy Hollow of the West. It is the most peaceful place that I know in America, and comes near being the most idyllic spot I have seen anywhere (which is a considerable admission for an Englishman to make). Here is an unbroken meadow, green as heaven, a mile long, waving knee-high with all delicious grasses and threaded with brooklets of crystal water. It is surrounded with a rail-fence that rambles in and out and round about and hither and thither in that sauntering way that makes a rail-fence such a companionable thing, nearly as good as a hedge. Beyond the fence the forest rises on all sides, surging gloriously up, ridge above ridge, a most friendly and comfortable sight.

The meadows lie east and west. To the east stands Mount Raymond, and to the west Signal Mountain (known also as Devil's Peak), the culminating point of the Chowchillas. The South Fork of the Merced flows along the northern edge, breathing easier after its boisterous rush through the cañon; and beyond it the glistening mass of Bald Mountain shows like an elephant's forehead to centre the gaze. On the south lies a particularly admirable belt of forest, flowery and ferny to a degree, through which the short trail climbs up to the Sequoia groves. Yellow pines, sugar pines, firs, oaks, and cedars stand ranked in emulous perfection, with a first-storey undergrowth of ceanothus, dogwood, wild-rose, hazel, and gooseberry, and a ground-floor tangle of lilies white, lilies red, lilies grave, lilies gay, dwarf ceanothus with delicious little blossoms of sapphire blue, chamœbatia the blessed, and dozens more.

In the Wawona Meadows one may experience what used to be called, in a pretty old English phrase, "a charm of birds." Embroidered upon the tenor voice of the pines, the deeper whisper of the oaks, and the talking rustle of ferns and grasses are the meadow-lark's bubbling cascade, the wild cry of the flicker, and innumerable chucklings, carollings, and cacklings from songsters of greater or less degree. Platoons of blackbirds wheel about in rhythmic manœuvres, dropping now and then by one impulse out of sight, as if the ground had opened to receive them. Swallows dip and dive over the lake of herbage, breasting the green billows like swimmers, and exploiting all manner of flavorable insects. All the earth's children, animal and vegetable alike, are rampantly at work or play. Starry hosts of mimulus twinkle, wild strawberries hide and tantalize, buttercups and wild-roses perform their little alchemies of remembrance; gay young dandelions flash their gold like prodigals, and hoary old dandelions ("all flaxen

was his poll") stand pondering on the brevity of
life. And ever the shining waves of the grass go by
and away, to die in soundless surf on the forest edge.
The soft wind blows you little cool kisses, and when
for a moment it dies away, the pine incense rises hot
and spicy, with almost a spirituous pungency.

For an hour or so at midday silence reigns. The
birds retire to shady siestas: everything drowses,
except the tireless wind and the grass, and even they
move sleepily. Then some one, somewhere, gives the
word, "Come on!"—and in a moment the world
moves on again, whistling and playing pranks like a
schoolboy. Trailside company is distractingly plentiful: there are pipings and rustlings overhead, excited scamperings underfoot, underground soliloquies
of amphibious brooks, indecisions of butterflies, imminent perils of pendent bees, trepidations of liz-
ards, absurdities of inverted beetles, perturbations of
ants, exasperations of gnats with assassinations of the
same; and everywhere green laughter of leaf and
grey reverie of lichen.

The high land-cliff of Wawona Point rises on the
northern boundary of the upper grove of the Wawona Sequoias. From it one looks down nearly
three thousand feet into the gulf of forest, in the
midst of which the meadows lie like a sheltered lake.
I found it especially a noble station from which to
watch the sunrise. Only two miles to the east rises
Mount Raymond, and his peak is the first to kindle.
For a few moments the illumination seems to be

stationary ; then it spreads slowly down, turning the blue shaded snow-fields to glistering white. Then it catches and goldens the spiry tips of the fir-forest, and they seem to tremble with delight, striving up and thrilling with the fervor of life.

As the radiance comes flooding down, the needles of a sugar pine on the ridge between me and the sunrise flash and shimmer with white lances of light, and the great Sequoias smile out, one by one, with solemn, age-old joy. Wawona lies still sunk in a bowl of purple shadow, but the sun's brush lays wash below wash of gold on the mountain-side. Next the light catches the old white stump that stands on the point ; then it suddenly streams through the gorge below him, and paints a long triangle of yellow that pushes down and down, reaching and grasping, until in a few moments it comes to the edge of the meadows. The quiet is intense and unbroken but for the voice of the river, which throbs up from the void below and seems to echo back and reverberate from the very sky.

To south and west the level plain of the San Joaquin lies in long streaks of fawn and blue; blue where every slight inequality of ground spreads an island of shadow behind it. Farmers wake, horses stamp and rattle for their morning hay, roosters shout their insane defiances to creation, car - bells jangle, newsboys wrangle, bacon sizzles in kitchen and camp, and I go down to breakfast.

CHAPTER XI

THE law of Nature which is expressed in that overworked phrase, "the survival of the fittest," has had a complete, and from the point of view of the survivors themselves (who are naturally the best judges) a highly satisfactory, demonstration in the quick declension of the old Mexican population of California before the present lords of the Golden State. The transaction took place with the automatic certainty of all such natural processes, but also with a rapidity which entitles it to the attention due to a phenomenon. It was a summary clearing of the stage for the quick action of the Golden Drama.

Nature needs no apologist for her writs of ejection, and her outgoing tenants have no recourse or appeal. In this case they attempted none, but, generally speaking, sank away as quietly as the streams that dwindle and seep out of sight under the energetic Californian sun. "The hour had struck, and they must go." And go they did, rich and poor, gentle and simple alike, bowing with what grace they might to

> " The good old rule, the simple plan,
> That they should take who have the power
> And they should keep who can."

But I, for one, have always felt the injustice of the contempt in which the dispossessed Mexicans have been held by their heirs-at-law. No doubt, nothing succeeds like success, and nothing fails like failure; but then, the point of view governs all, and one can always conceive an aspect from which the conquered might contemn the conquerors. For myself, I own to a sympathetic regard for "the greasers," whom, in general, I have found singularly friendly and responsive; — a virtue which, it seems to me, is entitled to a high rating under the circumstances.

Scattered up and down the multitudinous cañons of the foothills where the Sierra Nevada sweeps out in fringes of winter green or summer ochre upon the great central valley of California, an unsuspected number of Mexicans have found congenial homes. As miners, shepherds, bee-men, or nondescripts they live in these sequestered places, performing at least as well as the rest of us the Symphony of the Quiet Life, which consists in such matters as "living content with small means, talking gently, acting frankly, bearing all cheerfully, doing all bravely, awaiting occasions, hurrying never."

Troops of children, often lovely as young arch-angels, whose dark eyes and shining tresses have often disquieted my tough bachelor heart with long-ing, play around these humble doors. Mandolins tinkle through long evenings after easy days, and the smoke of everlasting cigarettes mingles with low-toned laughter and murmured conversation in the most musical of languages. Standing outside the hurly-burly, these philosophical non-combatants find leisure for the quiet pleasures and family employments and courtesies which we deny ourselves, or think we are denied. They have not travelled so far from Eden as we have. Can we be sure that we who have come farther have not fared worse?

When the hottest part of the California summer day arrives, the boasted energy of the Anglo-Saxon sinks to zero. The sun-baked rocks and boulders shed out a violent, blistering heat; the white sands reflect the light like a mirror; the breeze grows listless, flutters, and dies away; the traveller grows listless too, and his affairs become less important than the necessity of turning aside for an hour's siesta in the shade.

That, at least, was my conclusion as midday approached, when a few years ago the course of my affairs took me a day's journey into one of the less frequented cañons of the Sierra foothills, — the San Timoteo. As I wished to return the same night, I had started early from the little town in the valley, and had ridden a good many miles before the heat of the day came on. My horse, moreover, needed water; so when my eyes, following a narrow track that led off to the right of the trail, fell upon a plank thrown over a gully which by the débris it contained gave notice of the proximity of a house or camp, I at once turned him into the little side-trail. Riding down into the gully and up the opposite side, I saw, fifty yards

farther on, a dwelling. It was the regulation " lone "
miner's cabin, — an object which under all its variations constitutes a type ; just as, under all his diver-
sities, does the "lone" miner himself. It stood, or
rather stooped, hunched together with that air of pre-
mature age which in three months settles upon struc-
tures whose builders have attached more importance
to haste and economy than to T-squares and sound
workmanship. A wall of rock of considerable height
rose near behind the house, forming a buttress or spur
of the main cañon wall. A few fair-sized live-oaks and
cottonwoods inhabited the little bench of land, an
acre or two in extent, which, naturally clear of brush,
offered itself as a desirable building site.

On a rough shelf attached to the house was a *batea*,
— the wooden pan or dish used by Mexican placer-
miners in the operation of " washing out" by hand.
A pick, an axe, and other such articles lay near by ;
a mattress was spread upon the ground in the shade
of a tree ; and if I needed other evidence of the owner's presence, the sound of music proceeding from the
half-open door, and smoke issuing from the chimney,
undoubtedly afforded it. Both the air played and the
instrument furnishing the music were familiar. The
air was *La Paloma*, a composition as distinctive of
Mexico as *Suwanee River* is of this country, or *The
Blue Bells of Scotland* of the land of Burns. The
instrument I recognized as one which was known
to me in my youthful musical enthusiasms as the
mouth-organ, but is now, I believe, more ambitiously

known as the harmonicon. I listened until the end of the tune, and was then about to ride up to the door when I heard a boy's voice speaking rapidly in Spanish, answered by a man in the same language; and a moment later the air was begun again by two performers together. I waited again until the verse was completed, and then dismounting walked up to the house. The musicians, after a short colloquy, were beginning still another performance of the same air, but ceased at my knock, and an old Mexican presented himself. I use the term old in the qualified sense in which, it seems to me, it applies to all Mexicans of over forty-five years' age; but he was strongly built, and his face was remarkably intelligent and pleasing, though wearing that expression of half melancholy passivity which seems to be a mark of his race.

I explained that I had expected to find water in the cañon but had failed to do so, and requested permission to water my horse at his spring.

"Surely, señor," and with grave politeness he led the way behind the house, and pointed out a small covered well.

"At your service; it will be three miles before you reach water, señor."

"You have lived here long?" I asked, for the sake of conversation.

"Yes, señor, it is five years since we came from Guadalajara. Do you know Guadalajara? It is a beautiful city, like the fine American cities, señor."

Attracted by his friendly communicativeness, I remarked upon the music I had heard and asked whether he had brought his family from Mexico with him.

"Yes, señor; but there is but one boy."

"Then your wife is dead?" I ventured to ask.

"Yes, señor, in Guadalajara."

"Gracias," he continued, in reply to my expression of sympathy; "but it is God's will, señor; it is not good to complain; and I have the boy, and we are very happy. He is not strong, but he is very good. And clever, señor! You should hear him play."

"Yes," I replied, "I heard him play."

"Ah! but that is nothing; he was but playing then to teach me to play, too. It will be fine music, señor, when I can play like he can."

We had been walking back toward the trail as we talked, and I now stood ready to mount and continue my journey, having given up the idea of resting there, fearing I should be an intruder.

"The sun is still hot, and there is little shade, señor," said my friendly Mexican. "Perhaps you would like to rest at the house?"

I willingly assented, and he led the way, first slipping the bridle from my horse and tying him in the shade of a tree.

On entering the house I saw a boy of perhaps fourteen years of age, lying on a roughly made cot. A glance showed that he was deformed, and a pair of home-made crutches in a corner stood mute witnesses to the fact. But his face was remarkably beautiful, the eyes, in particular, very animated and eloquent; and his smile the most radiant and affecting that I ever beheld. It seemed to take you at once into his confidence; to love you as if by nature; almost to kiss you, in its pure, spontaneous affection. It thrilled me, and thrills me now when I think of it. I can call it nothing but heavenly.

" The caballero will rest, Rafael," said his father.

"Si, señor," and the boy looked at me with that sweet, bright smile.

I love children. One does not usually think of a boy of fourteen as a child, in that sense; but Rafael in his weakness was a child, and a very appealing, responsive child; and Rafael's smile was an invitation to love him as a child. I sat down on a low box beside him and took one of his hands in mine. In the other hand he held his little instrument, playing it softly, under his breath; and whenever his eyes met mine or his father's it was always with the heavenly smile.

" Play, Rafaelito," said his father; " the caballero does not know how you can play."

The boy drew his hand from mine, and after a few preliminary chords launched into the most original and brilliant variations on the same air which I had heard him play before. It was astonishing to see him, and would have been almost weird but for the extraordinary beauty of his expression. He lay, rather than sat, facing the little window, which was somewhat high in the wall on the same side as the door, and looked toward the south. The sun shone clearly in upon the lad, broken by the blurred, flickering shadows cast by the slow-moving leaves of a cottonwood. His eyes were fixed upon the sky, and shone with the steady, calm radiance of the evening star; while in strange contrast his sunken chest rose and fell as he played, with the painful agitation of a woman's breast when she sobs. The boy was rapt, ecstatic. The little room, with its humble household contrivances, took on the enchantment, and glowed with the spirit of the pulsating music. José, the father, crouched gazing at the floor in a dream, his elbows on his knees, his hands hanging down and twitching, one foot beating time. Such passion, such freedom, were in the boy's playing, — it was not a child playing a toy; it was a Paganini, but a heavenly Paganini.

Suddenly he ceased. José rose and came forward, a tremulous smile on his grave face. "Can he not play, señor, as I said, my Rafaelito?"

"It is marvellous," I said. "But it is not good that you play too much, Rafael; you are not strong, and it is bad for you."

"Oh no, señor," he said; "I must play. I love to play; it is my life." And he smiled his heavenly smile, his eyes glowing.

"It is true," said José. "He plays always, and it is not well that I stop him. You see, señor, there is nothing else he can do, and one must do something: one dies."

He took the water-pail and moved towards the door. I followed, and when we were outside I en-

quired how the boy had learned to play so wonder-
fully.

"Of himself, señor," José replied. " He was hurt by
the train when we came from Mexico ; he fell from
the step, and hurt his back on the iron. Then he was
in the hospital at Los Angeles nearly three months,
but they could not cure him. But they gave him the
armónico, to amuse him ; yes, they were kind, but
they could not cure him ; it was not God's will. And
when they let him go we came here ; and we are
happy. The claim, señor? no, it is not much, but it
gives always enough. At first, he would come always
with me where I work ; it is on the hill that the claim
is. But it is a year now that he is not so well, and he
stays at the house, and plays and plays. That is how
he plays so well. It is his life, yes, truly, his life, señor.
And then he said I must play, too ; and I try to play,
but I am not young like him, and I cannot learn fast.
But he is patient, and teaches me. And when it is
moonlight we sit outside the house, and we play and
play. He loves greatly the moonlight. And I tell him
of Guadalajara, and the music there, and the fine
churches, and he plays always ; and we are very
happy, señor."

He stopped speaking, and then, with a smile that
was a reflection of the boy's, said again, —

" He is an angel, my Rafaelito ; and we are very
happy, señor."

It was necessary for me to resume my journey,
and I returned alone to the house, José being occu-

pied for a moment outside, to wish the boy good-bye.

"Gracias, señor," he said, with his heavenly smile, as I again praised his playing; "and my father plays also; I have taught him, and already he plays well. Do you play, señor?"

I had to acknowledge that I had no accomplishment in that direction.

"It is a pity; it is fine to play; and father says so, too. Do you know, señor, I can always hear it, yes, when I am asleep, sometimes. I can hear it running and running like the water. And then when I wake I play it so, and it is another way, a new way, señor."

After a pause he went on, —

"And it is such good company for one. That is why I made my father learn; and then, if I am not here, — you see I am not strong, señor, — then he will play, and it will be as if we played together; is it not so?"

"Yes," I answered; "almost as if you played together. Good-bye, Rafael; but I shall come and see you again, and you will play again to me."

"Yes, señor; adios, señor." And he smiled his smile that was like a kiss.

I had finished my business and was riding back down the cañon in the cool peace of the evening. As the cold mountain breeze blew past me, it seemed a different world from that of the morning, with its throbbing heat and garish light. *La Paloma* still rang in my brain ; and as the light faded I ceased to urge my horse, and fell into a reverie in which I seemed to see again the face of Rafael, luminous and smiling, or gazing up at the sky with his rapt look as he played and played. The tall evening-primroses that grew beside the trail were like the boy in their pale, bright serenity ; and with a feeling of tenderness I leaned down and touched one here and there, as though it were he himself. The moon rose above the cañon wall, and poured its still radiance over the scene. I remembered that José had said that Rafael often played in the moonlight, and as I came near the place where the little trail led to the house I found myself listening quite eagerly. I had no intention of staying, in any case, but I had a strong desire to see the boy again, and thought I would quietly approach the house if I heard any sound, but without their knowledge, so that I could withdraw unseen. At a turn of the cañon the music suddenly reached me. They were playing together, as I had heard them in the morning: Rafael was teaching his father. I dismounted and tied my horse to a bush, and quietly walked to where I could plainly see without being seen. The moon now shone full upon the little opening, and its idyll of love and simplicity. The mattress had been drawn out from under the tree where I had seen it into the moonlight, and on it lay José and Rafael, side by side, playing.

"Did I play well, Rafaelito mio?"

"It is excellent, yes, *excelentísimo*," answered Rafaelito of the Heavenly Smile.

Although it had seemed likely that I should find it necessary soon to repeat my journey into the San Timoteo, two years elapsed before I was again in the cañon. I was far from having forgotten old José and the boy. On my way up I was pressed for time, and did not call at the house, but contented myself with riding near enough to see that it appeared to be still inhabited, and determining to stop there on my return at night. I recalled vividly the vision that my memory had preserved (as it always will), of the father and son playing together in the moonlight; and I hoped that I might repeat an experience that was so sacred in its touching simplicity. Perhaps I was unduly sentimental, but so it seemed to me.

There was a half moon that night, and I rode quickly down the cañon, enjoying the scents that filled the air from sage, laurel, and the hundred and one aromatic herbs and shrubs of the California brush. I passed again the tall evening-primroses, standing in silent beauty like spellbound fairy princesses, and their pale tranquillity again reminded me of Rafael. It was still early when I came to the little trail, and I had no doubt of finding my friends either in the house or, perhaps, playing in the moonlight as I had last seen them. But when I came near the house there was no sound of talking or playing, and I saw no light, though the door stood open. I tied my horse, and approaching, knocked, and called "José! Rafael!" There was no answer, and with a feeling of disappointment I struck a match and stepped within. Evidently the house was inhabited, and by the same owner, for there was but little change in the appearance of the room; but when I looked for the boy's bed, and his crutches, I could not see them. Something of a presentiment came over me; many things may happen in two years, and the boy had been a cripple. Going outside, I was upon the point of calling the father's name again, when I thought I heard, faintly and at a distance, the well-remembered sound of the playing. Yes, I heard it unmistakably; it came from beyond the house, intermittently, as the breeze brought it. Following it I soon found that I was on a well-marked path that led up a little side-cañon, of which the gully that one had to cross in reaching the house from the road was a continuation. The path I was on led, no doubt, to José's placer-claim; but what could be the reason of his being there at night, and where was the boy?

Following the path, which was steep and rocky, I came nearer and nearer to the music: it was again *La Paloma*. Then the trail emerged on a little opening, which was, in fact, the top of the spur of rock which rose behind the house. At a little distance I saw some one sitting, playing: it was José. He had not seen me, nor heard my approach. When I called his name he ceased playing, and came slowly toward me. The moonlight was on his grave, dark face; he did not at first recognize me.

"José," I said, "you remember me?"

I turned my face to the light.

"Yes, señor," he said, "now I know you; and you are welcome. I fear it was hard for you to find me."

"No," I replied, "I heard you play. You played when I was here before."

"Yes, I remember, señor," said José.

"And the boy, Rafaelito, who played so beautifully," I said: "I have not forgotten, José. Where is he?"

"Dead, señor"; he spoke quietly. "You would like to see the place? It is here, close by, señor."

He led the way, talking simply as we walked.

"We were very happy; yes, that is it, perhaps we were too happy, señor, do you not think so? One must have trouble, and the boy was not strong."

He stopped at the spot where I had seen him sitting. There was a little enclosure, the shape of a grave, not to be noticed at a little distance, marked out with roughly broken pieces of quartz. At one end a cross was marked upon the ground in the same way; and in the centre of the enclosure there was a small, shallow, wooden box, about a foot square, such as some articles of food are packed in; but a piece of glass formed the top, which was held in place by four pebbles of white quartz. Something glittered like metal under the glass; it was the beloved *armónico*, and Rafaelito of the Heavenly Smile lay beneath.

"When I work, — it is over there that I work, señor, quite near, — I can look and see the place. And always I come here in the evenings, and then I play. He made me learn ; he was very patient, my Rafaelito. And was it not fortunate that I learned, señor? it is as though we played together."

" — Yes, it is hard; but it is God's will, and it is not good to complain. *Vaya con Dios, señor.*"

PART II

THE HIGH SIERRA

"Let the noon find thee by other lakes, and the night overtake thee everywhere at home."

THOREAU.

CHAPTER XII

THE HIGH SIERRA: THE YOSEMITE VALLEY TO THE HETCH-HETCHY

ON a hot, still morning of middle summer I left the Yosemite Valley for a month's expedition into the High Sierra. The region I expected to travel would be entirely new to me, so it was advisable to take a guide; and as there would be no opportunity for re-furnishing with provisions until I reached Mono Lake, on the eastern side of the mountains, it was necessary to take enough pack-animals to carry supplies for two or three weeks.

The problems of guide and pack-train solved themselves very satisfactorily, and in this manner: I was returning one day to camp, after compassing, at the cost of a broken rod, the overthrow of an experienced trout who had long defied me in a reach of the river a mile or so below the village. Near the place where we settled our account I came upon a man of a cheerful and self-helping aspect, who was camped in a little meadow that ran to the river-bank. In conversation this proved to be one Bodie, who had been recommended to me as a good man and a capable guide; and before we parted a "deal" had been arranged whereby he and five animals were placed at my disposal for the month of July.

Mr. Field, whom I already knew as a pleasant comrade and a thorough photographer, whose excellent pictures illustrate these pages, was also to accompany the expedition, completing a triangular (or perhaps it would be fairer to say an octagonal) party.

It was the 3d of July when Field and I left the valley. The village had broken out in a rash of flags and bunting. Fireworks and a dance were billed to wind up the exercises of the Fourth, and I confess I felt no regret in turning my back upon these festive incongruities.

We drove out on the Big Oak Flat road, bound for Crocker's Station, where Bodie awaited us with the animals. This is the road which, from the southern side of the valley, one sees traced like a white ribbon on the northern cañon wall. I found it on the whole disappointing in the views it offers; but the Bridal Veil Fall was often in sight, and interesting glimpses were opened up of the wide scoop down which the Bridal Veil Creek flows to its famous plunge : while the remarkable fractures of the southern wall of the Merced Cañon would compel the attention of the least geological of men. From this road also El Capitan shows more magnificently than from any other point of view, fronting the west with a vast, door-like cliff that is truly imposing in its unbroken verticality. But many of the most wonderful features of the valley are not within the view from this side, while from the spot that has been ambitiously named New Inspiration Point, El Capitan itself is completely hidden and only a small segment of the Half-Dome is in sight.

Making up, however, for all deficiencies, an unusual haze that day filled the valley with an atmosphere like a vapor of opals, and steeped the landscape in a dreamy beauty, ineffably airy and spiritual. It was like one of those enchanted valleys of our childhood, populated by friendly fairies, gigantic genii, and companionable birds and beasts, where gallant lovers in peach-colored velvet were constantly occupied in rescuing princesses in silver and sky-blue.

The summer, moreover, was at its climax of flowers. Every forest opening glinted with cyclamens, columbines, and wall-flowers, these last of a peculiar sultry yellow like compressed sunshine. As we rose, the timber changed from yellow pine to spruce, from spruce to sugar pine, then to fir, and lastly to tamarack. At Tamarack Flat we stopped for an hour to rest the team, fagged with a climb of twenty-five hundred feet, and then, after making another rise to Gin Flat (a natural culmination), began the long descent.

The road passes through the Tuolumne grove of Sequoias. While we were paying our homage to some of the most notable trees, we encountered a tall backwoodsman who sat whittling and whistling beside the road. Your true backwoodsman savors of the forest as a fisherman smells of the sea, and I was struck by the woodcraftiness, so to speak, of this man's appearance. He looked like a kind of faun, and his occupation of whittling seemed almost necessary and symbolic. Long, lean, and shaggy, there was a fine air of wild instinct about him; he seemed a part of the landscape; and it was a shock to find him to be after all a prosaic and commercially minded creature, when, in reply to a remark upon the stateliness of the great trees that rose around us, he cast a calculating eye over the " General Lawton," and replied, "Don't know nothin' about that; maybe they's fine, maybe they ain't. That thar stick will cut up two hunnerd thousand foot of lumber, board measure. To my thinkin' it's all dad-blasted foolishness that a feller cain't cut a stick o' timber like that. What's trees, anyway? Ain't they lumber?" He spat viciously to right and left, throwing up little volcanoes of dust, and reiterated, "A dad-blasted foolishness, that's what it is: two hunnerd thousand foot, board measure." For some reason, the fact of this iniquitous waste of lumber being estimated by board measure seemed to aggravate the matter intolerably, and he continued dad-blasting and spitting angrily until, when we parted, quite a range of small craters surrounded him.

Running down a good road between walls of superb forest, we drew up by late afternoon at the little settlement of Crocker's, or, as it is given on the map, Sequoia. Without having ever seen, except from railway cars, a New England village, I thought I recognized the model of those quaint and sleepy hamlets which American poets and writers have cast into a type. A single street, or streetlet, of a hundred yards all told, dawdled past the doors of half a dozen whitewashed cottages, and then suddenly wavered off into the forest. A "hotel," a miniature store, and an amusing post office formed the business centre, and a few small dwellings and a barn comprised the suburbs.

In this Arcadian spot Bodie awaited us, and thence convoyed us to his camp half a mile away. Here we found our animals assembled — a horse, two mules, a big jack and a small jenny — hard by a lost-looking house, the residence of an acquaintance of our guide's. The goodman was away, but his womenfolk did the honors, and a couple of choleric dogs, together with a rifle that leaned against the house, represented him efficiently by proxy.

When the hour of supper approached, Bodie, to give us a taste of his quality, notified us that we were to be regaled with hot bread, and produced a brand-new Dutch-oven which he was contributing on his own account to the equipment of the party. When the bread was ready and we drew around the gunny-sack board, he sprang further surprises upon us : first a bag of sugared "cookies," then a jar of pickles, and lastly one of jam. I have no doubt he had provided these exotics with the kindly idea of mitigating for us the abruptness of the descent to camp rations; but I could see that he felt that his own dignity was compromised by such trifling, and I observed that he made a point of always referring to them slightingly as "them little dinkies."

This genteel repast over, Bodie repaired to the house and the society of the ladies, who, overlooking our presence, condescended to take the air on the door-step. It was easy to gather from the soprano laughter accompanying a bass monologue that our guide was something of a wag. We, for our part, lay at ease, smoking lazily and maturing our plans.

A serene rose-cloudy sunset, with a placid white moon drifting in a sky of Turneresque blue, promised a truly glorious Fourth. All around stood thickly "the green steeples of the piney wood," closing us in with a horizon of restful undulations. At length the stars piercing the darkening indigo of the sky reminded us that we were to be up at four, and turning into our blankets we were lulled asleep by the murmuring stream of badinage that still flowed on, encouraged by tributary rills of applause.

There was no sign of movement about the house when at six o'clock next morning our cavalcade filed out upon the road, though a rear-guard skirmish between the mules and the dogs plainly advertised our departure. As we passed through the village a withering sun was already bleaching the sagging bunting, but no sound of toy-cannon or fire-cracker broke the drowse of Sleepy Hollow. The character of Crocker's population does not belie the unemotional aspect of the place.

I watched with curiosity, not unmixed with anxiety, for the first disclosures of the qualities of our animals. The horse and the mules were the property of Bodie,

and he had guaranteed their dispositions; but he had
hired the two burros for the trip, and I knew from
severe experiences the surprises that are latent in
these incomprehensible creatures.

Almost before we were out of the village it became
plain that the big jack combined the worst idiosyncrasies of his species with the solitary virtue of
enormous strength and great tonnage. A big-boned,
knuckly beast with a lowering eye, I never knew him
to abate for an instant the attitude of sullen hostility
which he adopted at the outset. Not that any of us
ever attempted to get into relations with him; that eye
forbade it. Bodie's feelings toward him fluctuated
swiftly: at one moment he would extol his size and
endurance, averring, truly enough, that he was the
equal of any blamed mule in the mountains; half a
minute later he could be heard assailing him with
violent reproaches and threatening to break every bone
in his "dog-gone" carcass. To threats and praises alike
Jack opposed the same detestable demeanor, and I
seldom deprecated the sudden strappados which fell
upon him, and which Bodie justified by explaining
that "the surly son of a 'Pache riled him all up."

For strength of will I never met the equal of this
animal; it was colossal, and pure adamant. From the
first to the last day of the trip he steadfastly refused
to keep the trail with the others. Defiantly he would
turn off from the plainest path, his great parietals
bulging with obstinacy; and when a loud hail warned
him that he was observed, he would rush off and

ram himself savagely into the worst thicket or rock-pile he could find. By practice he had developed an abominable sagacity, and could judge to a nicety the space between trees or below branches that would ensure the maximum of damage to his load. Into these places he would charge, and stand shoving and straining with sullen fury, hoping to dislodge his pack; and the only way to force him out was by hammering him steadfastly on the muzzle. Even under that application he would stand out, until, the cumulative effect becoming unbearable, he would bolt back to the trail, trembling with rage, and a hateful spectacle of concentrated vice.

The jenny was entirely otherwise; a confiding little creature, as willing and placable as the jack was ugly and difficult; in Bodie's phrase, "a kind little divvle." Her we loved, and many were the residual beans and supernumerary flapjacks that fell to her lot. One fault she had, but it was so natural, and by contrast so venial, that we easily forgave it her. It was a trick she had of hiding. During breakfast she would stroll about the camp, receiving our remainders and enjoying the conversation; but when the time came that the detested "chores" engaged all our attention she would edge off and melt imperceptibly into the brush; and when she was wanted for packing it seemed as if even her tracks had evaporated. At hide-and-seek she was a genius; nothing was too small to hide her; and when we returned from a fruitless search over half a mile of rough country she was generally discovered drowsing or browsing close to camp, and would meet us with a gaze so mild and serious as to quite disarm our resentment.

Bodie's own mount was a handsome chestnut, clever, gentle, and self-reliant. In places where the mules and burros went timidly, Pet maintained his own bold gait, striding freely over glacial pavements where even the tap of their own hoofs kept the other animals shaking with nervousness. Considering that the natural habitat of the species is a region of plains and open distances, I admired the more the fine freedom of his stride on the worst and steepest of trails.

In his intercourse with his companions Pet never forgot the dignity of his rank. Nor did he refuse its responsibilities. Nothing pleased him so much as the opportunity, which came frequently enough, of rounding-up the pack-animals. Bodie usually rode in the rear, where he could best oversee the train, which sometimes was strung out over a hundred yards of trail; and it often occurred that the first warning of foolishness on the part of the pack-mules or burros would come from Pet, quite independently of his rider. With his tail switching and a contemptuous toss and snort he would check his pace and jump aside to head the wanderers back into the path. The rebels, seeing him coming, usually stampeded in all directions, and Pet would then take them in hand one by one, outflanking, countermarching, and concentrating with admirable strategy.

The two mules, one white, or rather of that unpleasant color known as flea-bitten, and the other
black, were used indifferently for packing or riding.
The black was a passionless sort of beast, a mere nu-
meral, vacant even of the elementary trait of obstinacy. The other, whom we named Clementine, was
noticeable for a ludicrous physiognomy that gave the
impression of a continual simper. She nursed an
elderly passion for Pet, and could not bear him to be
out of her sight, though he, for his part, detested her
and met her languishing blandishments with un-
equivocal kicks. Knowing that nothing would tempt
her to abandon his company, she was often allowed
to fall behind the rest of the pack-train while she dal-
lied with the trailside herbage. At such times, when
she became suddenly aware that Pet was out of her
view, she would charge wildly up the line, caroming
off everything that came in her way, until she arrived close behind him, whereupon his ears would
flatten and he would gather for a kick.

Bodie's feelings at such moments were those of an
artist watching helplessly the wreck of his handiwork.
Not the securest of diamond-hitches could withstand
the shock of the collisions which her packs had to
endure with trees, rocks, and the other animals. By
the time she reached the coveted place her pack was
usually under her belly, and the whole train must
halt while she was unloaded and repacked. Her
eternal simper was at such times hard to bear, and
you may be sure that her comfort was not much

considered when it came to the pull on the latigo-strap.

Our road lay through open forest country, charmingly diversified and flowery. The most beautiful of all the Mariposa tulips grew abundantly in sunny places, rosy red in color and fantastically painted with blots of maroon and purple. Golden mimulus, purple godetias and pentstemons, and lavender lupines grew among the brush, itself fragrant and flowery, that broke with rounded bosses the severity of the straight-stemmed pines and cedars. The white mountain-lilac was still in blossom, burgeoning in cloudy masses, and providing the last ingredient in a landscape of perfectly proportioned color. Chamœbatia also bore us company, like a friendly little mountaineer setting us cheerfully on our way.

A long, gentle descent brought us to the South Fork of the Tuolumne, which we found easily fordable. Until now I had not made the acquaintance of this river; but it had always attracted me, perhaps simply by the oddity of its name, like a musical mouthful of chance syllables (Too-ol'lum-ne); and although the stream I saw was not distinguished by any special beauty among the sisterhood of Sierra rivers, all lovely alike, still it was an event to meet it, and, as it were, check it off.

Jack and Clementine had already wasted so much of our time in stoppages and re-packings that I decided to make an almost nominal day's march of it, and to camp at Ackerson Meadows instead of pushing on to the Hog Ranch, which would have been no more than ten miles. The decision was welcomed by Bodie, and I found early in our acquaintance that he had all a good stockman's regard for the comfort of his beasts. When I announced also that during the expedition we should not break camp on Sundays I observed that the fact, though it occasioned him some surprise, gave him no distress. I, on my side, was not only willing, but anxious, to fall in with his suggestion of early starts, easy marches, and timely camps on other days, so far as possible; and when I proved myself quite his match in the matter of early rising I believe he came to regard me as almost a paragon from this point of view. We were nearly always up by four o'clock. I fancied that Field was not fully in sympathy with such virtue, but he never complained, and always turned out ungrudgingly.

It was not much after noon when we rode up to a little scorched-up house in a wide meadow, and were hospitably greeted by a hirsute Irishman who was "holding down" the ranch for the present owner, the successor of the original Ackerson. Choosing a spot for our camp on the edge of a swampy expanse which afforded good pasturage for the animals, we turned them loose, and, it being Saturday, made rather elaborate preparations for a day and a half of unearned ease. The remains of the "little dinkies" gave a festal touch to the evening meal.

While we lingered over the coffee, two young fellows appeared, carrying guns and heavily encrusted

with cartridges. An immature squirrel depended from
the belt of one of the sportsmen. In the course of conversation they remarked impressively that they had
bear-meat to spare, and offered to share it with us if
we would visit their camp, promising also to enter-
tain us with music. Later in the evening, when Bodie
had gone to swap items of news at the cabin, Field
and I were walking over to pay our call and receive
the expected boons when the skirling of a phono-
graph warned us away, and we hastily retraced our
steps and turned into our blankets early by way of
compensation. I confess I find it difficult to forgive Mr. Edison for this diabolical invention, and I
even welcomed as a mitigation the vociferous yelp-
ing of a coyote halfway down the meadow. The
conjunction of sounds formed what I should suppose must be an absolute novelty in tone combina-
tions.

Sunday passed in a kind of Nirvana of heat and
laziness. Returning from a walk through flowery
glades where beds of pale lilac lupine and foot-high
fern were spread upon a brown floor of pine-needles,
I found the rail-fence which enclosed the meadow
decorated with an extensive " wash." Jenny thoughtfully munched the sleeve of a blue jumper, while
Bodie, lightly clad, slumbered in the shade.

About sunset a solitary mallard visited us, flying
three times silently around the vicinity of our camp.
As it vanished with strong, steady wing-beats into
the dusky glory of the west, I fancied that it might

be the spirit of some departed Indian warrior, come
to revisit his old hunting-grounds ; one of

> " . . . the wandering spirits
> From the kingdom of Ponemah,
> From the land of the Hereafter."

Half-past three next morning found us astir, and
six o'clock saw us on the road, headed for the Hetch-
Hetchy. At Stone's Meadows we rode through a very
sea of some pretty, composite flower with yellow rays
and a black centre, that grew in countless multitudes.
In the hot, still morning these black-eyed Susans, as
they stood silently drinking in the sunshine, seemed
the very type of California's floral intemperance.

The finest city lot is dreary and undesirable in comparison with these emerald-and-topaz heavens. But
this lovely spot is now uninhabited, and the old cabin,
long disused and sunk into decay, kneels like a bro-
ken-backed camel on the flowery sward. These abandoned dwellings, which surprise the traveller in the
loneliest portions of the Sierra, are the relics of the
days of the sheep-men. By many a mountain meadow
and clearing you will find the little ten-by-twelve
hutches, doorless and windowless, with a tumble of
stones at one end where used to be the chimney.
Here, in the days when mutton was king, the gay
songs of *la belle France* were sung by black-bearded
Gascons to the gusty surge of accordions or the thin-
blooded skirling of violins. On the frontiers of the
Forest Reserves you may meet the little dark men

now, wandering from pasture to pasture with their placid charges, attended by two half-wild dogs and a weird little pack-burro. Whenever I encounter one of these sauntering pastors I seem to see a Jacob, and wonder in what Pyrenean village lives the Rachel for whom he is serving.

We crossed the Middle Fork of the Tuolumne by a bridge of rough planks, and a few more miles brought us to the Hog Ranch. The hogs have given place to cattle, and these, with a few horses, now roam over the green expanse and wax fat beyond the wont of their kind on superb pasturage. The ranch is like an English park, — a lovely valley, wide and grassy, broken with clumps of oak and cedar ; but the house is a filthy old shanty which, nondescript and ugly at its best, and now long fallen into disrepair, is an offence to the eye and reeks with skunk-like odors.

Thus far we had followed what is nominally a road, being practicable for robust vehicles ; but at this point a rougher country begins, and we entered upon our long trail. It made an inviting beginning, winding through shaded avenues deep in pine-needles and flowery with many brilliant blossoms. The most noticeable flower of this locality in midsummer is the godetia, which grows in low, close companies, painting the ground in places with islands of solid purple. Mixed among them are handsome lily-like brodiæas of a deep, pure blue, and the coral-red stars of the erythrœa, with many another. But the character of the landscape soon changed, and for some distance the trail led through open, rocky country, clad with a sparse growth of the unattractive and shadeless *Sabiniana* pine, which here appears at a greater elevation than is usual with it, by virtue of some particular and local conditions.

From an altitude of fifty-five hundred feet the trail made a long descent towards the north. Suddenly there opened far below us a valley like another Yosemite, its cliffs, meadows, and winding river gleaming through the pearly summer haze. The white torrent of a waterfall could be plainly seen even at that distance, creeping down a great cliff on the northern side. I knew it at once as the Hetch-Hetchy.

Down endless zigzags, "hotter 'n blazes," as Bodie truly said, among fine oaks and spruces, by creeks ferny, aldery, willowy, and through meadows blue, meadows yellow, meadows red, and meadows mixed of every color, we marched until we debouched at last upon the floor of the valley. Here met us a representative of the law in the form of a serious and taciturn young trooper, huge of limb and yellow of seven days' beard, a sort of youthful Oom Paul. He bore a large German pipe with a bowl like a small nail-keg, and remained canopied in clouds of plug-cut while he conducted his mild catechism: Names? A, B, and C. Good. Come out from the valley? Sure. Where was we heading? Could n't say exactly; generally, north and east, off there. What was we out for? Just taking in the country. Hunting? No. No? No. Guns in them packs? No, again. Going by way of Soda Springs? Might. When? Couldn't say. Know the country? Ask him, Bodie. Oh, that Bodie? Go ahead. And waving his pipe benevolently at us, Oom Paul turned away and sank into an extemporized hammock, while we filed out upon the level in search of a camping-place.

Any spot in this valley would be well-nigh ideal for the purpose, but it was still early in the day and we could afford to be critical. So we prospected for warm miles, with a special regard to the question of mosquitoes, which we had been warned might be troublesome here.

There are two waterfalls in the Hetch-Hetchy. One of them is a short-lived burst of energy that begins and ends with the melting of the snows that lie above the northern wall of the valley. This fall is seen by but few people, for the last of its water escapes before full summer arrives. I looked eagerly for this cataract, Too'eoola'la, which Bodie reported as far exceeding the other in power and beauty, declaring that when in full career it filled the whole lower end of the valley with its whirling spume. But we were too late; not a sign remained of what, perhaps two weeks earlier, would have been so splendid a sight. A spell of hot weather had upset the pail.

The other fall, the Hetch-Hetchy, is not so transitory. It draws its waters from a creek twenty miles or more in length, and from a number of lakes and lakelets lying up on the high country to the north. It does not leap out, as do the various falls of the

Yosemite Valley, from the lip of a sheer cliff, to drift
and dream in vapor; but pours down a twisted and
precipitous gorge, crashing from ledge to ledge,
writhing and bursting in a terrific catastrophe. Seen
from across the valley it is as if a broad vein of virgin silver, running from top to bottom of the two-
thousand-foot precipice, had been laid bare by some
great convulsion: such a treasure of solid metal as
flushed the imagination of the Conquistadores. The
Hetch-Hetchy Fall is thus of a quite different type
from the other great waterfalls of the region, but in
beauty it is fully their equal, and in features of wild-
ness even their superior.

Midway up the valley stands the remarkable cliff
called the Kolana Dome. This magnificent rock of
two thousand feet somewhat resembles in outline the
mountain known as Liberty Cap in the Yosemite,
and stands fronting the river with a face almost perpendicular, and rolling back the roar of the Hetch-
Hetchy Fall. Passing around the foot of this cliff,
and skirting a pretty pool which renders a perfect
reflection of rock and waterfall, pine and sky, we
stopped at a clump of small cedars near a deserted
cabin that stood on the bank of the river, and there
made camp.

The Tuolumne as it flows through the Hetch-
Hetchy takes on a character very unusual in California rivers. It becomes a placid, slow-moving stream,
wide and deep, gliding under outreaching branches
of oak and pine. Not a ripple breaks the shining

current, except where trout are leisurely dining. It would be a superb place in which to dream away a summer. The green and golden air laps one in unbroken content: it is like that land of the Lotos-Eaters "in which it seemed always afternoon." And with a boat or canoe, what afternoons one might have on that street of charmed water! Still more, what evenings, watching through the leafy screen the sunset flushing up the pearly walls; or drifting under spandrelled arcades of oak and sumptuous foliations of pine and cedar, the cathedral gloom lighted by windows that open on gold and amethyst skies. And then the mornings, steeped in the incredible freshness of the California dawn; brushing through knee-high meadows where yellow enotheras stand in companies like pale odalisques; or through thickets of ceanothus sweet as hedges of hawthorn, where robins are bustling and the powdery blossoms fall like snow; or fighting duels with chivalrous trout in the ripple where the gleaming current is drawn swiftly over into broken water.

The heat of the day had so evaporated our energies that no one would volunteer to build a fire. The spot where, by Bodie's choice, we had camped, revealed signs of recent occupation by another party, which was objectionable when we had the whole valley to choose from; and as we ate our cold supper and slapped at the mosquitoes by prosaic candlelight, we decided to remove next day to the other side.

With this move in view we had engaged to be up

by four o'clock or earlier ; but when in the early grey
I rose on my elbow and looked over to Bodie's sleeping-place, I was not sorry to see the deep quiescence
of his form, and willingly returned to light slumbers.
Half-a-dozen times at intervals I looked again ; still
no sign. Then Field got up, shouldered the camera,
and went off to keep an appointment down the valley
with a view which must be caught before the ripple
came on the water. Next I arose, and last of all Bodie,
with unnecessary explanations.

After breakfast, leaving him to pack, I retraced our
yesterday's trail for some distance, in order to review
with a fresher mind the features of the lower end of
the valley. A hot sun was already drawing up the
dew that lay on bush and sward. The haze of yesterday was gone, and every scratch and scoring on the
majestic walls showed as clearly as if it were cut on
steel under one's hand. The young leafage of the
oaks shone with a dull, clean burnish, like the skin
of an athlete. The sumptuous tassels of the yellow
pines, which here grow in remarkable perfection of
symmetry, shone with diamond-points that fell in
showers where squirrels leaped from spray to spray.
Birds were foraging cheerfully, in the certainty of
breakfast; and high up in a brilliant sky an eagle
swung, a mere point of black, like a planet circling
in space. In a corner of the meadow a company of
evening-primroses were gleaming palely in the pro-
tecting shade of the oaks. To me there is something
very poetic and sensitive about these flowers, with

their slender, moon-like graces : as 't were, I know not how. Next I chanced upon a bush of ripe raspberries, and while I loitered with these I was entertained by a party of lively young king-snakes that were either quarrelling or playing in the brush, chasing one another about with a rapidity of movement and a play of color that were quite bewildering.

I am always meeting people who report of this or that place that it is "thick" with deer, or bear, or such things; but I have never yet found the term justified when I came to the spot. Thus we had been told that the Hetch-Hetchy was thick with rattle-snakes. As a matter of fact none of us saw one there; and the whole time we were out we met only two, one of which was killed by Field at Lake Eleanor, and the other by me in the Till-till. In the Yosemite itself I have never seen a rattlesnake, though I killed two some distance up the Tenaya Cañon.

In general features the Hetch-Hetchy is a remark-able duplication of the Yosemite. The mountain-walls are of the same character, though they are not, on the whole, so high and cliff-like. There are the same clean-drawn, dome-like outlines, the same quiet beauty of winding river, the same level meadow-floor, dotted with stately trees and sprinkled thickly with flowers. There are the same pine-ranked precipices, and cloudy waterfalls, and huge cubed shatters of talus; and though there are no such geological marvels as the Half-Dome or the Sentinel, no such dominating mass as El Capitan, it is still a phenomenon that Nature,

with her magnificent carelessness, should have chosen
to use two designs so nearly alike.

The upper part of the valley is a park-like stretch
of level grass-land, with fine oaks as the predominat-
ing member in a partnership of oak, pine, and cedar.
The characteristic tree of the Hetch-Hetchy is the
oak, which attains there a notable perfection, leaving
the conifers the second place,— a condition which is
just reversed in the Yosemite, with its half-thousand
feet more of elevation. The southern wall rises at
this upper end to a great height, culminating in a
precipitous ridge, with an altitude of seventy-eight
hundred feet, which is named after "a party of the
name of Smith." At this point the valley may be said
to begin; above, it "cañons" to the long gorge that
is known as the Grand Cañon of the Tuolumne. In
this deep ravine the river rushes in continuous cascades for twenty miles: here, as it enters the valley,
it widens to a thoughtful stream that glides as peace-
fully as the idyll of a summer day.

The main trail crosses the river at the head of the
valley by a plank bridge near where Rancheria and
Till-till creeks join almost as they enter the main
stream. Thence heading east and north it passes
over Rancheria Mountain into the wilderness of laced
and braided cañons in which a week later we were
wandering. Near the bridge another trail branches
westerly, and following the northern side of the valley enables one to make a complete circuit. This trail
is a particularly interesting one, skirting the river,

which flows in a broad stream a hundred feet wide under overarching oaks and cedars.

About opposite Kolana Dome, the mountain-wall presses sheer and close to the river, and the trail is carried on a rocky ledge a few feet above high-water mark. Then it passes through levels where by mid-summer the brakes stand shoulder-high, and only the humped loads of your pack-train appear above the ferny lake. Crossing Falls Creek where it runs, a lovely white torrent, carrying all the water of the great Hetch-Hetchy Fall, it next enters wide oak-glades where every tree is a specimen of oak perfection, reaching out wide, full-leaved branches to join hands with its fellows. You ride through pillared arcades where the very air is green, as in a conservatory, and flowers thrive to giant size in the delectable mingling of shade and sunshine. Here lusty spikes of lupine drop their pollen on your horse's shoulder, and there you push through columbines that swing drops of wine and amber above the level sea of bracken.

I had found, on returning in expectation of dinner, that my companions had struck camp in my absence, and gone round by the bridge, leaving me to follow at my leisure. It was late afternoon when the sound of an urgent tattoo, performed *stringendo* on a frying-pan, fell sweetly on my ears, and a few moments brought me to the new camp, and diurnal but never monotonous beans. Bodie had chosen a spot close to the foot of our to-morrow's trail, which climbs out of the valley at the northwest corner. A picturesque log-house, doorless and ownerless, stands here under giant oaks, where a natural flower-garden of wild-roses leads down to the grassy meadow. After supper I strolled about my garden while the primroses opened their gentle, moon-like faces, and the hummingbird moths came whirring about, thick as cockchafers under a chestnut tree: and I think that no proud possessor of famous rosery ever enjoyed a more delicate entertainment of scents than did I in this Hetch-Hetchy solitude.

The breeze that had blown during the afternoon died away; the aspens ceased their excited little dances; the sun blazed down a final salvo of heat for warning of to-morrow; and after lying an hour gazing up through the starry foliage at the darkening sky, we took shelter under early blankets from the mosquitoes which rose in hosts from the wet grass of the meadow.

CHAPTER XIII

THE HIGH SIERRA: THE HETCH-HETCHY TO THE TILL-TILL

SIX o'clock next morning found us climbing the steep trail out of the Hetch-Hetchy, at a point about opposite where we had entered it. The upper end of the valley lay in the early sunlight that streamed between the eastern peaks, while the whole lower half was eclipsed in the vast shadow of Kolana. A heavy dew lay grey on the meadows, and the river ran green in the sunshine and steely dark in the shade. On the opposite wall the pinnacles of the pines already shimmered in light of a smoky hotness. I looked over to where Oom Paul's camp should be for the smoke of his morning bacon, but I fear he is no early riser.

A climb of some two thousand feet in a distance of not much over a mile brought us to the top of the ascent. Early as it was the sun was scorching, and we congratulated ourselves on having broken the back of the day's travelling while we were fresh. We now entered a cool forest of cedar and yellow pine, with here and there a sugar pine rising in conspicuous majesty. Squirrels and blue-jays made a lively stir. Little pools of clear water lay in grassy hollows, reflecting the white and blue of the sky. Purple gode-

tias flocked in every sunny opening, and tall lilies
and larkspurs glowed in the shade of the forest aisles.

A few miles of easy travelling brought us to another meadow golden with flowers. Here dwelt in
past times one Miguel, a Mexican who has been
translated by the cartographers of the Geological
Survey into the clan of the McGills. Traces of his
occupancy remain in a rail-fence that wanders in an
irresolute manner about the meadow, the old cedar
rails whitening like bones in the sun, or submerged
a fathom deep in idle herbage. Each of these meadows seems more delightful than the last. Sequestered
in deep forest and hushed eternally by its murmur,
they are heavenly places of birds and flowers, bits of
original paradise. The little brooks that water them
ring carillons of tinkling melody as they wind through
shady tunnels of carex and bending grasses. At morning and evening and on moonlit nights the deer come,
no longer even at the trouble of leaping the fences,
to regale on mint and lettuce that has descended
through many generations from the old settler's vege-
table-garden. All day the robins and the meadow-
larks repeat their canticles from the last remaining
fence-posts, and squirrels and chipmunks scamper
along the sagging rails, appreciating the convenience
of a literal railway.

A turn of the trail brought us sooner than we had
expected in view of Lake Eleanor. This is a handsome sheet of water, a mile and a half long and half
as wide, with timbered mountains sweeping down to

the shore at all points except the southwest, where Eleanor Creek flows out of the lake through meadows brilliantly green. On the northern side fine cliffs fall sheer to the water, rising at the eastern end to a conspicuous white dome. The lake was very still, and the reflection of the dark cliffs perfect, except when the blue was broken for a moment by wandering flaws of wind. In the middle a black speck that was creeping about warned us that we were not to be entirely alone.

A steep descent led us to the lake level, near where a small meadow bordered by a creek offered a good camping-place. Here retribution overtook Jack, who by this time had earned the hearty ill-will of us all. Leaving the trail in his usual offensive fashion, he was trying to push through an opening of the brush near the edge of the lake, where the ground was more boggy than he supposed. In a moment he was up to his belly in black mire. Field ran forward to hold him by his halter-rope, and Bodie, laying hold of his tail with one hand, gave him a terrific rope-ending with the other. The jack, half sunk in slimy ooze, could do nothing to retaliate, though he was frantic with passion and actually bit himself in his impotent rage.

Not the least of our guide's accomplishments was the lightning rapidity with which he could throw a meal together. The moment we reached our campground he would have the pack off the animal that carried the cooking tackle, and within five minutes a fire would be burning and batter mixed for flapjacks. Almost before Field and I had the other animals unloaded Bodie would be hailing us that the grub was getting cold.

Bread needed but little longer time, though he was rigorous with himself in this matter, and would criticise his product severely for the least shortcoming. The new Dutch-oven, primarily intended for the baking of bread, came to fulfil many uses: now it became the vehicle of a "mulligan"; anon it would hold our potatoes or coffee. I once happened to refer to it as the *sine qua non*, having regard to its varied uses. The term took Bodie's fancy mightily; it became then and thenceforth the "sinkienon"; and I have no doubt it is the sinkienon to-day, to the perplexity of other travellers under his convoy.

Its shape, a portly spheroid supported upon three Falstaffian legs, made the sinkienon something of a problem in packing. By experience we found that it travelled best seated on the top of one of the packs, securely lashed to keep it in place. In this position it resembled some stout captive, or Begum, in a howdah. It was always the last to be lifted up, and the first to be lifted down; and when Jack or Clementine ran amuck our first anxiety was ever for its safety.

In the afternoon heavy clouds gathered in the east, enhancing the solitary beauty of the scene. All the natural colors of the landscape seemed to be withdrawn, leaving only black, white, and a full chord of greys. Leaden masses of vapor drooped over the lake, and lay furled along the line of the black cliffs on the opposite shore. Far in the east a line of ragged, spiky peaks stood high up in the sky, lighted now and then for a moment by the westering sun through cloud rents of gloomy glory. A group of aspens on a low point were reflected on the dark surface of the lake as if drawn in Chinese white, and the heavy water moved uneasily under the massed lily pads near the shore. Everything promised a storm; but no storm came, and I relieved the disappointment by a swim in water of a delightful temperature, with a charmed stillness in the air, and the ripples flowing away from me as I swam in shining curves of black and white.

Among a clump of tall pines on the shore we found two soldiers camped. The mystery of the boat we had seen was explained when we found the old dug-out canoe in which these peaceful sons of Mars went fishing, or paddled serenely about upholding the majesty of the law. Half-a-dozen times a day they rowed across an arm of the lake to fill their buckets at an ice-cold spring. They are happy warriors whose lot it is to serve their country so.

My plans as to our route were not very definitely laid down. The intention was simply to strike easterly from this point, keeping north of the Tuolumne River, crossing the crest of the Sierra by one of the two or three passes that I knew to be practicable, refitting at Mono Lake, and returning by one of the passes farther to the south. In conversation with the soldiers we learned that the wildest part of the region, and therefore the most attractive, lay up in the direction of the Matterhorn peaks to the northeast. I had not provided myself with maps of that part of the Sierra which lies north of the "Yosemite" and "Mount Lyell" quadrangles of the Geological Survey, nor had Bodie, as it happened, traversed this part of the mountains. But he had no doubt of being able to find a way through to the east, by his knowledge of the general topography of the range.

The name of the Matterhorn peaks had a highly desirable sound. We pored for an hour by candle-light over the soldiers' maps, and decided that we must see the country that answered to such a name.

The next morning was clear and sparkling. Early ducks were breakfasting among the water-lilies, and the lake was still sleeping in the shadow of the eastern mountains, when we took the back-trail up to the summit. The roar of falls on Eleanor Creek, a mile away, reached us clearly on the still air. The brush was drenched in dew, and under a genial sun poured out its most pungent essences, and all the wayside blossoms had that divine freshness that flowers wear in early morning, as if they were newly brought from heavenly conservatories. There grows about here a giant kind of forget-me-not, with stems eighteen inches high and flowers three quarters of an inch across, a forget-me-not of the forget-me-nots, not to be forgotten.

At the head of the divide we found our new trail

bearing away to the northeast, near where it crosses a rushing stream called Frog Creek. Looking back to the west we bade a second farewell to the lake, now showing an oval disk of gleaming blue among folds of dark forested mountains. Far beyond, a glimmering haze lay over the arid valley of the San Joaquin, and a wavy band of neutral-tint just indicated the outlines of the Coast Range. It was an ideal painter's landscape.

On the north exposure of the mountain-sides around us magnificent firs stood like a picked regiment, every individual tall, straight, and handsome: the southward-facing slopes carried a mixed forest of yellow pine, sugar pine, and cedar, with stray outposts of the tamaracks. A waving sea of fern flowed over all the forest floor, interspersed with tall spikes of blue lupine and yellow and red columbine. These two dwellers in the greenwood grow nearly always in company and seem to have a conscious affinity. Lupine is a jaunty kind of lad, careless and bold; columbine is pretty and rustic, but a bit of a rogue, too, in her way; the lightest dancer with the neatest ankle in all the forest. They make a gallant pair, of the true order of lovers in Arcady.

Fording the creek, where ouzels were out-singing the singing water, a long descent brought us to Laurel Lake, a small round sheet of water, not one tenth the size of Eleanor, delightfully gentle and secluded. Around the margin grew a rich belt of flowering shrubs. Azaleas bloomed in billowy masses, and scented the air with their hot-house fragrance. Beyond the ring of verdure the firs and pines were ranked thickly on all the slopes, and the little lake shone like a turquoise in its double setting. To the north a ridge of bare granite rose above the timber, glistening hardly less white than the summer clouds that were beginning to appear above it.

The sight of that barren mountain made me restless. There is something in me, and no doubt in many of us, that longs ungovernably toward the wild and savage in Nature. It awoke now, and called to me a hundred-fold louder than these scented shades; and after a few minutes' rest we pushed on toward Vernon Lake. We had been told that there was a practicable cut-off by making east across country; but I have seldom found it pay to attempt to break new country of this kind with pack-animals, and we took the back-trail to the forks. From here the new trail continued north and east through fine forest, where many of the sugar pines measured from seven to eight feet in diameter near the base.

While Field returned to Laurel Lake to recover one of his cameras that had been left behind, I abandoned myself to the deep charm of the forest, here mainly of firs. It is in the fir-woods that the fullest peace and calm in Nature abide. The silence is superb. It is not the empty, aching silence of deserts and mountain summits, but a silence that is thoughtful, comprehensible, and companionable. Ever and anon there rings for a moment through the dim, still aisles the cadence of the " organ-bird,"—I know not what else to call it,—full of an indescribable poignancy that is like a pang of memory, or the exquisite remembrance of lost delight. A phrase, no more, but always of that haunting sweetness ; now here, now there. The spirit of some sorrowful, wild nymph is in that bird.

The trail now trended more northerly, entering a rough and rocky country with a more open forest. There was an unusual amount of fallen timber, and presently we came upon a recent windfall which completely obscured the trail. We made wide détours, only to encounter everywhere prostrate trunks whose shattered arms stretched up as if they appealed to heaven against the outrage of their destruction. One by one the scattered members of the party trickled through the huge obstruction. Jack, whom I convoyed, did himself credit for once by feats of surpassing agility, and making no account of his load (which, you may be sure, was not the lightest), leaped breast-high trunks almost gaily.

We emerged at different points, and after repairing damages cast about for our trail. It had vanished from the face of the earth as if it had never been. At length we discovered faint traces of what might have been an antediluvian trail, and following it arrived at a pretty meadow beside which stood a decrepit cabin. This we recognized as Beehive, — a cryptic designation to which nothing about the place offered any clue.

A hundred yards beyond the cabin the faint track we had followed petered out once more. There is something exceedingly annoying in this behavior on the part of a trail. Half an hour of the most careful search left us entirely at fault; and hungry and disgusted we gave up the puzzle and went into camp beside the cabin. We had breakfasted before five o'clock and it was then two in the afternoon.

By some peculiarity of land contour the wind attains here a specially powerful sweep. While we were eating lunch a sudden gust overturned a tall tree close by. It fell with a resounding crash that gave us a respectful admiration for the wilduproar tha tmust reign here when winter storms are raging, and infected me, at least, with a deep desire to witness such a Homeric combat. In our sunny, pacific valleys we know only one side of our mother's nature : we never see her in severity of snow, nor in her sudden passions and relentings, and we lose much thereby.

The reaction in our feelings that came with fulness of bread left us resigned to the breaking of our plans which had contemplated camping that night at Vernon Lake. It was necessary, however, to find our trail, and leaving Bodie to the passive industry of cooking beans, Field and I walked up the meadow to survey for the actual location of the missing lake. Its distance from Beehive had been reported by the soldiers at Eleanor as one mile. Bodie, who had fallen into a mood of pessimism, declared that we should find it six ; but I had already observed that our good guide held in scorn any opinion of the military that touched upon his own province. He was wont, indeed, to roundly assert that soldiers in the mountains always got lost if they ventured half a mile away from camp.

On the farther side of the meadow we met our lost trail, and followed it for two miles through a long swale of marshy ground where myriads of white and blue violets and purple cyclamens were rejoicing in the spring, which at this elevation was in full celebration now in mid-July. The Sierra spring is six or eight months long : one might almost say, indeed, in the words of the hymn, "There everlasting spring abides." Beginning in February or March, when the foothills blaze with the red gold of eschscholtzias, one might follow the spring upward, witnessing from week to week and meadow to meadow the perpetual miracle. All through the months when the lowlands lie parched and gasping, and the evening diversions of the city householder are reduced to the watering of his lawn, the green-gowned goddess is climbing the cañons and benches of the mountains. Resting here and there beside snow-banks and ice-fountains, she waves her wand over the sleeping flowery hosts and draws them up from under their green counterpane. And when September draws to a close, and farmers in the valley begin to scan the heavens for signs of early rains, still around the high alpine lakes, themselves like azure flowers, she is waking violets, cyclamens, and castilleias, when winter rushes upon her and smothers her under sudden snows.

Reaching the summit of a gentle ridge we looked expectingly for our lake, but in vain. Deep cañons rifted a wilder country than we had hitherto seen. In one of them the lake must lie, but to-morrow must settle in which. We returned to camp, and I could see that our report gave Bodie a sardonic pleasure, as corroborating his assertion of the soldiers' lack of trail-craft.

Mosquitoes descended upon us in swarms while we ate our supper. They also follow the spring, and here they were in the full zest of the joy of life. Three smudges and the same number of pipes, all working industriously, hardly abated their ardor, and we could but sit and endure while we waited for them to succumb to the chill of the falling temperature. The animals, neglecting the excellent pasturage of the meadow, came and stood with us in the lee of the smudges, gazing at us with glistening eyes. Our favorite, Jenny, with superior strategy, would invite the tormentors to settle freely upon her; then kneeling quietly down she would suddenly but carefully roll over upon them, and arise gloriously besmeared with the blood of the slain.

Upon the trunk of a pine close to our camp I noticed some peculiar marks, partly obliterated by the growth of the bark. They did not look like letters, yet had evidently been cut by the hand of man. As I was going over to examine them I found near the tree two or three heavy flat stones, and guessed that I had chanced upon the grave of some old backwoodsman. A simple dignity invests such a place of sepulchre akin to that of the field where the great triad of Israelitish patriarchs were buried. How much better than the vulgar haberdashery of undertakers are the healthy tassels of kindly pine that wave and sigh over the remains of this nameless squatter.

By six o'clock next morning we were again on the move, passing up the long meadow among groves of twisted aspens that were even now only half upright after their burial under the snows of the previous winter. (Bodie's abbreviated name for these trees was "quaking ass," — so it sounded, — and when I first heard him use the term I imagined that he was making some reference to the jack.) Crossing a low divide the trail passed out on to expanses of barren granite, polished to a glassy surface by glacial action. The animals went nervously clattering and sliding over the glistening rock, from which the sun was reflected with painful intensity. A few twisted junipers grasped the crevices and grew into weird conformations that seemed to express equally the pangs of hunger and the pains of savage storms.

As we rounded a shoulder of mountain, suddenly our lake was before us ; a true Sierra lake, lying open and cold in a cup of granite. Its altitude is sixty-six hundred feet, only a few hundred feet higher than Laurel Lake; but it is of a very different character. The bare granite drops unbroken to the water on the east; around the west a fringe of trees finds a footing ; and at the northern end is a strip of vivid meadow, where should have been our bivouac last night. At the upper end of the lake an antique raft was moored, built of a few logs chained together, the work of some bygone fishermen who would not be denied of the mighty trout that lounge about the deep middle of the water.

This all looked inviting enough, but it was much too early to think of camping; and, moreover, I knew that lakes by scores and hundreds lay before us; strung like beads along every cañon; sunk like secrets in every dark belt of forest; smiling frankly open on high granite plateaus and under eaves of perpetual snow. So, leaving the lake at the south end, and crossing a wild little creek that scours and swirls away over polished rock at cascade speed, we climbed by zigzags over a barren mountain to the east. A magnificent view opened from the ridge to the south and west, the great cliffs of the Hetch-Hetchy rising clear and bold in middle distance, with the forest ocean beyond rolling away and away into blue infinitude.

Here our trail plunged again into heavy timber. These abrupt and frequent transitions are a peculiarity of the Sierra, dreamy forest and explicit granite alternating continually, and both alike painted with cheerful meadows and gardens and ribbons of flowers. In this case, however, the long descent brought us to a tedious region of brush, through which we toiled for hours under a sun that beat down upon us in dizzying blasts of heat. Far below we could see a green and pleasant valley, and winding through it a gleaming creek; but the trail seemed to threaten to pass it by, keeping obstinately along the southward-facing mountain-side. At length a sudden steep descent took us down to the level, and we guessed that we had chanced upon the Till-till, a small valley lying above and to the northeast of the Hetch-Hetchy, corresponding in a way to the position of the Little Yosemite with regard to the Yosemite Valley.

The usual abandoned cabin proclaimed some departed settler. By preference I always avoid the neighborhood of these cheerless objects, with their purlieus of mouldering gunny-sacks and rusty cans, and crossing the creek we came to a halt under a handsome cedar beneath which lay the shed antlers of a deer.

The day being Saturday we made preparations for a two-nights' camp. The principal difference lay in our setting up a rough tent by simply running one of the lash-ropes between a couple of trees and throwing the largest pack-canvas across it, anchoring the sides with rocks or pegs, as convenient. This tent was really only a ceremonious adjunct, of no particular use, but erected in deference to a convention as signifying unlimited ease and comparative permanence.

On this occasion, however, it served a real purpose. Clouds had been gathering all the morning in the north, and thunder rumbled at intervals. Towards evening the storm broke suddenly, while we were employed over the weekly clothes-washing For an hour deluges of rain and hail fell alternately, while we sat in patriarchal wise in the door of our tent, or made sallies in turn to sustain the sputtering fire under the sinkienon. Later, when the mosquito hordes arose in unusual vigor, we lighted a virulent smudge at the windward opening of the tent, and sat looking out at the lee end, reeking and weeping together in the pungent smoke.

The Till-till is a camping-place of unusual attractiveness. It is an enclosed valley of the richest verdure, sown with flowers and planted with a charming variety of trees. All around are timbered mountains, sweeping up on the north to a castle-like summit of crags. On this high peak the thunder-storm delivered its main assault, and it was a fine spectacle to watch the dark gathering of the clouds about it, and to see the glittering spears of lightning leap and quiver against its majestic cliffs. A long promontory of glacial-polished rock divides the valley lengthwise, and rooted in its crannies I found a quaint collection of dwarfed pines and junipers, as wild of shape and aged of look as if they might themselves have been ground under primeval glaciers; six inches of knotted stem to six feet of sinewy root. About the meadow stand delicate aspens and stately pines, and knee-high cyclamens form fairy groves among the tall reeds and grasses. The river abounds with trout, and even the grass of the marshes shivers with wriggling fish. I suppose that to rigorous sportsmen such abundance would be contemptible, but as for us, we fished and ate with no qualms of that sort.

By sunset the storm had passed, and the clouds broke into masses of ragged gold and swept gorgeously away like a procession of kings. Then a timid little moon came up above the southern wall, pouring down her silvery peace upon rain-laden grass and glistening rock and river, a symbol of the meekness that inherits the earth.

I awoke during the night, and lay for a long time watching with admiration too deep for that word the cloudy panorama of the skies. The moon was full and yellow, and the light about her, combining with the intense depth of the open spaces of the heavens, made her seem to be sunk as in a well, dark and clear, from whence her light streamed down with a steady, concentrated effulgence. Vast wings of cloud, feathered with little plumy sprays, rose to beyond the zenith, and against their lower edges the ranks of pine and fir on the high mountain ridge were etched in sooty blackness. The world was very still, as if the operations of Nature were for a time suspended, pausing to fulfil the solemn beauty to the uttermost.

I remember that I had at the time, and have had on similar occasions, a vivid impression of having been purposely awakened; and I sometimes wonder whether there may not be in circumstances of unusual beauty or impressiveness an actual force or presence, which in some mysterious manner passes the locked gates of the senses, and, laying upon us its thrilling hand, wakes us that we may not miss the unearthly pageant. Bodie, however, had a simpler explanation of my wakefulness. He "guessed there was a rock sticking into me."

CHAPTER XIV

THE HIGH SIERRA: THE TILL-TILL TO
LAKE BENSON

FOLLOWING a Sunday of sheer laziness, day-break found us stirring, and by six o'clock we had breakfasted, packed, and were passing up the dew-drenched meadow. At the east end of the valley the trail divides. One branch doubles back to south and west, and connecting with the Rancheria Mountain trail, enters the Hetch-Hetchy at its upper end. We took the other, which swings northward and climbs by zigzags around a peak whose perpendicular crags are built up in tiers like the pipes of a gigantic organ. To the west stood the strong cliffs of the Hetch-Hetchy, and southward a break in the long, flowing ridge of Rancheria Mountain showed the gleam of snow on a higher summit, which Bodie figured would be "off around White Wolf and Smoky Jack."

The morning was cloudless, and blue mist was pouring into the cañon with the sunshine. Through it the meadows of the Till-till and the great ledge of shining rock gave back quick lights like an opal. The sun waxed hot and hotter, and packs shifted with disgusting frequency. There was no sign of the trail having been travelled this year, but tracks of bear, deer, and mountain-lion were unusually plentiful, and grouse boomed in the scrawny, low-growing pines and junipers. A dull and simple-minded bird is the grouse of the Sierra. You may almost walk upon him before he will rise, and then he will but fly to the nearest branch and sit there in plain view, nearly tumbling off in his anxiety to get a good look at you. If you stop to pelt him with stones he does but gaze with deeper interest, quite unable to grasp the idea that the missiles that whiz past are directed at him.

Crossing the divide after a hard climb we passed under a high ridge, forested along the crest and sweeping down in slopes of grass and bracken such as you may see among the Welsh and English mountains. To the east a long barren cañon ran straight for miles to its head, where a line of snowy peaks rose sharply against the sky. Then came a long semi-meadow, edged with aspen and tamarack and sprinkled with violets, cyclamens, forget-me-nots, and, most exquisite of all, myriads of the large lavender daisies (*Erigeron*), which came to be, more than any other of my flower companions, my daily delight while I was in the high altitudes where it grows.

I could willingly devote a chapter to this most charming flower, so greatly did its beauty enter into me during my wanderings in the High Sierra. As with people, so with flowers, simplicity is what makes them lovable: and the compositæ are all for simplicity. I suppose there is no flower that is so beloved as the common daisy; and if it were decreed that all flowers but one, which we might choose, were to be taken from us, this would be the one the world would elect to keep. All over the Sierra these choicest of daisies stand through the summer in countless myriads, giving the chance traveller his friendliest greeting, or in lonely unvisited meadows and forest ways smiling lovingly back at the sky. It is the flower that remains in one's memory the longest, loved far beyond the rarer beauties of those solitudes.

An old cabin stood decaying on the edge of the meadow, and a mile or so farther on, another, its back broken by a tall fir that had fallen across it. A coyote sat on his haunches near by, so engrossed in the moral reflections appropriate to the scene that he did not see us until we were close upon him. Then he loped away with a ridiculous pretence of believing he had not been seen, though every shout sent him scurrying faster. A Clarke crow perched on a tamarack uttered remarkable sounds, expressive, I thought, of malicious pleasure as he watched his retreat. There were all the elements of a fable in the scene.

The trail climbed up among rocky ledges where clumps of pentstemon were blossoming with purple trumpets. Beautiful flowers are these, too; but without the fearless grace of the daisies with their open skyward look. Suddenly at a rise there came into view a long line of notched and splintered peaks only a few miles away, opening southward on a still higher and more distant line which marked the crest of the Sierra. A deep gorge opened below us, with lakelets and meadowlets strung along it, and lines of timber tracing every crease and rift of the granite, black on white, like a charcoal drawing. Down into it our trail seemed about to plunge, but swung abruptly off to the north by a little lake of ale-brown water, half full of fallen timber. Here I met my first Sierra heather (*Bryanthus*), with one spray of rosy blossom still waiting for me. I had been eagerly watching for the little plant which bore such a friendly name, and recognized it at once. I could not forbear kissing the brave little sprig of blossom, and stuck it in my sombrero for remembrance of bygone days on English moors and mountains.

Entering an amphitheatre of granite cliffs we wound steeply down a ledge trail into a cañon that trended northeasterly. Little pools clear as the very air, and pure and fresh as if just poured from a giant pitcher, filled all the rocky basins. These Sierra lakes and streams give one almost a new conception of water, not as something to drink or bathe in, nor as a feature of the scenery, but as the very element. It seems all but intangible, a mere transparent greyness, through which every boulder and splinter of rock on the bottom is seen almost more clearly than if there were no water there.

Passing down a rocky defile we dropped by the middle of the afternoon into what we guessed to be Jack Main Cañon, and fording a wide stream just below where it bursts from a gap of the mountains, went into camp on the farther side with ten or twelve miles of tolerably hard trail to our credit.

I have not been able to discover who Jack Main was, but I certainly commend his taste in cañons. A meadow incredibly flowery shares the valley at this point with a goodly river, — the same, as we found later, which flows into and out of Vernon Lake, and which lower forms the great Hetch-Hetchy Fall.

At this time, and for many days following, we were off the map, and were reduced to the sheerest guessing with regard to our whereabouts. Many and long were the debates around our camp-fires, where three distinct opinions usually developed, and were argued with all the obstinacy which is apt to mark discussions none of the parties to which have any real knowledge of the question in hand. In general terms, our problem was how to reach Soda Springs, somewhere away to the southeast. We were separated from it by a maze of rugged cañons, unknown to all of us, and all running transversely to our desired course.

The close of these discussions was marked, as regards our guide, by a docility that was almost childlike. He was willing, even eager, to defer to my judgment. Did I wish to follow this cañon farther? by all means we would do so. If I really believed we should cross that divide, he was mine to command. It was my party. He had told me he did n't know this piece of country, but he was my devoted guide, and he and his animals would stay by me. When once he could get sight of Mount Conness, however distant, he would be able to locate us with ease and to pilot us handsomely to Soda Springs.

We camped among a clump of tamaracks at the head of the meadow. For a quarter of a mile below, the valley was an unbroken sheet of dwarf lupine, and was literally as blue as the sky. Botanists would find in these Sierra meadows an amazing revelation of Nature's profusion. The wildling flowers stand as thickly as the grass of a well-kept lawn, waving in unbroken sheets of color from wall to wall of the cañons and around the margins of unnumbered lakes. In years to come pilgrimages of enthusiastic flower-lovers will wend to these delightful spots, where now only wild bees stagger in orgies of honey, and fairies dance by the light of the moon.

Investigation showed that we had camped better than we knew. Only a hundred yards above us was a charming little lake which had been hidden from us by the screen of trees. On one side it was fringed with aspens and firs; on the other, the rocky wall dropped perpendicularly to the glassy water.

The country about us here was the wildest we had yet seen, and considered as a prophecy was highly encouraging. Barren mountains rose high and close all around us, domed, peaked, ridged, and not even alloyed with timber except for the few scarred junipers that held the ledges, and seemed as old and gaunt as the mountains themselves.

In the evening I climbed to a high point whence I looked down upon the lake, lying eclipsed almost as if in a well under the shadow of its western cliffs, but still mirroring the glory of the sunlit peaks in the north. Far below, the camp-fire twinkled cheerily. The sound of Pet's bell floated musically up to me. Bodie, a black speck in the dusk of the valley, strolled down the meadow to review the transport department, and I caught on the breeze a stave of pensive sentimentality which seemed to reveal unsuspected deeps.

Slowly the light faded until only one great peak was left, shining like a beacon, solitary, white, pyramidal. As the sky darkened this glowed more brightly, seeming to collect and focus all the remaining light in the heavens. Then suddenly the grey shadow leaped upon it, and it appeared to sink and crumble like a burned-out log. I climbed down and stumbled through the darkness back to camp, where I found my companions transformed into two mosquito-proof bundles, to which I quickly added a third.

Next morning we marched up the cañon, skirting the north shore of the lake. Granite cliffs still walled us in, and the trail lay over areas of glacial rock over which the river rushed in white cascades down a wild and treeless gorge. Little half-acre gardens, shoulder high with grasses and flowers, occur even in this rough country, providing constantly fresh subjects of admiration and delight. By way of contrast I was never tired of noticing the quaint behavior of the junipers that were sparsely dotted about on the ledges of the cañon walls. There is a general resemblance in their deportment to the accepted portraits of Bluff King Hal, but while some are jovial fellows, holding their sides while they guffaw with inextinguishable laughter, others are like vicious Quilps and Calibans, sneering and fleering down so savagely that it is a pleasure to remember that they are rooted to their places.

A few miles and we came to another lake, lying in a meadow surrounded by rocky walls, and with a fine pyramidal peak at its eastern end. As we reached the higher altitudes, the mosquitoes became constantly more malicious and diabolical. Here they came at us ding-dong, like very Bedouins, biting savagely at every exposed part, careless of death so they could but once taste our blood. There is a deep pleasure in the reflection that untold millions of the creatures in these solitudes must live and die with that intolerable craving never once gratified.

The country here was sparsely wooded and the trail partly blazed and partly "monumented." There is a humorous disproportion between this high-sounding word and the frail thing it represents. Two or three scraps of rock leaned together or placed one on the other to a height of a few inches, or a loose fragment perched on the top of a permanent boulder, constitute a "monument" in the language of the trail. It is by these feeble tokens that the track is marked through treeless country and over expanses of rock that hold no more sign of having been travelled than would a city pavement over which half-a-dozen persons a year might pass; and as they are often so far apart as to be hardly visible from one to the next, it behooves the traveller ignorant of his way to bear a wary eye. At the parting of main trails the monument may tower to three or four feet, but in general and over wide areas it is "like a tale of little meaning, tho' the words are strong."

From time to time I had caught glimpses of the great peak which I had watched at sunset. Now, fording the creek in rather deep water with a powerful current, that threatened for a moment the safety, without disturbing the equanimity, of our brave little Jenny, we made straight towards it. A white torrent came roaring over a cliff-like rise that fronted us, and beside this we climbed, the trail ascending like a stairway. I fancied that our straining animals eyed us indignantly as they clambered from ledge to ledge, all but Pet, who strode along as freely as if he were on a boulevard. Even here parterres of flowers, mimulus, pentstemon, and columbine, grew among the tumbled rocks, and mats of bryanthus hung in eaves over the margin of the stream.

As we gained the summit of the divide yet another lake came in sight, lying against the shoulder of the peak we had just rounded. From its shape we guessed it to be Tilden Lake, — a winding, river-like sheet of water, romantic to a degree, nearly two miles long, running in bays and reaches of placid silver between rocky shores. Files and companies of hemlock, dark almost to blackness, marched out on the promontories and clouded the magnificent sweep of the mountain sides. Looking up the lake to the northeast, there rose my great mountain, a superb shape, massive but symmetrical, beautifully sculptured with pinnacles and turrets and marbled with clots of snow. It was Tower Peak, rising to an altitude of 11,700 feet, one of the summit crests of this part of the Sierra. A little to the west stood another stately mountain, built up in unbroken slopes of granite that ridged up to a culminating precipice like the climbing surge of an ocean wave.

Bird-life is scarce in this high region, and I was surprised to see two swallows playing over the lake, which lies at 9000 feet. A fine adventurous spirit they must have, and a brave spring of romance there must be in their sturdy little hearts, to find out this lonely spot for their summer idyll. "Even thine altars," said the Psalmist. Most true.

In the absence of maps we had no idea how near we were at this point to the divide of the Sierra. Tower Peak was not more than four miles away in an air-line, and on its northern face were the headwaters of the Walker River. I had not taken sufficiently into account the westerly trend of this part of the range, and we had all been misled by a preconception that the run of the cañons was more easterly and westerly than in fact it is.

The lake continued in a chain of smaller lakes, and

leaving these our trail swung to the south down a long, rocky cañon. We found ourselves now in a perfect maze, marching and countermarching, crossing divide after divide and creek after creek, until about two o'clock, tired, hungry, and puzzled, we straggled down a long descent and went into camp beside a loquacious stream in a grove of aspen and tamarack.

By the simple mathematical feat of moving the decimal point of supper two hours forward we secured a long evening of unbroken leisure. O the delight of those Sierra evenings! The blessed quietude, that lies on you like a soft pressure, and cools like a woman's hand; the hushed talking of the stream as it runs around the bend, or laps and drains under sodden eaves of moss; the delicious rose of sunset-lighted snow-peaks; the always friendly companionship of trees; the purling soliloquy of the fire; the surprise of the first star, and the wistful magic of moonlight; the pleasant ghosts that sit with you around the fire and call you by forgotten nicknames; the old regrets that hold no sorrow; the old joys that do; the good snow-chill of the wind drawing steadily down the cañon; the quick undressing and turning in, and the instant oblivion —

— And the offensive suddenness of four o'clock in the morning, when we got up by half moonlight that cast our reluctant shadows on frost-whitened ground. Before six o'clock we had forded the river and were scaling the southern wall of the cañon,

amid a heavy forest of fir, mountain-pine, and hemlock. The divine freshness and zest of the morning
combined with the genial exhilaration of coffee and
the cordial of the first pipe to raise our spirits to the
point of song, and we were not surprised nor yet
abashed, when Jack for once broke silence and halted
the cavalcade while he joined our chorus in lugubri-
ous octaves.

Crossing the first divide we were in full sight of
a deeply cleft crest which we took to be the Matterhorn peaks, but later found was the Sawtooth
Ridge. We were near enough to them to note the
terrible precipices that fall from the spiky pinnacles,
trimmed even now in mid-July with snow-fields.

The opposite wall of the next cañon rose impos-
ingly high and sharp, crowned with two dominating
peaks. At each ridge we hoped to secure an outlook
to south and east, by which we might gain a rough
idea of our position from the bearing of the peaks
of the Cathedral and Lyell groups; but always the
high wall closed in our view, and we were fain to
plunge into the cañons and climb the ridges one by
one, with very little idea of how many more awaited
us.

It was a day of flowers, especially a day of daisies.
Almost equal to the impression produced by the
power and magnificence of the mountains themselves was the pleasure I found in the continual
appearances of these companions of the way. The
characteristics of climate that render California re-

markable for her abundance of flowers are not confined to the valleys of the state, but invade the
mountains even to the limit of perpetual snow. Nor
is it only in the forests and mountain meadows that
the flowers congregate. Every ledge and cranny has
its bush of pentstemon, or sprinkle of mimulus, or
waving fringe of daisies. Around each pool and lake
grow bryanthus and cyclamens, and from the midst
of uncompromising boulders the great willow-herb
(*Epilobium*) bursts in torrents of lively purple. Even
on wind-scoured pavements the inch-high dwarf
phlox will contrive to flourish, covering itself with
pathetically tiny blossoms like pale little faces of
children.

A dwarf variety of the manzanita also appeared
here, blooming at this altitude two months later than
in the lower valleys. Instead of the strong, elbowy
shrub of the foothill and Yosemite levels, it is here
a flat-growing, matted plant, creeping horizontally
along the ground, its brittle twigs interlaced like a
basket. Its Greek name of *Arctostaphylos* matches
well with the brushy tassels of bloom, that are like
little classic vases cut in alabaster.

In the next cañon the trail divided just before
reaching the stream, and again we were put to guessing. The usual difference of opinion was in evidence,
and on Bodie's advice we took the westerly branch,
which climbed through a gap and rounded a pinnacled peak. Here a cluster of lovely lakelets lay in deep
pockets of the mountains, ringed with hemlocks.

The beauty of these high Alpine lakes is perfect and delightful; but awful, too. There is a solemnity in their high-raised, unsullied purity and quietude, a divine openness like that we see in the faces of children.

Why does complete beauty, in which there is innocence, make us sigh? Is it that we are conscious of separation and reproach, and sigh, perhaps, less for the innocence that must be than for that which has been lost? There is solemnity, too, in the changeless passage of Time in these high solitudes. Like perpetual flowers these lakes have lain for unmarked centuries, giving back blue to the blue heaven or whitening to sudden silver as the roaming wind goes by. Through innumerable nights the slow courses of the stars have passed over the dark crystal of their waters. Years go over them like hours, seasons are no more than beats of a pendulum. Possibly the whole course of human history has run while these unnoticed pools have lain watching the inscrutable sky, awaiting the world-changes that to us are science, to them, perhaps, life (for how impossible it seems that through all the slow birth and growth of human intelligence, age by age, the earth itself should contract no consciousness, and suffer only passionless change).

Circling around the base of the pinnacled monster that guards the pass, the trail dropped steeply by a wild cañon where the ground was boggy with runnels of water from melting snow-banks just above us, and entered unexpectedly a dense growth of timber, where it was lost among windfallen trees. Casting about for it we came upon a larger oval lake, under the east shoulder of the mountain. This we found later to be Benson Lake, lying at 8000 feet, and the mountain Piute Mountain, with an altitude of 10,500 feet; but at the time we knew nothing of names or elevations, and every lake was a new surprise, so that our wanderings had almost the zest of original explorations. Our geographical senses were exercised continually in forecasting the probable run of the streams and cañons we encountered; and we were beginning to be occupied also with the question whether our supplies would hold out until we found the means of replenishing them either at Soda Springs or at the settlements on Mono Lake.

Here we pitched camp on a blue carpet of lupines and under the lee of a curving beach of white sand. This lake is about two hundred acres in extent, enclosed on three sides by rocky walls, quite precipitous in places and rising to four conspicuous peaks. The other side, the northern, is a beach of fine hard sand backed by a strip of meadow that merges into dense forest. One or two clumps of fir are wedged into gorges of the eastern wall, and push down to the water's edge. A stream lively with trout rushes into the lake at the east end of the beach, which lies in crescent bays. A strong breeze blows continually from the south, sending the waves lapping noisily up on the beach, the wet sand of which bore a remarkable collection of autographs in the tracks of bear, deer, and other game, together with those of large wading birds. The smaller birds also were more in evidence here than we had lately found them, and the place seems to have attractions for a variety of creatures usually of very different shades of opinion. While we sat at supper in the dusk, a heron came sailing above our camp and alighted sociably in the top of a small tamarack close by, where it remained for some time observing our arrangements with interest, and quite careless of our notice.

Sitting on the shore of this delightful lake as night came down I revelled in the deep quietude of the place, while I watched the wavelets creeping in endless ranks out of the dusk and running playfully at my feet like kittens. The tree companies behind me seemed to move back and withdraw into the gloom. At half-past eight, one peak in the east, a sort of prong or tooth of granite, still caught the sun-glow, and towered up, a pile of rosy magic, into the clear, cold sky of early night. After my companions had turned in I sat for an hour or two by the fire, seeing again in the embers the long sunlit cañons, the grateful shadowy aisles of forest, the daisied meadows, the headlong cascades, the strong free sweep of the granite sea; and up there, two thousand feet overhead, where the bulk of Piute Mountain impended over me like a cloud, those little lakes, stark and open to the cold sky, with the ghostly snow-glimmer around them, waiting for the slow dawn of another day of the eternal solitude.

Before I turned in I took another look at the lake. The wind had changed to northerly, and the nearer half, sheltered by the ridge of sand, reflected placidly the surrounding mountains and the diamond glitter of the stars. The farther part was a dull gleam of steel. The moon was not yet up, but the high western peaks were beginning to catch her first light, and glimmered from an enhanced height with a look of unutterable age. The whisper of the creek pushing out into the lake kept all the air quietly athrob. Then from far up on the western precipice came the sharp report of a falling boulder, pried over by the sudden leverage of the frost. The sound grew into a hoarse rattle, and then to a thunderous tumult that reverberated in the hollow cup of the mountains like the roar of a monster trying in vain to escape. Gradually it lessened and sank into murmurs and mutterings, with word-like pauses and replies, dying away at last under some black rampart far down the lake. Then the singing voice of the creek took up again its quiet recitative.

CHAPTER XV

WE breakfasted next morning by half-moon-light, and by six o'clock broke camp. Field and I had prospected out the trail, the losing of which we nowise regretted, since it had thrown us upon this delightful lake, destined, I am sure, to become one of the favorite lakes of the Sierra.

The trail bore at first due east, and we started out upon it with confidence, believing that our perplexities were over. Fording the stream and crossing a low divide, we passed close under a remarkable peak, in shape a vast arch topped with a transverse elongated dome which terminates in a cliff of not far short of a thousand feet. A broad belt of snow lay along the foot of the cliff, and below that a huge promontory of talus ran off at a keen angle.

Rounding this mountain, my rose pyramid of last night appeared straight ahead. A snow-field lay under its summit, and from this the water streamed in countless rills, falling from slab to slab and filling the air with musical murmurs. Along the gullies flowers still grew thickly, columbines and larkspurs waving above thick beds of bryanthus and purple pentstemon. This latter is a handsome, generous-looking flower, larger but more ethereal than the much-admired crimson species of the lower valleys. Daisies sprinkled all the grassy hollows, adding a lovable grace to the stately gravity of the mountains.

It was not without a vast amount of grunting and complaint on the part of the animals, and several repackings, that we reached the top of the pass, for the trail was the steepest we had encountered. In the very neck of the pass was a small round lake surrounded by a meadow of the usual "short-hair" grass of high altitudes. It was intensely silent, lonely, and desolate. Three plovers were flying to and fro over the water, silently playing some ghostly kind of game; the wind silently trembled the brittle heather; the sky silently watched the lake, and the lake silently mirrored back the sky; the mountains stood silently around, pondering and intent. There was something spell-like in the absolute soundlessness, as though it never had been and never must be broken. Even the mosquitoes came silently to the attack, rising in grey, imp-like clouds from their ambush in the grass, and settling on us in a gloomy, predestined fashion that was most demoralizing.

This, as we later found, was Murdock Lake, lying at 9500 feet of elevation. At its north side rises a thousand feet higher my sunset pyramid (Volunteer Peak on the map of the Geological Survey). On the other side the trees march down to the water's edge, and framed between mountain and timber runs the rag-

ged line of the Sawtooth Ridge. Field and I climbed
up on the shoulder of the hill to the west of the lake,
and obtained, as we expected, a wonderful outlook,
— an uninterrupted view for many miles of the crest
of the Sierra, a tumult of peaks and precipices that
rose and fell with the wild passion of the waves of a
stormy ocean. The foreground and middle distance
were a rocking sea of granite, running in abrupt
points and hollows, and clouded with patches of
forest.

On leaving the lake at the southeast end, the trail
divided once more. One branch turned northeasterly,
the other to the south. Knowing that we were already farther to the north of the Tuolumne River
than we wished to be we took the latter, which we
followed first down a wooded cañon and then along
a grassy valley with a pretty, winding stream. I soon
observed that the trail was making more westerly
than I liked, but contented myself with keeping a
look-out for any sign of a cross-trail. Mile after mile
we went on until we reached the foot of the cañon.
There the trail, throwing off all disguise, turned
frankly westward and then northwestward, exactly
contrary to our required direction. Still, with a miserable perversity which it amuses me now to recall,
we kept on. It appeared later that we all had been
possessed by the same insanity, each of us perfectly
aware that we were heading the wrong way, and
each doggedly keeping the knowledge in his own
breast.

A few miles to the south I could see the precipitous walls of a gloomy gorge which I felt sure must be the cañon of the Tuolumne. I pointed this out to my companions, but they were gloomy too, and we marched on in devoted obstinacy. Then came a long, steep descent, down which we scrambled wearily; and threading our way through a jungle of vegetation, found ourselves in a small, aspen-bordered valley on the margin of a considerable stream spanned by a bridge, near which were traces of a recent campfire. Ignoring the bridge we forded the stream, and hastily unpacking our weary beasts went into camp once more in No Man's Land.

We had seen from above that the trail, after crossing the stream, climbed the steep side of a forested mountain on the west. After an hour's rest and a light meal Field and I explored this continuation of our trail for a mile or two farther, hoping, if not to find a cross-trail, at least to get some light on our whereabouts. As we gained an outlook to north and east we confirmed our suspicions that we had been travelling all day nearly in a circle, and that the creek we were camped on was none other than the one that flowed through Lake Benson. We were in fact again on Piute Creek, and only a few miles southwest of our last camp. We also suspected that the wooded mountain over which the trail continued to the southwest was Rancheria Mountain, and we knew that if that was so, by following it we should certainly find ourselves back in the Hetch-Hetchy.

Near the summit a new trail led off to the northwest, but that promised nothing better than a return to the maze of mountains and cañons among which we had lately been wandering.

Two or three times in the last few days we had come upon scraps of pencilled writing left wedged between boulders, or stuck into crevices of the bark of trees. They had been sometimes in the nature of serio-comic soliloquies, sometimes of complaints or disparaging comments upon the topography of the country: such as, —

"What the blazes am I going to do now? H. J."

"Oh, where is the old trail at? H. J."

"This is something fierce. H. J."

It was here that we found the last wail of this unknown brother in distress. A leaf of a note-book was stuck among the stones of the monument that marked the fork of the trail, and on it was written, —

"All in. Can't get through. Going back to the valley. H. J."

With these somewhat gloomy items of intelligence we returned to camp. Bodie, with fine recklessness, had prepared a thumping dinner, topping off the hot bread, steaming murphies, and sustaining beans with a fancy course of rice and syrup, in which he had let his imagination run to the length of stirring in a short dozen of prunes which he had excavated from some corner of the grub-pack. Then, in a comforting scarcity of mosquitoes, we made a noble camp-fire, discussed the situation, and determined that we must retrace our steps in the morning and hunt out the easterly trail which we had somehow missed.

It was not without disgust that we started next day on our back-trail. Breakfast had revealed the fact that it was becoming a matter of urgency for us to make Soda Springs quickly. Our last potato stared us rudely in the face, and Bodie reported flour for only two more loaves. We looked carefully as we went along for any indication of a cross-trail. The scanty timber was all tamarack, a tree which, with its thin bark and excessive resin, is a simple one to blaze, but also easily becomes a snare to the traveller, since any scar made by falling trees or branches quickly fills with resin and is then difficult to distinguish from an orthodox blaze.

Coming nearly to the head of the long valley we found a distinct blaze marked on a tamarack on the farther side of the creek. This, then, was our clue; but a huge barricade of windfallen timber had wiped out every other trace of a trail. For an hour or more we worked like foxhounds at this problem, feeling sure that we were on the right track, but unable to pick up the trail beyond the windfall. At last Bodie, skirmishing far ahead on Pet, struck faint signs of an old track, more like a deer-trail than anything else, and we took to it with some misgivings. It headed up by the south side of our pyramid, passing close beside and around it. I now observed that the upper one thousand feet or so is built of thin perpendicular slabs, regular in size, and squared as if cut by a mason ; the same formation, I suspect, as is found in the so-called Devil's Post-piles. The top slabs had weathered apart, and some of them were leaning outwards ready to fall and add to the vast accumulation of débris at the foot.

Crossing a snow-bank we came upon another charming Alpine lake, narrow and winding, and dotted with rocky islets. Dark-foliaged pines stood about the margin, and on the south towered a great mountain, its rifted seams and gleaming snow-fields reflected deeply on a surface like liquid steel. It was Rodgers Lake, lying at an altitude of 9500 feet : a true Sierra lake, lost and inviolate among a wilderness of stately peaks. It stands high on my mental list of the places I hope to revisit.

The trail leaves the lake at its northern end and enters an amphitheatre of granite cliffs. The ground was soaked with snow-water that trickled down on every side, and some care was necessary to avoid getting our animals mired down. Then came another lake (Smedberg), hardly less delightful than the last. In the meadow surrounding it a few long-stemmed buttercups greeted us, though the lupines were not even yet in bloom. Here we ate a frugal lunch, drinking from the drip of a friendly snow-bank.

The scenery here is of the wildest, the very scrap-pile of Nature. Even the trees are of strange and painful shapes, a few dressed scantily with shivering scraps of foliage, but for the most part barkless, white, and polished like bone by scouring storms.

Their appearance would call up one's pity, but that they are pines; sympathy for that royal race seems a superfluous impertinence.

As we rose from our meal I became aware that a group of five buck, with horns in velvet, had been standing overlooking us from a rock hardly fifty feet above where we sat. There was the click of twenty hoofs on the granite, and in a moment they had vanished " into air, into thin air."

A few miles more of strenuous climbing, and we crossed the high divide of Benson Pass at 10,130 feet. There occurs here a curious ridge of loose white sand, the result, I suppose, of an extreme degree of disintegration due to unusual stress of weather in this bleak pass. Once more we looked out upon a sea of mountains, no whit less rugged and intricate than those we had threaded. The air rang with the metallic tinkle of a thousand rills that streamed from the snow-fields around us. A curious effect is produced by the melting of the surfaces of evenly sloping sheets of snow under the direct rays of the sun. The crust, harrowed by the constant trickling of water, appears as though a fine comb had been drawn over it, the myriad channels all maintaining a perfectly parallel alignment.

Turning then southeasterly we entered a narrow, bouldery gorge with high, snow-laced cliffs on our right, somewhat lower barren ones on the left, and a bold white ridge barricading us in front. Isolated pillars of rock of grotesque shapes rose from the

sandy floor of the cañon, which from its peculiar
character we hoped might be Alkali Creek Cañon,
debouching upon the Tuolumne River a few miles
below Soda Springs. But at the foot the trail swung
again to the north, and we had no choice but to go
on, anxiously scanning the east side of the cañon for
a cross-trail. At last we espied the blaze on the farther side of the creek, forded, and with fresh heart
struck once more southerly.

But another disappointment awaited us. After
climbing a steep ridge the trail headed again northeast, dropped into yet another cañon, and crossed
another divide. Mile after mile and hour after hour
passed in this puzzling work. We were making east,
certainly, which was so far to the good, but north-
ing also, which was entirely to the bad. So on we
marched, fording creek after creek, crossing ridge
after ridge, hemlocks giving place to tamaracks and
tamaracks to hemlocks as we wandered up and
down.

About sundown we emerged in a new cañon with
a wide, strong stream, and, completely tired out, determined to camp, leaving to-morrow or some later
to-morrow to solve the riddle. We had been twelve
hours out, on the very roughest trails in the mountains, and had eaten hardly anything since five o'clock
that morning.

A supper of flapjacks (no longer, alas, "men's
sizes," — a *jeu d'esprit* of our good Bodie by which
he was wont to designate the plump "jacks" that he

delighted to deal out to us in times of plenty), and a grateful pot of tea brought us quickly refreshment of body, and, more gradually, peace of spirit. A miserably cold wind blew strongly down the cañon, but not strongly enough to quiet the mosquitoes. Lighting a trio of smudges we spread our blankets between them and turned in, still out of our reckoning, but somewhere in the United States, as we supposed.

We were astir at dawn, — by this time a matter of habit, — and made a leisurely breakfast. Since we did not know where we were, nor yet where we were going, it seemed superfluous to hurry. Moreover, there was a feeling in the air that to-day would almost certainly bring us into the neighborhood of Soda Springs and fresh supplies. At the lowest computation, the distance we had made must have put us well into the angle that is formed, roughly speaking, by the main crest of the Sierra and the Tuolumne River. Still, it was a solemn moment when we saw Bodie convert the last of our flour into the morning flapjacks, and we gazed upon each spreading disk with some emotion.

Again we betook ourselves to our eternal cañons, ridges, and divides. The trail led through a dim forest of hemlock and fir, where mats of the dwarf blue lupine in the openings gave back the hue of the sky in almost solid sheets of color. In damper places the giant variety grew to a remarkable size, waving heavy clusters of blossoms head high to the animals. Here I noticed the first appearance of a new kind of heather, which I identified as the *Cassiope* to which Mr. Muir refers so often and so lovingly. It is a delightful plant, graceful and delicate, yet with the sturdy demeanor of the mountaineer. The blossom is a white bell, borne in clusters in heather fashion, but larger and rather more open than the *Erica* of Bonnie Scotland. My much loved daisies grew prosperously in every glade and meadowlet, enchaining my affections daily more and more by their air of high-bred simplicity.

To our great comfort the trail, after traversing a succession of open meadows strewn with boulders, headed straight southeastward, and persevered in that direction, following a long, straight cañon. Remembering the past, we held our spirits in check until, after some miles of steady marching, we came in sight of a group of splintery peaks with a quaint, pencil-pointed horn beside them. We recognized them at once as the Cathedral and Unicorn peaks, and knew that Soda Springs, the much desired, the necessary in fact, lay a few miles on their hither side.

With light hearts we pushed on down a gentle slope, and about noon arrived at the foot of the cañon. Crossing a trouty stream, another mile brought us to the Tuolumne River at a point where there occurs a wide fall known as the White Rapids, — the first of a succession of falls and cascades by which the river begins to drop from the high levels of its upper course to enter the great gorge which widens lower down into the Hetch-Hetchy Valley. Here Bodie was himself again, and willingly resumed his abrogated functions.

Now that Soda Springs was within reach I was in no hurry to get there. I loved it not for itself but for the supplies it afforded; and in any case we should have to pass through the Tuolumne Meadows in order to reach Bloody Cañon, the pass by which we intended to cross to the eastern side of the Sierra. But we were here within a few miles of Tenaya Lake, one of the most renowned, because one of the few visited, lakes of the Sierra. So while Bodie with Clementine rode to the Springs, a few miles to the east, Field and I forded the river below the rapids and struck into a southwest trail for the lake, where Bodie was to rejoin us.

A change came over the scenery at this point by which we might have guessed, if we had not known, that we were not far from the Yosemite. In the sixteen days we had been out we had described what amounted in effect to a circle (though of a highly irregular kind), of which the Yosemite might be regarded as a narrow southern chord. We entered now upon domes and swelling contours, imposing in their gravity of line, though far less stimulating to the fancy than the wilder peaks among which we had been wandering. To a geologist no doubt every half-mile of all this cliff and cañon would be as a page of a book. I only see the vast aspects, and wonder at the finished product.

It is an overwhelming thought that in the view of Him to whom " one day is as a thousand years, and a thousand years as one day," the age-long processes of Nature may appear but momentary. How sublime would be the spectacle, so regarded, of the tremendous plane of ice, shearing with irresistible sweep these knotted mountains, and casting off to right and left like shavings the forest-bearing moraines!

A mile after crossing the river the trail skirted a narrow lake, of a peculiar greenish hue, named after some forgotten scion of the tribe of McGee. Then for some miles we traversed a rough tract of country where huge boulders powdered a granite plateau, mixed with a thin tamarack forest which in some miraculous manner has secured a foothold and forces a subsistence from this unpromising inheritance.

I was much entertained by the sagacious behavior of Pet, whom in Bodie's absence I was riding in place of my regular mount. Field was in the lead on the black mule, who was usually assigned to that post for his virtues as a trail-finder, — his only, but admirable, characteristic. Following him came Jack and Jenny. Probably Jack noticed that Bodie was away, and presumed upon my milder rule; anyhow, he was particularly disagreeable, and pointedly refused to keep in the trail. Contumacy was in the very flop of his ears. After I had headed him off several times he became violently angry, and revenged himself by charging about among the trees and rocks with the plain intention of doing as much damage as he could to his packs. It was deliberate malice, and I rope-ended him accordingly.

Pet, who at every opportunity asserted his superiority to his four-footed companions by ranging himself with the bipeds, entered into the quarrel with great enjoyment. With tail switching he closed up on the recalcitrant burro, almost treading on his heels, and harassing him by biting him on the flanks: all the while keeping a sharp eye on his heels, you may be sure. Whenever the miserable jack, wrought to a pitch of frenzy, bolted from the trail, Pet would toss his head with malicious delight, gather himself for a jump, and waltz over the obstructions in the gayest of spirits, appearing unexpectedly before the enraged animal whichever way he turned, and crowding him backwards with his neck twisted almost to the point of dislocation. All that I had to do was to attend to the protuberant parts of my body, ducking my head to avoid branches and shielding my knees as best I could from contact with the huge boulders. It was as good as polo, but it was hard on the packs. The sinkienon, bound *à la* Mazeppa, and wedged between the horns of the pack-saddle, rode out the storm in safety, and the photographic plates, packed in strong wooden boxes, also came through undamaged; but the weaker brethren suffered some contusions, and the coffee-pot sustained a compound fracture of the handle, necessitating amputation.

Jenny's behavior was correct and ladylike as ever.

Her place in the line was always following Jack, and I believe the meek little thing had a real feeling of loyalty to him. Whenever he became obstreperous she would turn off the trail after him for a few paces and then stand looking on with cocked ears, and an embarrassed expression like a third party at a quarrel. Once when I had to make a long détour in heading Jack into the trail, we had gone on for some distance before I noticed that Jenny was missing. I rode back half a mile, and was beginning to think I had missed her when I caught sight of her standing on a big boulder upon which she had scrambled, certainly with some difficulty, in order, I suppose, to be in plain view. She was patiently waiting to be called for.

As we neared Lake Tenaya the mountains showed more and more the capped and plated formation that is so noticeable in the domes of the great valley. The "monumented" trail passed over wide expanses of glacier-polished rock that glittered like glass and reflected the sunlight and the heat into our faces with unpleasant ardor. It was a relief to see the glint of blue water between the tree-stems, and shortly we emerged at the lake side. Following the edge of the lake to its northern end, we made camp in a thin grove of pines that fringed a meadow, and had hardly got things shipshape when Bodie appeared. He had made a quick trip of several miles more than we had covered, and had secured the needed supplies : not much, nor luxuries, but enough to restore the valuable flapjack to the bill of fare, together with sundry other items which had passed into history.

Lake Tenaya is one of the largest and most accessible of the Sierra lakes, and its repute stands high for beauty. Certainly it is a lovely sheet of water, clear as the element can be, and surrounded by fine, and at one end striking, mountains. Directly from its eastern side Mount Tenaya towers up two thousand feet above the lake, whose altitude is 8100 feet. To the northwest, a smoothly sculptured mountain of granite called Murphy's Dome sweeps up to almost an equal height. Between them, at the head of the meadow, stands a quaint little truncated cone some eight hundred feet in height, shaped like a fez, or a candle extinguisher. A winding creek steals through the meadow, carrying the water of Cathedral Lake. Farther to the west Mount Hoffman rises magnificently to close upon 11,000 feet, and almost due south, and only five miles away in an air-line, Clouds' Rest marks the eastern end of the Yosemite Valley. From the lower end of the lake issues Tenaya Creek, the stream which as it enters the valley widens into the pretty pool that is dignified with the name of Mirror Lake, and which joins the Merced River at the upper end of the valley itself.

With all my admiration of Lake Tenaya, however, I invite the appreciative tourist who may visit its charming shores to believe that along the almost unvisited High Sierra there lie scores of lakes equally or more delightful. I do not forget that tastes in scenery differ, but I think that the genius of a lake, unlike that of a river, accords best with the wild and desolate aspects of Nature. It is quietude embodied, and the voiceless solitudes of the upper world of barren peak, high thin air, and stainless snow-field are best suited to its lonely spirit. So I can hardly believe that any lake-lover would not agree that those lost, solitary, created-and-forsaken pools of silent loveliness, hidden away among the crags and fastnesses of the high back ranges, exceed in true lake charm even this handsome sheet of more accessible water.

To-morrow would be Sunday, so we should not move camp. Field, nevertheless, turned in early, with a sunrise picture on his brain. Bodie soon followed, soothed by the knowledge of being again in his own territory, and of grub-packs replenished to a point which would carry us safely to Mono Lake, where there are stores and civilization, of a kind. I for my part sat by the hour at the camp-fire after the last mosquito had retired, watching in the still mirror of the water the heavens and the earth gazing at one another, like lovers entranced. Every star was duplicated, and breathed with the breathing of the lake. The Milky Way was reflected in a dull smear of grey. The mountains merged and ran into grotesque shapes; at the lower end they became alligators, lying snout to snout. Once the silence was broken when a grouse drummed on the mountain side: I imagined him gazing in sleepy wonder from his roost at the red fire with its winking double in the water.

I walked around the little bay on the white, crunching sand, to note for myself the impressionist effect, and found it rather fine: — red, yellow, black, and grey, with murky brown lights on the under side of the smoke that trailed away over the lake. It was very quiet, and Nature was very big. It seemed an impertinence for man to light his puny picket-fires on her frontier. Pale sheet lightning began to play, flickering over the great mountain opposite like firelight dancing on the walls of a room. It reminded me of how I used to think, as a child, that when I was rich and grown-up (the same thing), I would always have a fire in my bedroom to lie and look at. For once, at least, I had two; and luxuriously I threw on another log to make a blaze to undress by. It is even so that many of our childish dreams come true, — with a difference.

CHAPTER XVI

BODIE: "WELL, SIR — "

THE town of Bodie, — or is it, perchance, a "city"? — lying a score of miles to the north of Mono Lake, was in its earlier days a place of ferociously bad repute. Although, so far as I am aware, Bret Harte does not mention it, his genial ruffians must have known it well. But in these dull times, when not only law but order reigns over the Sierra, the place subsists, so far as pungency of reputation is concerned, upon its past; the real has toned into the realistic; and bad men are spelled with capital letters in a poor attempt to revive the glories of the past.

Some local patriot with a fancy for alliteration, bent upon retarding in this case the obliterating process, has promulgated a legend of a "Bad Man from Bodie with a Butcher-knife in his Boot." I had been entertained with this epic, and when I encountered an individual who actually bore the name of the reprobate town I was naturally interested, and my eyes sought his boots in an endeavor to identify him with the Bodie "of that ilk." A very short acquaintance showed, however, that in his case the badness and the butcher-knife were mere pleasantries of speech, and fuller knowledge resulted in a sincere liking which the critical intimacy of camp-life has confirmed, and cemented with respect.

I think it was when we were camped in the Tilltill that, glancing over one Sunday morning about five o'clock to Bodie's sleeping-place, I saw the smoke of reverie already ascending from his placid form. It came out in subsequent conversation that he had been engaged in benevolent reflections upon how he would like to "dump a thousand or more of them young monkeys out of the Bowery and them places down in a medder like this here, kind of on a suddent, so's they would n't know it was coming. And, say, how'd it be to put in a bunch of milk cows, and a band of burros for 'em to ride? Whoopee!"

It appeared from occasional similar remarks that the Bad Man's thoughts somewhat frequently took this peculiar range when they were for a time released from the cares of his profession. To a remark bearing upon the beauty of the scenery or the weather, or the goodness of the water or the beans, this sympathetic human chord, or *vox humana*, in him never failed to respond, though in an oblique and apologetic manner. Once, indeed, he recounted to Field and myself an instance of practical philanthropy on his part, discounting it at the start by giving us to understand that it was only a sporadic outbreak.

Grasshoppers were under discussion in some connection. "Well, sir," Bodie remarked, "there's one good act, as you might say, that I did once in my life, and them insects remind me of it: though I don't blow about it, you understand." Being assured that we understood, and urged to relate the particulars of this solitary episode, he continued : —

"It was when I was up in Montana, in the Big Hole River country, along in the eighties. I had quite a little bunch of cattle in them days, and it so happened I had four or five cows come fresh along about together, and of course the calves was little and could n't take near all the milk, so I had a heap more than I could get away with; that is, until the calves should grow bigger. I used to take and milk them cows on to the ground, for to free them of the milk they carried that would have hurt them. Many 's the gallon of good milk I 've seen run away down them prairie-dogs' holes : it was sure a bonanza for them little cusses, unless some of them got drownded out.

"It happened one day, branding, I threw a steer kind of awkward so he broke a leg, and of course I had to butcher him. Well, sir, that day, or the next, — I forget which and it don't matter, — along comes a family that was in mighty bad shape. They was driving, of course, and the whole outfit was as poor and peakied and pitiful as ever you see. There was seven of them, father and mother and three girls, all well growed, and two younger boys, and they was all thin, and dirty, and their clothes was all dirty and tore. Say, d' you ever notice that people what 's dirty is generally thin? I don't say always, mind you, but generally. Well, that's the way these people was. Good people, too, they was, honest and decent: aye, and the man he told me, — and I believe it, too, — that two years before he would n't have took twenty-five thousand dollars for his holdings, away down in Kansas somewhere. Them grasshoppers had done him up. Two years running they came, and they cleaned him out like a tenderfoot in a 'Frisco poker-joint.

"Well, sir, the whole family was moving along, going anywhere to get out of that country; and if you'll believe me, they was bringing along with them an old runt of a cow that was poor as sin, like the rest of them, and give no more milk than what you could milk into that lard-pail over there, the little one. They had that and they had some corn meal, and that was dead plumb all them people had to eat; literally nothing else on earth did they have. And their horses was poor, and the old wagon squeaked, and they was all naturally broke up.

"Well, sir, I see this outfit coming along, and I calls out to them and asks them where they come from and where was they going; and they up and tells me the whole rigamaree. So I says to them, 'Turn in right here,' I says, 'and bring your horse-pail, and here's another horse-pail of mine, and them young women had best go over and milk them heifers over there. And,' I says, 'I killed a beef yesterday, and you can take all you want of the meat, for there's a heap more 'n I can begin to use.' Well, sir, say, you'd ought to have seen that outfit; it did me good to see 'em get busy. They stayed by me and camped four or five days, and washed up, and mended up, and heartened up, and filled up, — say, I wish 't I'd thought to have measured them: it was sure wonderful how they fattened on that range.

"And then it come to be, what was they going to do next? Well, sir, right then I thought of old John Goldfinch, that lived away down thirty or forty miles. He was an Englishman, and a good, straight, square man as ever I see, and I knew him well. He had two ranches, John had, with houses and barns on them, and all a man would want; and I says to this outfit, 'Go over to old John Goldfinch,' I says, 'and you tell him just what you told me, and tell him I told you to tell it to him, and he'll sure help you out.' And so they did; and John, he says to the man, 'Why, you're the blooming feller I'm looking for': and he puts them in one of them houses, and gives the man and the oldest boy a contrack right off for a thousand of poles he wanted cut up in the hills, and grub-staked them, and started them farming on shares.

"Well, sir, I was over that way a year or so after, to old John's. I'd forgot all about them people; never give 'em another thought. There was a girl about the yard, and when I looked at her I kind of thought I'd seen her face somewheres before, but I

couldn't just place her. And then she goes in, and
out comes a woman and another girl. It was them
same people, clean, tidy, prosperous, and smiling all
over their faces and round to their backs with good
living and kind feelings. They knew me, and say,
maybe you think they wasn't glad to see me. Why,
that man, he said he'd struck luck right from the
time they'd met me, d' you believe it? He'd had
good crops, and potatoes was worth ten and twelve
and a half cents a pound that year, paid right there
at his own dooryard. And flour was twenty dollars
a hundred then, too, and he'd got potatoes and
flour to sell, and a plenty to eat besides. And that
old cow, say, she'd have took a prize; she was a
Holstein, and milked like an artesian well as long
as she got her wages. And that's how it was with
them; I had to go over and eat supper with them
that night, and they gave me the whole song and
dance.

"Durn them mules, I hain't heard the bell for half
an hour. If they'd get headed up the trail we'd be
in a divvle of a fix."

The native modesty of this ministering angel forbade, except in this instance, his relating any incident
that threatened to reflect credit, even indirectly, upon
himself. But his occupation for many years as a
"packer" on the mountain trails had often brought
him across the tracks of those historic bears of the
Sierra, some of whom were known not only by sight
but by name to the exasperated sheep-men whose

mutton they slew and whose rifles they held in disdain.

"Well, sir," he remarked one day when the degeneracy of the present muttonless race of Yosemite bears was under discussion, — "well, sir, I remember when there was sure-enough bears in these mountains: bears I mean, not woodchucks. Once down in Kern County, in San Emigdio Cañon I think it was, twelve or fifteen years ago, I was packing for some sheep-men; that is, carrying the supplies for the herders' camps. There was a Mexican herding a band of sheep at a dry camp, — good feed but no water. We wanted to use that mountain for the feed while it was green, on account that sheep don't need water so long as there's good green feed. The herder kicked about the bears bothering him a whole lot: he said they got in the corral 'most every night, and killed his sheep and scattered the band. It made it hard for him, you understand, for it would take him all day to get the sheep together again, and then he could n't be sure that he got them all.

"So one day he says to me, 'You've got to give me a man to help me as long as I'm on this mountain, or else I'll have to be moved to some other place.' Well, sir, it happened an Irishman comes along. He had n't never herded sheep before, but I took him to the camp anyway, more to make company for the Mexican than for any good he'd be with the sheep.

"That same night a she-cinnamon comes into

camp with two cubs about half-grown. The Mexican had got his bed by an old pine tree that was broke down: he'd built him a rail platform out from the tree, and he slept on top of that, not to be bothered by the sheep and skunks. I don't know where the green Irishman was sleeping, but it was somewhere close by. Anyway, the herder's dog runs out at the bear, and she chases him back into camp, *pronto*. Then the dog runs under the bed to get out of the bear's way, and the bear goes after him; but there wasn't near room enough under there for a bear and dog fight, so the bear she just took and fired the bed and the man and the whole shooting-match up in the air, and scattered them all over the ground. Then she began slapping and cuffing at the man, like it was a prize fight, but the greaser was on to bears, and he sabed enough to cover up his head and make out he was dead.

"While all this was going on the Irish runs up to where there was a big pine tree, about four foot thick, and begins grabbing and hugging at it, trying to climb up out of the way. It would n't have helped him any if he could, for that matter, because a bear will climb a big tree, though he can't climb a little one. But the Irish did n't know nothing about bears, except he knew he hated to be eat up by them. The Mexican he calls out, 'Throw some fire at her; throw some fire at her, why don't you?' But the Irish was busy trying to skin up the tree about then, and he calls back, 'I'll not do it: I'm a-doing well enough where I am.' By that time the bear had gone back to where the cubs was. They was acting kind of dazed with the excitement, and the old bear cuffs them and hustles them to make them run away; that's how they do; and then they all skinned out.

"Well, sir, next morning I was eating my breakfast at my own camp down in the lower cañon, and I see a man coming down to the meadow. He was coming down a big high mountain, and making fast time. 'Hullo!' I says, it being the Irishman, with his blankets on his back : 'Hullo, where are you going?' 'Going?' says he, 'I'm going back to where I come from, that's where I'm going. I wouldn't stay up on that mountain not if you was to give me the whole Kern County. Why, there was four big bears come in there last night and *chewed the greaser*. No, I don't want no breakfast,' says he; 'how far is it in to Bakersfield, that's what I want to know?' 'Sixty-five miles and better,' I says. 'So long,' says he, and off he goes on a two-twenty gait.

"I was in Bakersfield myself, a day or two after, and, say, that Irishman had sure enough got in there the same night when I saw him in the morning. He'd walked forty miles, and a rancher with a wagon had give him a lift the last twenty-five.

"Anyway, I never knew an Irishman have any luck herding sheep, or killing bear either. There was Johnny O'Donnell, up in the Big Hole country ; a bear had got into his corral one night, and picked up a hog that must have weighed all of two hundred, and hopped out again and never so much as knocked a rail off. So Johnny baited for him the next night with another hog, and he clumb up into a big tree right over the corral to get the bear.

"Well, he waited and waited. It was pretty quiet and lonesome, and after a while what does he do but go to sleep, up there in the tree. Well, the bear come, sure enough, and Johnny he wakes up sudden and scairt, and falls down out of the blame tree and breaks his arm, and the gun, too. The wonder is he did n't shoot himself instead of the bear; that would have been the real Irish of it, to a finish. But he did n't, and he scared the bear and saved his bacon all right, and Johnny and me used up the hog that he had baited with.

"But you 'd never believe how plenty they used to be, specially down lower in the sheep country. There was a man down there I knew that killed five one night. He was another Mexican, too. It was down on the old Tejon Grant, and he was always complaining to the foreman about the bears coming into the corral every night, killing his sheep and crippling and wounding them. You see, it is n't only what they kill first-hand, as you might say, but the sheep get scared and stampede, and pile up and suffocate against the corral, like I 've heard people will do at a theatre fire.

"Well, the foreman fixed him up with a rifle and about fifty rounds of cartridge. He had got his bed set up on four posts in the middle of the corral, about ten feet clear of the ground. That 's the way herders mostly do, and it's a good way, too. I never have no use for skunks, and they are always plenty around sheep-camps. This herder had got his bed up extra high just on account of the bears, they was so annoying.

"Along about eleven or twelve o'clock, — moonlight it was, and clear, — a bear hops into the corral, and he ups with his gun and he hits him the first shot and wounds him. The bear rolls over and commences to holler and scream outrageous. Then another bear jumps over to see what all this hollering was about, and the Mexican lets drive again and gets him : that was number two. About that time number three happens along, and he plugs him. Then along comes number four and passes in his checks, and pretty soon number five chips in and cashes his.

"The Mex. had been doing considerable shooting, on account he'd plugged them half-a-dozen shots apiece all around, so as not to make no miscue when he got down on the ground. His ammunition was pretty near gone, and he could n't tell but what there was more bears out on the warpath looking for a scrap. So he waited for half an hour or an hour, maybe, but no more bears come along; and he climbs down at last, pretty much excited, and without so much as waiting to put his boots on he starts down to the ranch-house, three miles away, and wakes up all the men on the ranch and tells them what he'd done.

"Of course they all thought he was lying; but young Neale (that was the son of one of the owners

of the ranch), him and some more of the men con-
cluded to go up and find out how much of a liar he
was. So they went and looked, and sure enough there
was the five bears dead in the corral, and as many as a
dozen or fourteen sheep lying around trampled and
suffocated.

"I knew young Neale myself, and he gave me the
straight story, so I know it's a fact.

"One other time down in Kern I had planted a
herder in a new camp. That afternoon he butchered
a sheep at the foot of a tree and hung the carcass up
to one of the limbs. His camp was made at the foot
of this same tree, and he meant to come along next
day and get part of the mutton. Well, sir, along in
the night in come three good-sized bears into camp,
and commenced chewing up the sheep. The herder,
(an old man he was), and his dog ran out at them,
thinking in the dark they was cattle; but he soon
sees his mistake when one of the bears hits the dog
a lick and breaks his leg.

"There was a little table arrangement at the foot
of the tree, built out of small logs. It might have
been twenty feet from the table up to the first limb,
that the meat was hung from, and the old fellow
jumps up on the table and catches hold of the tree
and the rope both, and climbs up in his night-clothes.
The wind was blowing hard, and it was bitter cold,
near freezing. But there he was, and there he stayed,
shivering with the scare and the cold till them three
bears made a clean-up and vamoosed. Then he

comes down and builds three or four big fires to warm himself and keep the bears away. That day he built him a crow's-nest in a live-oak, about fifteen feet up from the ground, and after that he used to sleep there as long as he stayed.

"The next year it happened I had to plant another herder with a band of sheep in that same camp. He was a French boy, and a greenhorn, just out from the old country: did n't speak a word of English even. He'd butchered a sheep and it was hanging from this same crow's-nest in the live-oak, and the boy was sleeping there too, like the old man used to. The mutton was hanging maybe eight feet clear of the ground.

"Well, the first or second night an immense big grizzly jumps the corral and first of all eats up the offal. Then he stands up on his hind feet and commences on the carcass, and eats off the head and neck and the fore-shoulders, clear up to the liver. The boy was all the time lying in bed, five feet or so above the bear, watching him chew the mutton. I guess the bear did n't see the boy; if he did he did n't take any stock in him, and the boy laid there mighty quiet and still, you bet. Anyway, there was the big grizzly so close he could pretty near touch him, chewing away and cracking the bones like they was walnut shells. When he gets through he walks off, and leaves the other half of the carcass hanging. I tell you that was a pretty badly scared boy, and him a parlyvoo and a greenhorn, too.

"Well, sir, I was past there that day to see how the new boy was making out, and he showed me the half mutton all chewed up, and tried to tell me about it. He was so excited I couldn't make out much of what he said, but it was all '*l'ours*' over and over, and I knew a little French from being Canadian. Anyway I could easy see what his trouble was. I knew the bear would surely come back that night to finish the mutton; so I got two other men with me, with rifles, and we went over to the camp and built another crow's-nest about thirty yards away.

"About dark we got up in the tree. I had fixed it that we would all shoot at the same time, and I was to give the word. The boy was down at a little spring to get a pail of water while the daylight lasted, when along comes the bear. The boy hollers in French, '*Voilà l'ours qui vient!*' and the bear raises up and looks ugly at him. At that I gave the word and the three rifles popped all together. The bear fell over, and the boy lit out lively for his tree. No, he wasn't carrying no water-pail.

"The bear rolled over and over, hollering and yelling most unearthly, and after a while he got away into the brush. It was too dark to trail him that night, but next morning we went after him with dogs. We found him two or three hundred yards away from where we had shot him. He was pretty much crippled up, and we easy finished him.

"He was quite an old bear; his teeth was all wore out, and his claws was wore short down, and the fur was rubbed off in places. He was a bear what had done a heap of mischief, too : Pinto they called him. The sheep-men all knew him, and they used to say Pinto killed more mutton than all the butcher-shops in Bakersfield. We gave the skin to the boy, and he sold it for twenty dollars. That was quite a strike for a sheep-boy, and like a loony he had to go showing the money around. So in about a week I heard that Curly Ike down to Swiftwater had got it away from him."

Thus far the good Bodie. But the two grizzlies most eminent in their time, and whose legends circulate most regularly around Sierra camp-fires, were Clubfoot and Old Joe. The former had the misfortune early in his career to put his foot into a trap, and paid for his freedom with a toe. But the incident taught him caution, and his amorphous imprint soon became dismally familiar to ranchmen over a wide extent of the foothill region. His history has already become nebulous, and I found that the glamour which is fatal to moderation of statement has settled about his name. Only the last scene of his life emerges plainly from the trailing clouds of glory into which he vanished. It is known that he made a brave end, turning up his remaining toes somewhere "up north," where he was taken at a disadvantage in the act of dining royally upon beef of his own killing.

Old Joe reigned about the same time over a region a little to the south of Clubfoot's territory, and there his twelve-by-nine footprint was recognized with respect by backwoodsmen and cattlemen of the Mariposa country. The famous hunter Jim Duncan was engaged about that time upon his stint of a hundred bears, and was particularly anxious to check off Old Joe on his rapidly increasing tally. As John Conway, now the patriarch of Wawona, who was himself a crony of Duncan, expressed it to me, —

"Jim's score was doin' nicely, but they was mostly blacks and cinnamons, and Jim he just naturally hankered after Old Joe. One dark cloudy day, down on Alder Creek, Jim was out hunting with his old muzzle-loader. He stopped along by some big pines, just resting and standing quiet, and he looks up and there comes Old Joe, walking along in easy range and not seeing him. Jim he looks at Joe, and he puts up his gun, and draws a bead, and — and then, by thunder, he crawfished! Yes, and I would too, if I'd have looked at Old Joe along any old muzzle-loader."

Thereafter, the terror of Old Joe lay heavier than ever on the foothills, and the ranchmen paid their tolls almost with alacrity. At last, however, his oppressions roused the sheep-men of the Hornitos region to fury, and they conspired under the leadership of one Hadlick to overthrow him. Half-a-dozen of them proceeded to Pothole Meadows, whence he had been last reported, and where there was a big corral, the traces of which remain to this day to vex the souls of tourist gentlemen interested in mutton. A couple of sheep were killed, and the carcasses, after being trailed around, were hung up in an oak tree about ten feet above the ground. Then, having staked their mules out in the meadow, the men gathered around the fire and passed an hour or two in a symposium of verbal bravery at Joe's expense.

When darkness fell they stopped talking and lay down quietly with rifles ready to hand, and waited for events. About nine o'clock the jacks came tearing into camp on the lope, trailing their picket-ropes, and stood with their tails to the fire, their necks stretched forward, and their ears working like metronomes, gazing out into the darkness. Presently Old Joe arrived and walked up into the light of the fire, while the mules bolted back into the meadow, where they stood shivering and snorting, their terrified eyes shining greenly in the firelight. But Old Joe was not the bear to take tough mule when there was fresh-killed mutton hanging in plain view. After a few moments of what looked like ostentation, but may have been only indecision, he walked up to the tree where the sheep were hanging, reached up and took down a carcass as if he were a butcher, and walked thoughtfully away. And all the while Hadlick and his merry men lay watching, and no man durst put finger to trigger.

I ventured to suggest to Mr. Conway, in extenuation of their inaction, that I had heard similar cases ascribed to a species of hypnotism. "I don't know about that," he rejoined, "but if that's what you call being scared plumb out of your senses, I reckon that's what them fellers had."

"No," he added, in reply to my inquiry as to the circumstances of Joe's departure, "no one knows what came of Old Joe. He was never killed, anyway not in this section of country. I reckon he just naturally got old, and went off up into the jimmy-sal,[1] and died, as you might say, in bed. But you can bet he died with his boots on."

[1] Jimmy-sal: *chamisal*, . e., greasewood-brush.

CHAPTER XVII

THE HIGH SIERRA: LAKE TENAYA TO MONO

THE old Tioga road winds its tortuous length of fifty miles through as rough a stretch of country, I suppose, as any road in the United States. Leaving the Big Oak Flat road near Crocker's Station, some fifteen miles northwest of the Yosemite, it makes for its objective point, the derelict Tioga Mine, on the crest of the Sierra, in a whole-hearted style that comports well with the spirit of the boisterous days in which its lines were run. Its main direction is easterly, parallel to the courses of the Merced and Tuolumne rivers; but in mid-career the opposing bulk of Mount Hoffman forces it to a wide southerly détour where it skirts Lake Tenaya. Then swinging again to the northeast, it crosses the Sierra at Tioga Pass, 9940 feet above sea-level.

After a quiet Sunday, enlivened by a brief but stirring thunder-storm, we marched out early on Monday morning upon this rude highway, heading for Soda Springs. Passing under the eastern shoulder of Murphy's Dome, it was seen to be continued in two or three subsidiary flatted domes. Bodie's archives of local lore failed to yield any record of the departed son of Erin who has bequeathed his name to this barren mountain and the creek which comes down on its farther side. He or some other patriot has taken care to commemorate his friends pretty thoroughly in this part of the Sierra : the Raffertys, Delaneys, McGees, Brannigans, and Donohues are all remembered in the names of lakes, mountains, and creeks, while Ireland herself has both a creek and a lake "named for her." I own that I prefer even these uncompromising names to the sentimental titles that are attached to many of the points of the Yosemite Valley itself.

As we passed close to the little conical point of granite which was so conspicuous at the head of the lake, there was an excellent opportunity to study the peculiar Yosemite formation at close range. One has a vision of Nature in the rôle of housemaid, scouring away through patient centuries at these granite blisters with a glacier in her hand, polishing and finishing them to perfection. At the north end of even this little mountain a vast quantity of talus has accumulated, much of it looking as white and clean as if it had fallen yesterday ; as probably it did, speaking in centuries. On all the surrounding slopes great rounded boulders lie about by thousands, the untidy emptying of the pockets of the ancient glacier.

We were reminded by the appearance of four vaqueros that we were now for a few miles in more travelled country. Soda Springs is the farthest outpost of civilization in this region, and hither all the trails of this part of the mountains head in. The men were Mexican sheep-shearers, who, as we learned in five minutes' exchange of news, had come up from Inyo by one of the southern passes, bound for the ranches of the San Joaquin.

Cigarette - ends were shed around them as we talked, like autumn leaves. One of them, with an amount of forethought unusual in his race, had used some interval of rest to provide himself with a stock of "tabacos," which were disposed, in readiness for instant use, in the band of his sombrero. This store was freely drawn upon by his companions, who when they needed a new cigarette had but to jerk their horses over and pluck one from him, as if he were a tree yielding that desirable fruit. They rode tough, undersized ponies with enormous Spanish saddles which clothed the little animals like overcoats, and gave them a tournamental appearance that, in conjunction with the slouching negligence of their riders, was highly comic.

In conversation with them we were able to assure ourselves that we should find any pass by which we might elect to return, after our visit to Mono, open from snow ; which is not always the case, even by the end of July, unless the preceding winter has been a mild one in point of snowfall. Bodie also refreshed his knowledge of the movements and general well-being of sundry Jims and Bills "down Inyo," and "over Mono" ; after which, with the inevitable valedictory, "Well, guess we'll have to be moving," and a chorus of "Adios !" the cavalcades sorted themselves and parted east and west.

Like huge blisters the domes rose on all sides, each more remarkable than the last. A very noticeable one is Fairview Dome, along the base of which the road passes, with another facing it, on the extreme summit of which a great pebble of perhaps fifty tons has been left by the ancient glacier, carefully balanced, like a pea on some prodigious ostrich egg. On both these mountains, which rise about a thousand feet above the general level, the glacial polish can be seen glittering to the very top.

Bodie was that morning a man of many moods. First of all snatches of *Ben Bolt* were borne past me upon the breeze. This outbreak of sentiment I had just succeeded in tracing to the pensive influence of the hemlock forest through which we were riding, when the theme of his song abruptly changed, and I heard him relating, in a novel kind of *allegro* recitative, the prowess of one Casey, a Hibernian Ulysses of strange and varied exploits. This, too, seemed appropriate enough, in the haunts of bygone Murphys and McGees; but when he broke next into *A Life on the Ocean Wave*, I abandoned the attempt to follow his mental processes.

It was a saddening feature of the scenery along many parts of our route that we passed frequently through wide areas of tamarack forest where the trees were dead, as the result (so I afterwards found) of fire, though at first sight the cause was not apparent. This was the case in parts of the region we were now traversing. On questioning Bodie as to the cause, his brief reply was, "Insecks"; and he proceeded to express his contempt for certain "Government guys" who, he said, came out every year or two from Washington to examine and report upon the matter. This seemed to confirm the statement which I have sometimes heard advanced, that the man of action is prone to hold him of mere theory and investigation in slight regard.

I found the same principle illustrated when, guiding the conversation into his own field, I took occasion to quote Kipling's line about "the mule-train coughing in the dust." "The feller what said that," he rejoined, "don't savvy what he wants to say. Mules don't never cough, not unless they've got a cold on 'em. Sneezing's what he means, and I don't care who the jay is." As I seemed to recall having myself experienced a kind of compound of the two operations, I was not prepared to argue the point, and judged it best to abandon this field also to him.

Discoursing thus of many things, at five-animal range, I being, as usual, in the lead and he in the rear, we found ourselves emerging upon a wide expanse of level grass-land. This was the Tuolumne Meadows. Here comes in from the south the so-called Sunrise trail, which is the direct route to this point from the Yosemite Valley by way of the Little Yosemite and the high mountain region east of the Tenaya Cañon. Straight ahead rose Mounts Dana and Gibbs, with Kuna Crest a little to the south and the point of Mount Conness, more distant, in the north.

Dana was our to-morrow's quarry, and we marked
him for our own. Cathedral and Unicorn peaks also
came now suddenly into full view, close on our right;
the former crested with half-a-dozen splintery pinnacles, the latter with a single sharp, horn-shaped cone,
and both broadly banded with snow. Out yonder to
north and east, under a hood of pale, hard sky, lay
the Mono country and Nevada's dry and burning
plains.

Fording the river, which here runs a wide, handsome stream, we made for the camp of the little de-
tachment of soldiers, four in number, who are kept
here during the summer on outpost duty. On the
way we passed the springs themselves, an outflow of
cold mineral water, bubbling up generously, close to
the bank of the river.

It was with no little interest that we traced by the
soldiers' maps the course of our wanderings all the
last week, locating the cut-offs we had left undone
that we ought to have done, and the trails we had
done that we ought not to have done.

Striking again into the road we followed it, rising
steadily, for five or six miles. At about 9700 feet we
found a southerly trail which we held for a mile or
so, and then camped on a small creek which comes
down from the saddle between Dana and Gibbs, and
at the very base of Dana himself. On the west rose
the magnificent shape of Kuna Crest, plentifully be-
snowed. Along the base stretched the moraine of
the old glacier, the most perfect instance of a lateral

moraine that I have seen. By the trees growing upon it I gauged its average height as not far short of a hundred feet.

It was somewhat too late in the day for us to make the ascent of Dana, so Field went off to look for a small lake which Bodie reported as lying under the northern face of the mountain. A sudden rain coming up, Bodie and I rigged up our big canvas and sat tight. Our guide was in a rare literary mood, and buried himself in our travelling library of three elderly magazines: I devoted myself to the pleasures of anticipation, for to-morrow I was to taste my first authentic mountain of this region.

There he was, 13,050 feet undeniable, showing from our camp a handsome red-brown cone with its longest side thrown out to the northeast, where it terminated in a fine precipice. Forests clothed its lower buttresses, and sheets of snow gleamed on the higher slopes. On the northern side much more snow must be lying, as I could see was the case with his lesser brother Kuna, whose north and west faces were in view. I acknowledge I felt some excitement, though Dana is held to be a very easy mountain to climb, and Alpine Clubs would no doubt deride it. But after all, one's first thirteen - thousand - footer ought to be something of an event, and I hope never to be *blasé* of my mountains.

A vivid after - glow flushed the snow on Kuna Crest to a delicious rose, and burned on Gibbs and Dana in a strange, deep, rusty red that needed explaining. It was entirely a new note of color among the all-prevailing granites, and seemed to signify that a change might be looked for in geological features.

Lying snugly rolled that night in my blankets, I noticed the sky, which was now clear of clouds, filled with a greater myriad of stars than I ever observed before. The velvet firmament was almost white with their innumerable multitudes. I suppose that there are countless numbers of stars yet unrevealed in the empty spaces of the sky, and I wondered whether we may not be in fact surrounded with an unbroken curtain of light.

The next morning Field discovered that he had left one of his lenses behind, halfway up Alkali Creek Cañon, where he had last used it. Bodie handsomely offered to ride back for it by way of Soda Springs and a cut-off trail. We appreciated this friendly proposal all the more since we knew that he entertained grudging sentiments with regard to photographic implements in general, as being objects unruly to pack, and the occasion of frequent stoppages and disarrangements of loads. As to climbing the mountain, he had done that once before, and "climbing wasn't his long suit, anyhow." So at half-past six Field and I started for the summit, while he mounted Clementine and by diligent rope-ending persuaded her away from her attendance on Pet, who I could almost fancy fetched a sigh of relief.

Under a cloudless sky we followed upward the course of the little creek. If I had not known that I was in California I could easily have believed that it was a Highland burn that came shouldering down between bossy, over-curving banks of rough mountain grass, pouring steadily over ledges and boulders, swirling in elbows, draining and sucking through matted roots of heather, and tossing crisp, hissing drops a yard into the air. Then into the blessed forest, with its million-and-one friendly presences, trees and birds, flowers and roving zephyrs, and that old feeling of interrupted action, and hidden, whimsical woodland creatures.

Gradually the forest thinned until we passed out on to the open mountain-side, clothed with mats of dwarf willow and tussocks of wiry grass, and with ribbons of water furrowing the ground in a network of pipe-like channels. A few dwarf pines were scattered here and there, holding their hard-won ground determinedly, like the advanced outposts of an army. The stark poles were tossed about the ground where the storms had wrenched them down, and many of those that stood erect were like skeletons, white and bony. At eleven thousand feet, even the Old Guard, that dies but never surrenders, had been beaten down to the ground, but still they fought upon their backs, under impenetrable shields of flattened and felted foliage that a man might walk upon.

Small rugs of meadow were spread in hollows, spotted with daisies, small but precious. In one of these meadowlets a few thistles were growing sturdily, looking as much at home as if they were on Ben Nevis; and among the boulders an alpine phlox formed little round cushions covered with hundreds of blossoms, ridiculously tiny but marvellously perfect.

So far the way was remarkably easy; it could hardly be called climbing, being nothing but a straightforward march up the saddle between Mounts Dana and Gibbs. At 11,800 feet we gained the crest of the divide, and with extreme curiosity I looked over to the eastern side of the Sierra. From where we stood a cañon broke steeply down between walls of brickburned rock. Sheets of "screes" swept down on either side, laced with streaks and pennons of snow. Almost at the head of the cañon lay a small lake of a strange, peacock-blue color, the bluest thing I have ever seen, as Bodie had predicted I should find it. Dark masses of timber filled here and there the hollows of the southern wall. Below and in the middle distance was a confused tumble of buttes and foothills; and beyond that lay a pale, circular sheet of blue-grey water, with a white island in the middle. It was Mono Lake, and strange and ghostly it looked. To the south of it stretched a line of grey volcanic craters, and beyond again, the uneasy ridges of the Nevada desertranges faded into the distance.

It was a sight that I had long wished to see, — mysterious Mono; and that day, under a bleached desert sky pencilled with lines of pallid whitish cloud, it looked mysterious, solitary, and desolate enough to satisfy my best expectations.

We were still twelve hundred feet short of the peak of Mount Dana, which rose to our north above a vast slope of broken rock, interrupted here and there by cliffs. It is certainly an easy mountain to climb; I can hardly conceive that there is anywhere a peak of equal height that is so easy of ascent. To reach the summit was simply a matter of pegging away at the tiresome slope, using a reasonable degree of care in picking our footing, for the blocks were of every shape and size, and often shifted under our weight. A broken leg would not be difficult to come by.

The strange color of the mountain as we had seen it from camp was now explained. Both Dana and Gibbs are entirely different in formation from the country we had heretofore traversed. They are not built of granite, but of metamorphic slates, red, green, and purple in color, often handsomely veined and marbled, and splintering smoothly into large cubes and rhomboids, and tile-like smaller fragments. It is an interesting formation, and its rich display of colors, contrasting with the brilliant green of the meadow-patches, makes up a fine combination from a landscape point of view.

As we neared the summit we encountered ever larger snow-fields. The sun was hot, and the water ran in a myriad streams, clinking merrily among the rocks under our feet as if a hundred kobold blacksmiths were laboring there. To me there is something very delightful in the subterranean voices of hidden water, songs almost with words, liquid lyrics of delight. When I knelt down and put my ear to a splinter of stone that hung suspended like an inverted cone between larger blocks in one of these music galleries, I was quite charmed at the exquisite tone that sounded from it. No silver bell nor string of violin ever gave out a purer note. There was something solemn in the crystalline earth-music, solemn and sweet and lonely, and I went on with a feeling of pleasant awe.

Climbing at last along the edge of a snow-bank that followed a northwesterly ridge, we gained the summit. A wonderful view rewarded us, — a complete circle, three hundred and sixty degrees full, of mountains and lakes, with a strip of desert to the east where the plains of Mono flickered in parching heat. Immediately under the peak to the northeast is a remarkable plateau, about two square miles in extent, almost perfectly smooth, and covered with small broken rock. This plateau breaks away precipitously to the east, and slopes more gently on the west to a narrow snow-filled cañon that divides it from Mount Dana itself. At the head of the cañon lies a small glacier.

To all other quarters of the compass the whole prospect was a sea of peaks and ridges, whitened with snow, gloomy with precipices, and sprinkled with lakes of every size and shape. One long, trough-like valley led away westward toward the peaks and domes of Yosemite. Over all, the sun shining in a sky of broken clouds sent a thousand purple shadows flying like flocks of swallows. Southward a blue haze half obscured and half revealed a multitude of splendid peaks. Among them Mounts Lyell and McClure gleamed whitely glorious, cuirassed with glaciers, and Ritter, knight of the black shield, overtopped even them and us by a few score feet.

It is remarkable how nearly alike in height are the main summits of the Sierra in this middle part of the range. There are four mountains that rise above thirteen thousand feet, — Dana, McClure, Lyell, and Ritter, — yet the last named, which is the highest, rises to only one hundred and fifty-six feet above the thirteen-thousand mark; while a considerable number of peaks have an altitude of over twelve thousand five hundred feet.

The comparison of this mountain topography to the sea is so essentially true that its triteness may be excused. The resemblance is exact and vivid to the broken forms of ocean water at the first lessening of the violence of a storm; and when now I looked out over the vast extent of mountains, I received the same impression of confused but powerful action, of the leaping of passionate surges, the suck and sob of streaming hollows, the implacable gathering and advance of ridges in infinite *échelon*, that I have experienced in looking out from the deck of a ship in mid-ocean the day after a gale had blown.

It was strange to find among the blocks and boulders of the very summit a lovely plant growing. It was polemonium, bearing a beautiful flower of that heavenly pure blue that I know only in the forget-me-not besides. The blossoms are large, profuse, and clustered, and have a delightful scent. For its luxuriance of size, color, and perfume, it might well be the trophy of a hot-house; and to find such a plant at this altitude, when all other flowers, even the hardy alpine phlox and daisies, had dwarfed and dwindled until they ceased, was a notable surprise. Some angel, no doubt, comes to take earth-pleasure in this lonely garden of the mountains.

We lingered for two hours about the summit, revelling in the superb prospect and the serenity of this heavenward station. Then, having duly contributed to the monument of piled rocks that marks the point of the mountain, and waving *au revoir* to Mono in expectation of being there to-morrow, we started on the return. The first part was accomplished in chamois fashion, leaping down from slab to slab in erratic courses, and only stopping to recover breath and the perpendicular when knees and nerves became shaky together. The ascent had taken five hours, the descent occupied two. Neither Field nor I is of the number of those who consider mountains as a sort of gymnastic apparatus, except incidentally; and we suffered no distress when we learned that the mountain has often been climbed in two hours from the locality of our camp. We had done just two and a half times as well.

Bodie had returned from his twenty-five-mile ride, lens recovered and supper already under way. Surpassing appetites, coinciding with the knowledge of unlimited supplies near at hand, justified a lavish repast in which the last precious dust of the tea-canister was involved. A transcendent fire, fanned every moment to leonine roaring by blasts that roamed down the eastward pass of the mountains, hardly tempered the chill of ten thousand feet of altitude. We unrolled our blankets early, and, discarding only our boots, crept in and lay, feet to the fire, chatting and smoking in tolerable comfort.

By half-past six the next morning we were passing around the eastern face of Kuna Crest, where it rises to a handsome peak. It is altogether a fine mountain, with a long ridge trending southeast and northwest, and maintaining an average height of over 12,000 feet. A faint trail led at first through rough meadow country, and then passed into tamarack forest which here showed no sign of disease, though the trees were whitened and scarred by storm and stress of climate. This hardy conifer has an unusual range of habitat. There are trees of the species in the Yosemite Valley at four thousand feet, and here they were growing at over ten thousand. Though uninteresting in appearance and below the level of its family in physique, one gets to like this tree as one lives with it, for its every-day virtues. It fills the part of the ordinary citizen or man-in-the-street, unpretentious and undistinguished, but carrying on the routine work of the tree-world in a conscientious, methodical manner, leaving the choice places to choicer spirits, and populating great expanses of unhopeful mountain with its serviceable armies.

One or two old cabins, long tumbled into ruin, stood beside the trail. Heaps of stones and rubbish were piled against them, the remains of capacious chimneys. A glow of sentimental warmth seemed still to hang about these mounds of débris. I conjured up again the figures of the bygone miners and sheep-herders who had sat around the fires that once roared in them, — swart Gascons from the Landes, out-screaming the wind with impish piccolos and boisterous accordions; down-east Yankees, "sudden and quick in quarrel," mitigating the solitude with euchre and deep potations; the ubiquitous Briton, dreaming over Fleet Street or the old village in Surrey or Connemara as he stared into the glowing caverns of the fire. Now it is the little striped chipmunk that sits ruminating there, if such a bundle of nerves can be imagined ever to be in such an attitude of mind; and the only sound is the voice of the Clarke crow, uplifted in soliloquy as weird as that of the Raven.

Some three miles of steady but easy climbing brought us to the head of Mono Pass. A pile of rocks marks the summit, and the bench-mark of the Geological Survey gives the altitude as 10,599 feet. A trail comes in here from the south, leading by way of Parker and Agnew passes to the so-called Devil's

Post-pile, and so out by Mammoth Pass to Pine City on the east side of the Sierra. In the neck of the pass lies a small lake fed by snow-banks, and beyond it a group of long-deserted shanties, a windlass, and a mound of tailings mark the grave of somebody's hopes and capital. Here blows an eternal wind, strong, steady, and hissing cold. I always feel a solemnity in these great airs of the mountain summits, these winds of God. Like formless but mighty presences, the great sighing billows of the air-ocean surge on their vast courses, singing in majestic recitative their *Benedicite, Omnia Opera!*

We halted to cinch up saddles and packs as securely as might be before beginning the four-thousand-foot descent of Bloody Cañon. Then with a final backward look to the west we plunged down the steep eastern face of the Sierra. A few hundred yards below we encountered a considerable snow-field. The snow, softened by the midsummer sun, was treacherous and annoying, and it was with difficulty that we prevailed upon the animals to commit their precious bones to the uncertain footing. Several times they all, Pet excepted, made a concerted bolt back up the trail, and for a time the welkin rang with sounds of battle, castigatory drummings upon equine ribs, and all the confusion of a general mêlée. At last they went floundering and staggering across, sinking to the hocks in the rotten snow-ice. A quarter-mile brought us to another but smaller snow-field. This we skirted; and escaped catastrophe thereby, for it turned out to be hollow beneath. The water running from the upper snow had cut its way under this bank, leaving it a mere shell from wall to wall of the cañon. In its present softened condition it would certainly not have supported the weight of the loaded animals.

Just below lay a charming little lake, blue as heaven, and swept ever and anon with handfuls of wind that sent delightful gleams and shudders over it. It bears the inscrutable designation of Sardine Lake. I hailed Bodie with an inquiry as to the reason for the name, and received his illuminating reply in one word, "Canned." I learned later that years ago an ill-fated mule bearing a cargo of the delicacy consigned to a merchant in some mining-camp of the Walker River region had fallen off the trail, and after a series of spectacular revolutions had vanished in the icy waters.

In the upper course of the cañon the walls rise precipitously. It is in fact a gorge rather than a cañon, and it is easy to guess how it came by its name in the days when great bands of cattle were driven across the Sierra by this route, lacerating themselves as they scrambled among the jagged rock-débris through which the so-called trail is laid. When one recalls the behavior of a herd of excited cattle driven along an ordinary highway, and then imagines the scene of action transferred to this fearfully steep defile, filled with shattered rock and narrowing at the top to a mere cleft, with yelling vaqueros urging the

bewildered and terrified beasts into a panic, it becomes a marvel that any of the animals should arrive
at the head of the pass alive and unmaimed. The
bones that still lie strewn up and down the trail tes-
tify to the fate of many a victim of Bloody Cañon.

I was charmed to find growing in this wild place
a great variety of flowers. In the drip of snow-banks
and among the tumble and shatter of slaty rock, there
bloomed the choicest specimens that I had seen
of many varieties, and with a remarkable range of
colors. In particular I noticed columbines of pale
rose and yellow, and even pure white; pentstemons
crimson, pink, purple, and blue of various shades;
and yellow and red mimulus, all surprisingly large
and perfect, as if grown in a hot-house. A botanist
would be enraptured with them. Here I met also another conifer, the limber pine (*Pinus flexilis*), a species which is confined, I believe, to the eastern flank
of the Sierra. Its whitish twigs and its foliage are
very similar to those of *P. albicaulis*, but the cone
is larger and clay-yellow when ripe, and the tree is
altogether bigger and more pine-like in habit of
growth.

Below Sardine Lake the cañon began to open and
the blue hills of Nevada came in sight. Then the
forest began in earnest. Owing to the rapid fall
in altitude the various conifers meet and overlap
very interestingly. Within a short range one passes
through the successive belts of the albicaulis, contorta, flexilis, and Jeffrey pines and the two firs. The

juniper also grows here to a handsomer tree than its stubborn wont, and it appeared to me that all the vegetation inhabiting the locality attains an unusual perfection of growth.

Two miles and two thousand feet below Sardine Lake lies Walker Lake, a beautiful sheet of water, narrow and winding, nearly a mile in length, and wooded on all sides. Along its northern margin spreads a delightful meadow, fringed with aspen and willow, and exuberantly flowery. Long grasses were mixed with pale blue iris, larkspurs, lupines, daisies, and half-a-dozen kinds of those yellow compositæ of which, for some reason which seems to have to do with their color, none but botanists take the trouble to learn the names. Wild roses also there were, of a color as deep as was the joy of meeting them; and evening primroses, stately-tall.

The lake is a beautiful one, partly rocky and romantic, partly reedy and rural. Looking back, the mountains towered grandly, snow-laced and stern, close above this Eden; while from this point eastward began the domain of the sage-brush and the desert, hardly more than an hour's travel from snow-banks and alpine crags. It is a condition highly interesting, and entirely characteristic of California, the land of violent contrasts.

At the lower end of the lake a band of cattle were feeding. To us they wore a pleasing air of novelty. For three weeks we had had neither meat nor milk of them, except the canned apologies, and at the sight the latent butcher within the breast awoke and whetted his tools.

After leaving the lake the northern wall of the cañon becomes bare of timber, except for a sprinkling of small oaks, and is dotted with the usual desert brush. The southern wall continues well forested, and Jeffrey pines and tamaracks kept us company along the trail, each striving to outdo the other in endurance as they approached the desert level. I backed the Jeffrey, as being the nobler, more pine-like tree, and was gratified to see him eventually win out, growing sturdy and green far out on to the Mono plain.

Suddenly we encountered a barbed-wire fence, and the trail widened into a sandy track that no doubt calls itself a road. A clear brook ran beside it, bordered with wild roses and tiger-lilies. Then appeared cultivated enclosures, and in the distance a few scattered farm buildings were visible. An Indian woman, pappoose on back, was performing some primitive agricultural rite about a plot of garden ground fenced with willow poles, where nothing could be discerned to be growing. A girl in a trailing blue "wrapper" turned upon me a countenance of such intense blackness that I at first mistook it for her hair. My salutation, first in English, then in Spanish, elicited no response beyond a grunt *staccato* and a stare so sincere and prolonged as to become embarrassing. The Mono Indians are famous for their skill in basketry, and this stolid woman, it was likely, could weave baskets of amazing fineness of texture and admirable shape and design. I was anxious to secure a specimen, but felt myself at a disadvantage and was fain to abandon my intention so far as these representatives of the tribe were concerned.

Crossing a meadow of knee-high grass watered by a network of rivulets, I found my party, whom I had allowed to out-travel me by a mile or two, just going into camp at Farrington's Ranch. So great is the topographical contrast between the eastern and western faces of the range that while on this side it had taken only a few hours to descend from the crest to cultivated plains, on the other it would have taken as many days.

I despatched Bodie straightway to the ranch-house, where he was no stranger, to buy a loaf of stove bread and a pitcher of milk. We ate and drank our fill of these simple rarities with enormous gusto. Then I lay at length among willows, wild roses, ants, and sagebrush, and gazed dreamily off at the line of volcanic craters a few miles away across the valley. Unmistakable craters they are, grey and ashy, topped with burnt-looking rocks, the lips that once spouted the imprisoned flame and fury of the earth up into that blue sky that now smiles so serenely. Will they ever again break silence? Stranger things have happened on this old earth.

Suppose that as I lie here, indolent with ease and the fullness of bread, I should fancy that I see a faint smoke ascending from that grey cone. It cannot be : and yet, it certainly is. Strange : what next? The smoke grows thicker and is unmistakable. After a few minutes a deep sigh or moan of the earth, such as I have heard preceding earthquakes, breaks the heavy hush of the air. I gaze fascinated at the smoking peak, awaiting I know not what. My mind is filled and teeming with all the unimaginable horrors which since childhood I have associated with earthquakes and volcanoes, — Pompeii, Lisbon, Sodom and Gomorrah, Pelée, The Revelation. And then — but never mind what might happen then. What does happen is that Field sits serenely smoking the while he peruses the five-days-old newspaper brought by Bodie from the house for our delight; the bell on the black mule tinkles with a cracked, High-Church sound behind the bush under which I lie; the wind blows, the clouds sail. Still, I remember that the wise man who, sadly reversing the better order, became foolish, wrote before the melancholy change that there was no new thing under the sun (he might have said, or old either), and that what had been would be again. So after all, who knows?

We had received friendly welcome to supper at the ranch-house, and revelled again in stove bread, with butter sweet and cool as primroses, steak of the juiciest, lettuce of the crispest, onions the most seductive and undeniable, and such a platter of potatoes as may not often be seen upon this planet, towering in plump spheroids of dazzling whiteness and discharging fragrant cumuli of steam that assailed the very ceiling. The atmosphere abounded in taken-for-granted hos-

pitality and friendly badinage, in which certain legendary love-passages of Bodie were haled into the
light, he nothing loath although professing ignorance.

Later in the evening Field and I were summoned
from photographic labors to partake of — pineapple
sherbet! frozen with snow brought from the mountain peaks. Stumbling back to our camp thereafter
through the soft, warm darkness, we contemplated
with deep joy the prospect of a night *sans* mosquitoes,
and an extra hour of sleep, or of that pleasant semi-
coma which refreshes the mental faculties even more,
in the morning.

CHAPTER XVIII

THE HIGH SIERRA: MONO TO GEM LAKE

PHYSIOLOGY and psychology meet in the border-
land of dreams, and the onion is a potent and
treacherous vegetable. All night I walked precipices,
'scaped hair-breadth 'scapes, and glissaded down
league-long slopes of pineapple sherbet into sardine-
populated lakes; and when the sun rose sudden and
red above the low Nevada mountains, I fortified myself behind my knees and slowly returned to myself.
I remembered having once been awake and seen the
narrow waning moon swimming low down, like
an ancient galley-boat, in the early morning sky,
while a band of horses galloped and thundered
around me, neighing wildly over some nocturnal excitement. I remembered, too, that I had had a bad
headache. But a dip in the creek changed all that;
and with shining morning faces we presented ourselves at the breakfast-table, ready for fresh im-
prudences.

During the morning Bodie and I drove over to the
store at the lake to lay in fresh supplies for the days
to come. One meets out-of-the-way characters, naturally, in out-of-the-way places. As we ploughed
along the dusty road we came up with a wagon and
team driven, as it appeared from the rear, by a stout,

grey-haired woman, wearing a man's soft felt hat. Her knot of greasy hair wagged with the wag of the conveyance upon a villainously dirty yellow neck-wrapper, and her broad back somehow expressed an ignominious and abominable complacency. As we passed the wagon we found that the driver was a man, with a swarthy, clean-shaven countenance of the fakir type. The swarthiness was principally the result of dirt, and I use the term clean-shaven as applying to the manner of shaving, and having no reference to real cleanliness.

A hundred yards ahead we passed another wagon, driven by an older man, less completely obnoxious, perhaps, in feature and person, but of a truculent and bullying aspect. The two "outfits" seemed to bear a sneaking relation, though there was nothing that could be said actually to indicate any connection between them.

I found that the sentiments of repugnance aroused in me by the men were strongly shared by Bodie. On my asking for a diagnosis, he unhesitatingly classified them as "wagon-tramps," a profession whose name was new to me, but of whom he averred the existence of a large fraternity, well organized for purposes of mutual aid and protection in the practice of their calling. This consists in thieving in the grand larceny manner. Where your foot-tramp ventures to pick up a bridle, the wagon variety boldly steals the horse: where the smaller rascal demands the housewife's pies and coffee, this comparative degree appropriates half-a-dozen sacks of barley from the barn.

"The woods is full of them," Bodie poetically complained. "Along about March or April, spring anyway, these skates start out with their wagons. They just keep moving along, moving along, beating their way; always fat and hearty, never paying for nothing they can steal, and that's pretty near everything they want. See that dirty, long-haired blatherskite behind there: ever see a feller of that pattern farm? keep store? work honest with his hands? No, sir, not with that hair and hide. Say, them cattle ought to be roped on sight and the hose turned on 'em, or the crick, and the hair clipped off 'em way down to their teeth. And I'd like to handle the shears, I would." Thus honest Bodie; and I fully agreed, though with a reservation as to the last article.

It was a weird yet fascinating land through which we drove. Mono Lake and the region surrounding it are unique within the United States. Here, at an elevation of sixty-four hundred feet, is a body of water eighty or ninety square miles in extent, highly mineralized with the alkalines, borax and soda. Many streams from the mountains pour into it great quantities of pure fresh water, but without mitigating in any degree its peculiar quality. It is a veritable Dead Sea. No fish nor reptile inhabits it, nor does any wandering bird or animal come to its margin to drink its bitter waters. The shores are whitened with alkaline incrustations, and the branches and twigs of dead trees that rise above the surface are petrified to the semblance of bone.

The lake was anciently of much larger extent, and the old shore-lines are still plainly marked upon the higher ground, the highest one that is clearly distinguishable being nearly seven hundred feet above the present level of the water. Two islands and a number of islets lie out in the middle of the lake. The largest, Paoha or Herman Island, is about two miles long by one and a half wide. It is largely made up of volcanic ashes, and hot water and steam issue from a number of vents at the southern end of the island, hard by where rises a spring of fresh cold water. The smaller island is purely volcanic, of black basalt, with a crater of three hundred feet height.

On the principal island indications of oil have recently been found, and the inevitable derrick is already in evidence, with millionaires, diamonds, Paris, and divorce courts looming in the mental background.

It did not enhance for me the attractiveness either of the lake itself or of the Indians of the locality to learn that these latter subsist in part upon the larvæ of a fly which breeds in this blighted water. The larvæ are washed up at a certain season on the shore in such quantities as to form, I am told, heaps and windrows two or three feet in height. Lo, the omnivorous, has discovered a weird gusto in this unholy edible, which he dries in the plentiful sun and then grinds to a powder which he denominates *cuchaba*, and mingles with his flour of acorns and other heterogeneous aliment.

To the south of the lake stands the range of dead volcanoes, grey and menacing, their sides covered with powdery ashes mixed with pumice and obsidian. Even these forbidding slopes some varieties of plants, and even trees, contrive to inhabit. The highest of the volcanic peaks rises twenty-seven hundred feet above the plain. Facing them on the west rise in strongest contrast the splendid peaks of the Sierra, laced with joyful streams, spangled with lakes, and glorious with forests: life against death; water against fire; beauty for ashes.

The road was deep in sand, merging into interminable wastes of sage and greasewood brush. Rabbits and doves abounded. Here and there lay huge isolated tufæ, covered with ugly blisters, knobs, and corrugations. One of them that was near a settler's cabin had been ingeniously converted into a storage-room, or it might even be called a house, for it was nearly as big as the cabin. The inside had been hollowed out and a door fitted to the aperture. It resembled an enormous mouldy chocolate-cream, and would have been a handsome dwelling for Diogenes.

On the hillsides grew scattered trees, mostly a new variety of pine, the *monophylla*, single - leafed, or piñon pine, from which the Indians gather great crops of those small edible nuts which I have observed in fruit-stores waiting long for purchasers. It is a useful-looking, bushy little tree, thickly foliaged with greyish-green needles. The cones are small and compact, and by no means generous in appearance; but they are filled with large seeds which form almost the staff of life of the Indians of the region.

The post-office for this locality bears the appropriate name of Crater. I was expecting to receive letters there, and found Uncle Sam established in a rather pitiable little shack of a house, the only one for a mile or more in every direction. He was a genial soul, however, and discoursed with us in friendly wise, while he sorted out my mail, upon such matters as should be of universal interest: as, the price alfalfa hay was fetching over to the San Joaquin; and, had Bodie "heerd how was Jedge Dickerman's bay mare as had cut herself to slithers on a ba'b-wire fence down to Bishop?" Further, he opined that Mono must look good to us after what he called, with a probably unconscious Biblical allusion, "them etarnal mountins." In this Arcadian post-office one mails one's letters in the bureau drawer, and from the excitement aroused by my request for a five-cent stamp I gather that they are regarded as philatelic rarities of high finance.

There are one or two little settlements along the lake-side, situated naturally at the points where streams from the mountains enter the lake. These hamlets are quite idyllic spots, riotously verdant, with neat houses and every appearance of modest prosperity. Thickets of wild rose six feet high, and heavy crops of alfalfa, clover, and timothy give proof of the magical effect of water upon this otherwise dreary desert. Yet to me there seemed always something menacing in the neighborhood of that blue, sinister lake, like the inscrutable smile of a poisoner.

By the roadside an Indian woman was sitting, surrounded by children, dogs, pots, gunny-sacks, and ashes. To my enquiry whether she had baskets for sale she replied briefly, "No makeum basket," and closed the incipient transaction.

While we attended to our business at the store, which is also a saloon, there entered our two supposed wagon-tramps, bearing demijohns and other accoutrements proper to bibulous travellers. These and themselves they proceeded with a businesslike air to fill with strong liquors, and after haunting the "stoop" for a few minutes in a furtive manner, climbed into their respective rigs and passed upon their way. I did not grieve that ours lay in the opposite direction.

Next morning I awoke at half-past three, and lay luxuriously smelling the morning scents and watching the dawn. I might have been in Syria or Egypt. A long narrow line of burning desert red ran along the low east, shading suddenly into the ultra-blue of the night sky, hardly yet lightening to the day. The moon and the morning-star shone together, clear and earnest, with a few other stars of the greatest magnitude still beaming in the zenith. It was almost theatrically scenic, but for the heavenly largeness and purity of the air, and the low cool blowing of the dawn-wind. I saw the Pyramids, and the Sphinx, and the Flight into Egypt. Then I got up and reversed my bedding, and lay down again to revel in the phantasmagoria of the high mountain wall to the west, turning from night dimness to shadowy grey, then flushing and burning to red, redder and yet redder, as the level arrows of the sun began to stream between the peaks of the distant Nevada ranges. And when the flashing disk came soaring up, and turned his shrivelling rays upon our bivouac, I sighed to think of that long, toilsome climb back to the High Sierra levels, which lay before us.

Leaving the hospitable Farringtons with kindly farewells, and little dreaming how soon and how strangely the charming young daughter of the house, whose brightness and gaiety bloomed like a rare flower in that sequestered spot, was to be summoned away, we took the road to the south. It passed at first through a long valley meadow, with the living snowy mountains on one hand and the dead grey ones on the other. Behind lay Mono Lake, flickering mirage - like under the desert sun. Swallows, most beloved of birds, skimmed joyously over the pastures, and meadow-larks bubbled and blackbirds chirruped from every fence-rail.

After a mile or so we left the road for a trail that struck more westerly, and were soon skirting the grey, sage-covered foothills. Then the pines met us, their long picket-lines thrown bravely out far into the enemy's country. Parker Peak and Mount Wood, straight ahead, towered up magnificently, solidly snow-covered for half their height. These mountains form a noble gateway to Parker Pass, the next pass to the southward of the one by which we had crossed the range.

A handsome stream, Rush Creek, came pouring down, clear and arrowy. We were to keep it company for some days, and excellent company it proved to be. I do not know a more attractive stream in the Sierra. Even here on the lower levels it flowed full and strong and whole-hearted, and I wished that its fate had been rather to sink away into the desert sand than to merge and stifle in that dreary lake.

Crossing a slight rise we came unexpectedly upon Grant Lake, lying unlakelike among rolling, sage-covered hills, but with fine snow-clad mountains beyond to the south and west. A little square cabin stands by the shore, half lost among the tangle of brush and boulders. The door was open, and I went inside. There were tokens of recent habitation in the new ashes on the hearth, though furniture there was none except two plank shelves attached to the wall. The fireplace was a quaint concern, built of slabs of rock set between natural rough posts of wood. The little habitation might have been transplanted bodily from the plains of Languedoc.

The lake shades off at its southern end into a wide swamp of tules, bordered by a meadow of waving grasses mixed with wild roses, iris, and many other flowers. A solitary sandhill-crane stood among the twinkling shallows of the lake-end, philosophically waiting, secure that his own should come to him. The crane seems to be a bird of admirable patience and quite gigantic leisure.

Grant Lake is altogether a pleasing and peaceful spot, with a quiet, unexciting beauty of its own. Passing down the meadow where a bunch of portly cattle were grazing, or, having grazed, were considering the possibility of grazing again, the trail wound among sandy flats where grew myriads of the thistle-poppy (*Argemone*), mixed with the common low-growing thistle. The creek accompanied us in a friendly manner, running with a smooth, swift flow between banks lined with quiet willows and whispering aspens. As we began to rise more steeply the sage-brush ended, unregretted, and the pines received us once more into their illustrious kingdom.

Conversation flagged somewhat. I think that in my own case this was due to a feeling of regret that we were now inward-bound, complicated possibly with a slight indigestion. Bodie's voice reached me occasionally, rebuking Jack, who insisted upon marching alongside instead of in the trail, and some twenty feet away, as if he were an officer. This preference resulted frequently in his encountering some impediment which his obstinacy would not brook to evade but urged him to push through, with disastrous effects upon his pack. When the barrier was plainly impassable his habit was to turn round three times, as if he worked on a pivot, and then stand looking at us with a coldly indifferent air which implied, "I don't care; you've got to get me out; and I'm going to do it again, too."

A grove of unusually large aspens merged suddenly into pines and junipers as the trail entered a narrow cañon, with rugged mountains closing around us. After a mile or two the cañon opened to another irised meadow where a cascade foamed down a side-cañon; and half a mile farther we could see the whole river pouring wildly down the western mountain-side in a broad scarf to enter Silver Lake.

This lake lies under a fine craggy mountain, whose steep gullies were laced with snow almost to the water. It appears to be visited by a good many people from this eastern side, being easily accessible (it lies at seventy-two hundred feet of elevation), and a notable fishing ground. At the lower end were two or three tents, and on the lake was a boat from which two anglers were industriously casting. We sought a camp-ground at the upper end, and with some difficulty found a few square yards of level on the river-bank above the lake and close to the foot of the fall, which provided an eloquent background of sound for the meditations which an early camp and inspiring surroundings invited.

The mountains were sombre, rugged, and finely turreted. On the eastern side of the lake they plunged in precipices almost to the water's edge; to south and west they were equally imposing and rose in cliffs of uncompromising verticality for three thousand feet.

While Field photographed and Bodie succumbed to a siesta, I fished the stream with good success. The trout rose well to both fly and spoon, and were of good size and mettle. Bodie had recounted to me legends of trout of two feet length and over, and that such magnificoes do navigate the deep, still waters of this lake I see no reason to doubt. Moreover, the flesh of these trout is salmon-red, as becomes a lordlier race, and is of surpassing flavor, as we all agreed at breakfast next morning.

When I returned to camp I found it pervaded by a novel and grateful odor which proceeded from the sinkienon. I cautiously raised the lid, and beheld a semi-liquid conglomerate of ruddy or saffron hue, such as I have seen in the unlawful flesh-pots of wandering Egyptians. It was a "mulligan," long-expected, come at last; and as we ate we blessed once more the kindly hostess of Farrington's, and came and came again.

When we turned in, a south wind was blowing strongly, with a scent of rain in it, whereat I somewhat rejoiced. Thus far the whole trip had been made in sunny weather except for two or three spasmodic thunder-showers; and I longed for a day or two of storm, or at least of cloud, so that wild scenery might receive the enhancement of wild weather.

I awoke to a glorious cloudy morning. Lowering vapors were lighted redly on their fringes by a sun that struggled to raise an excited countenance above the opposite wall of mountains. Hardly an hour ahead of him the little thin moon was slipping through the wrack as if she thought herself pursued. Evening primroses, like other moons, gazed mildly down at me as I lay and watched the changes of the sky reflected in the smooth-flowing river six feet away. The wind had ceased, and even the aspens stirred not a leaf.

By seven o'clock we were on the trail. It led at first up the steep face of the western mountain, among junipers and open brushwood, and close beside the fall. The lake lay leaden grey among the gloomy hills, and rain was already falling from the eastern clouds. The wind had risen again, and boomed softly in our ears, mingling with the rush and roar of the fall. It was a morning full of half-tone poetry and clear but not acute sensations. I wonder whether I am singular in finding myself, as I always do, ten times as much alive on a soft grey day, or even on a hard grey one, as on a sunny blue one. If, I thought, I were a poet, or a painter, now, now I could do great work.

And then came the blessed rain, driving down, driving down. Ah, welcome, welcome! O wild, free spirit of my beloved Cumberland mountains, I feel thee near! O friends, long departed, with whom I knew them, ye are near, too! Now, see, far off the sun is pouring down a grey-gold flood of light upon some lonely lake, — I see it by an inward sense; nay,

I am there. How still it is, and holy : the vision of a vision.

We rounded the head of the fall in a wild amphitheatre of castled cliffs that poured off into vast slopes of screes. A few junipers huddled on the rocky ledges. The rain streamed fervently down. Our animals scrambled and staggered upwards with bitter complaints, but mercy there was none. As we reached the crest the wind rushed heavily against us in angry surges as though it would sweep us over the cliff, and flung the stinging rain and hail level in our faces. Wild water, wild sky, wild earth, wild air, — it was superb, the pure - drawn joy of life. And here, in the neck of the pass, lay Lake Agnew, darkly, wildly beautiful. High mountains closed it in ; at its head a long white torrent thundered down over black ledges of slate ; and over all crouched a sky shredded into grey rain. Ever and anon the wind swooped screaming down, and the little lake seemed to shrink and shiver like a terrified child.

At the head of the long cascade yet another lakelet was hidden, with rocky islets breaking its surface. This connected with still another, lying under a black precipice, and surrounded with huddled clumps of tamarack. Opening from this is a larger lake with a magnificent snowy peak showing beyond it to the west. It was Gem Lake, and the great mountain was Lyell, king of the middle Sierra.

The trail ran high above the water around the northern end of the lake before it dropped to a small meadow at the western end. Huge junipers were scattered along the cliff ledges, many of them mere skeletons, white and polished to the bone by the storms of many centuries. At this altitude of nine thousand feet winter reigns and rages for half the year; and the weird brothers stand grappling the rock with literal death-grips, their aged arms streaming out with horrified gestures, as if they would fight off the grisly enemy to the last.

By a rocky point where a few clustered pines made a shade which, however unnecessary to-day, might be grateful to-morrow (which would be Sunday), we pitched camp. Bodie, good man, rejoicing in abundant pasturage for his beasts, opened the grub packs with alacrity, and, outdoing himself in despatch, quickly hailed us to a majestic steak, replete with the juices of Mono's best herbage.

The evening was mild, threatening more rain. I set fire to a sizable log that lay on the shore, and sat for an hour or two listening to the pleasant monologue of the lake. The wind, which had ceased about sundown, now rose again, and sent the ripples first whispering and then chattering up on the little beach. The sky was overcast, and occasional drops of rain fell hissing into the fire, which throbbed and roared like a blacksmith's forge under the heavy swirls of wind. The sparks blew out in a steady stream over the black water. It was a fine, hearty end to a splendid day, and I brought my blankets down from camp and spread them close to the water's edge, so that I could easily lift up and see what might be going forward in the way of weather or scenery if I should chance to awake during the night.

As it happened there was a good deal going on in the way of weather. I might have slept an hour or two when I awoke to find the rain pouring down heavily, and distant thunder rumbling in the south. Pulling up an extra canvas over my head I lay and listened for a while to the tattoo of the rain and the muffled growling of the thunder; then gradually I dozed off once more. A terrific burst of thunder right overhead awoke me again, followed by others that roared and crackled all around the lake. I almost seemed to see the shattering impact of the sound-waves as they broke against that black precipice, as I have seen great breakers burst on a stormy coast and rush wildly up the face of some high cliff.

The rain poured steadily down, and I retreated further into my fastness, in present comfort but with some anxiety as to how long it was going to last. I was fearful of damage, moreover, to our photographic properties, which were not protected against such heavy rain; but I was a hundred yards away from camp, and the prospect of a dash through rocks, darkness, and a deluge was depressing. So I lay and suffocated myself into a state of coma, in which I was dimly aware of the tumult without and of a small but determined stream of water trickling down the bed within. I sleepily followed its course with my mind's eye, like a demonstration of the elements of hydraulics, observing how it slowly filled the hollows and ran rapidly down little cañons, intent upon finding its level, which coincided with the position of my feet. When next I awoke there was no sound of rain, and I could see grey light marking the squares of my plaid blanket. Molishly emerging I beheld a sodden earth, a scowling sky, and Field, driven untimely from his soaking bed, standing like a fire-worshipper on the highest coign of the adjacent rocks, eager to embrace the first rays of a melancholy sun.

Breakfast put a better face upon matters, and a warmer sun allowed us to dry our clothes and bedding, though much after the fashion of Irish haymaking, dashing in and out between showers of rain and hail that kept dropping upon us as soon as ever we spread them out.

Wandering up the course of the stream in the afternoon, I encountered a shepherd with his band of innocents. I had seen yesterday with some surprise a cloud of dust rising from a shoulder of the mountain a mile or two to the north, and after much cogitation had decided that it must be caused by a landslide. Later in the evening, however, I had heard, borne on the wind, the deep *toom*, *toom*, of the great French sheep-bell, and knew that the dust that had puzzled me marked the passage of a band of those "hoofed locusts" (as Mr. Muir calls the unconscious devastators), which, denied entrance into the National Park, range all summer about the eastern flank of the Sierra. These animals seem to have a ventriloquial quality of voice that disguises their exact locality, and the first notice I had of their near approach was the barking of the two dogs as they caught sight of me and rushed to the attack. One of them was a superb collie of an unusual silver-grey color and of great size; the other a composite canine, simply a dog. I was not sorry to hear the voice of their master crying, "*À bas, Roland! Suzette!*"

The shepherd was a pastoral-looking youth, French, blue-eyed, with a pleasant slow smile and a language mixed of his native tongue, English, and Spanish. With his wide-brimmed hat and sauntering, country air, he would have made a pretty Silvius if fitted out with a beribboned crook in place of the stout cudgel he carried, with which he mechanically thumped the log of fallen timber across which we conversed.

"It was rain the night that is passé, ver mooch rain."

"But yes, it is certain: and we got wet. And you?"

"Ma foi, yes, m'sieu'. Sacré! quel tonnerre! quel éclair! quelle pluie! I was — how you say? — droon, moi."

"It is said that to drown is not unpleasant," I ventured.

"Eh, bien, to me I do not like it. It wets."

"It is true. Think you the rain is over?"

"Quien sabe, señor?" And after some further debate, and with gesticulations of profound consideration, we parted.

It is a strange life that these wandering shepherds lead. In the spring they leave the valleys with their flocks, a couple of dogs, and a burro loaded with simple provisions, among which is sure to be included one of the great round cheeses made by loving hands of mother or sister in dear France, and brought or sent to console the absent Jacques or Armand in his exile. For half the year they wander from valley to mountain and from cañon to meadow, in and out and up and down, each night gathering their slow-moving flocks around them, and camping patriarchally with their faithful lieutenants, a true democracy of labor. The only sounds they hear, beside the great monologue of Nature herself, are the everlasting conversations of the sheep, the bark of their dogs, and the deep boom of the sheep-bell.

The bells, like the cheeses, are characteristic; — solid, old-world things compounded of steel and silver, and often curiously ornamented. Their tone, while it is of great carrying power, is musical and mildly melancholy. Often, too, the herders carry with them some beloved instrument, — flute, or accordion, or even violin ; and you may chance to hear, in some lost cañon or by some lonely lake, the *Marseillaise*, or some wildly sweet Provençal air, played with a fervor of love and longing that exceeds the utmost of skill.

Near by our camp was a heap of stones that supported a rough cross, made of straight pieces of pine-bough fastened loosely with baling-wire. This hum-

ble monument marks the grave of a solitary who
came years ago to this high and lonely spot, seeking
to evade arrest by the grim sergeant. But the hand
was on his shoulder, and here he died. Through the
short summer the birds whistle and the grasses wave,
and all the long winter the silent snow falls and the
storm whirls, over his place of rest. I noticed that a
few wild forget-me-nots were blooming among the
stones of this tiny cemetery. Some friendly angel
may have planted them there, out of pity and such
strange sorrow as angels may feel.

The evening clouds were remarkably beautiful, of
golden-rose, smoky greys and purples, and greenish
yellows, with a further background of dull, thundery
blue. Again I sat late by the ruddy fire. It was
pleasant, drawing toward the end of my Sierra wanderings, to think how many of these friendly pines
and hemlocks had been reddened by my camp-fires.
And will be again? Quien sabe? as Armand says.
But the little black wavelets plashing on the beach
keep saying again and again, Yes, yes; — yes, yes;
— yes, yes. So be it, with all my heart.

A few showers fell again during the night, but we
had rigged up a shelter, and Field and I were only
aware of them to the extent of turning over, smiling
comfortably, and going to sleep again. Bodie, who
had declared that there would be no more rain, suffered the fate of the prophet who is rash enough to
back his opinion to the length of acting upon it.

CHAPTER XIX

THE HIGH SIERRA: GEM LAKE TO THE
LITTLE YOSEMITE

THE morning dawned propitiously for a move over the Donohue Pass to the Lyell Fork; but while we were in the act of packing, clouds again came driving up from the south; the mountains became grey and veiled; and in a few minutes rain was falling heavily. For myself, I wanted nothing better than a long rainy day in such a spot. Promptly unpacking, we raised our canvas shelter, and, seated on our bedding rolls, settled down to enjoy ourselves with the virtuous feeling of having been willing to be energetic but denied the opportunity.

It was very, very lovely. The lake was silent, drifting toward me and meeting the grey margin with a mysterious soundlessness. A solitary water-bird flew with sharp, curving wings over the water, and the sound of the creek running into the lake beyond the stony point, where the ripples spread in shining arcs, was mixed with its own echoes. The clouds gathered and parted, ever pouring up from beyond the southern mountains. Is there no end, dark angels? On the soft wet green of the hills sudden shifting gleams were cast from a sky broken by wan, troubled lights.

Black slate glistened on the mountain-sides, and the long screes plunged into the water in purple avalanches. It was Scotland or Dartmoor.

The tamaracks' dark foliage glowed unwontedly bright against the sodden black of their bark, and the little tufts of alpine phlox growing matted among the upturned slates waited with half-opened blossoms in patient shyness. Lichens and mosses, yellow, grey-green, and Indian red, touched the cold stones with disks of strongest color. The red twigs and sallow leafage of the willows twinkled with diamond lights when a beam of pallid sunlight struck athwart them. Where a two-minute shower fell between me and the hazy sun, a silent dance came on the surface of the lake, like the short second movement of the Moonlight Sonata, and beginning and ending as suddenly. On the wet wind came the distant sound of the sheep-bell and the far-off, dreamy cry of the sheep. I could see them streaming endlessly over a pine-clad shoulder of the mountain half-a-mile away, making to the next valley.

The weather clearing somewhat by the middle of the morning, we packed again and started for the pass, leaving the lake and its lonely grave desolate under brooding clouds. Farewell, unknown friend; sometimes I shall revisit in memory your quiet place of rest. Farewell! farewell!

We now started westward through tamarack forest, following generally the course of the stream. Rising rapidly, and skirting two or three lakelets, we

entered a wild and rocky gorge. The trail, poorly
blazed and showing no sign of having been travelled
that year, taxed all Bodie's trail-craft to follow it. As
we reached the first divide a glorious sight burst upon
us. Right ahead rose Mount Lyell and his fellows, —
McClure, Ritter, Kellogg, Banner, and half-a-score
beside of the giants of the range, more clustered and
heaped together than at any other point of the whole
chain. Over the majestic prospect was poured a tumult of light and shade that raised it from a landscape to a pageant.

The storm-clouds that wrapped the peaks revealed
every moment, as they changed and parted, black
crags and high-flung summits, or snow-fields massed
in unbroken sheets of gleaming white. The unusual
quietude of the river, which here, moving through
level meadows, reflected the mountains in its dark
waters, enhanced the dreamlike feeling of the place ;
and the silence, in contrast with the impetuous movement of the clouds, seemed a fine summary of the
eloquence and power of Nature.

At this spot it began again to rain upon us, and
the immediate prospects were for more. So we went
early into camp beside the creek, rather than cross
the pass in the face of a possible heavy storm, which
at nearly eleven thousand feet might prove a severe
experience. We had heard at Mono that a party of
people who had tried to cross a few days before had
been forced to abandon the attempt through stress
of weather and the difficulty of crossing the treach-

erous snow. Thunder boomed among the peaks and the rain thrashed down in staggering drifts, setting a thousand rills coursing among the channels of the granite.

Bodie somehow accomplished a loaf of bread, under circumstances which he truly said "gave him no show"; and we sat snugly dining, smoking, and congratulating ourselves under our improvised shelter. The afternoon passed in alternate rain and clear, but without any glimpse of the sun. It was dismally cold. The mountains changed and changed, from glorious gloom to gloomy glory; the river swirled and roared along; and the clouds trooped sullenly past, like that line of kings that frighted Macbeth.

By evening the weather cleared, and I wandered in the gathering dusk about the neighborhood of our camp, smelling the vigorous piny essences poured out from rain-soaked bark and foliage, and feeling the thrill of intense life in the hardy dwarf pines and tamaracks. I am constantly surprised, in spite of experience, at the flowery and luxuriant vegetation which one meets in these high places. Exploring up a little creek that entered the main stream beside the camp, I found myself among cyclamens, columbines, daisies of wonderful size, and many other delicate and beautiful flowers, growing with long waving grasses in gardens set among a tumble of granite boulders. Here, at the end of July, a Californian would think himself in April or May. It is like the quick summer of Arctic latitudes, sudden, vivid, and brief. It is hardly a month since winter ended, and six weeks hence the snows may again be falling. A few miles away, and but two or three thousand feet above, are glaciers, and snow-drifts fifty feet deep. (Bodie says a hundred, and perhaps one may as well guess generously; it is stimulating and yet harmless, which is unusual.) Even the sturdy dwarf pines hereabout are close upon their last straggling verge. Yet in this little sheltered cañon early summer is in full career, rank and riotous.

It is this peculiarity which gives to the High Sierra its most unique charm. It may be that in the Himalayas, or the Mountains of the Moon, or some other such place of legendary import to most of us, the same condition might be met with; but it is a constant delight and surprise to encounter this rare conjunction in our own friendly mountains.

The next morning dawned heavy and rainy-looking, with the fiery sunrise that an old rhyme, by which I used to divine the weather prospects of school holidays, declares to be the shepherd's warning. However, by the time breakfast was over it looked more promising, so we hurriedly packed and started for the pass. The trail here is the mere ghost of a track, the shadow of a shade, and Bodie, who had covered the ground before, took the lead. A perpendicular ridge pinnacled with seven sharp spires shot up superbly on our right, and I passed it with regret; but in view of the weather, time was just now an important consideration, and the snowy monsters ahead, growing every moment nearer, consoled me, and we pushed rapidly forward.

The way led alternately through masses of piled and shattered granite and brilliant little meadow-patches, sparkling with rain and starred with hosts of flowers. At last the sun shone weakly, but we rejoiced with trembling, for July here is as changeful as April on the plains. Over broad areas of glacial rock, strewn with boulders and laced with gushes of snow-water, we picked our way with the precarious aid of so-called monuments, hardly discernible in the general wreck and shatter.

We were here at timber-line, where only the dwarf pines, tough as whip-cord, can endure the winter's rage, and even they are beaten and felted down into mere rugs that spread horizontally a foot or so above the ground. The flowers that grow in these highest meadows are astonishingly rich in color. Lupines of the bluest, and daisies of a deep lavender approaching purple, mingle with glistening buttercups, and castilleias of scarlet at its highest power. I have hitherto refrained from mentioning the last-named flower (generally called Indian paint-brush), having conceived something of an aversion to it at the outset. Its construction is peculiar and unflowerlike, and it is somehow uncongenial to me; while the astonishing profusion of the plant, which accompanied us everywhere in our wanderings, high and low, irritated me with a sense of almost persecution. But I am compelled at last to do justice to its color-power, in which regard it outdoes even the geranium and nasturtium. It was here of a red so fierce and refulgent as to really require a new word to express it. The red poppy is a pale invalid beside this roistering gypsy. It pours out color, throbs with it, seems to shed it off like something palpable; and I can imagine that an essence or sublimation, too fine for our senses to perceive, goes up from each of these myriad blossoms which could be kindled into flame,—the essential, elemental Red.

Passing through a turfy valley, where the stream widened into still pools, clear as air, we were in full view of the great cluster of mountains known as the Lyell group. A solemn and magnificent company they were, and I felt much as if I looked upon a gathering of the kings and emperors of olden history,— Charlemagne, the Great Rameses, the greatest of the Cæsars, Alexander, Sardanapalus. Farthest to the south one splendid peak ran up in a steep, swinging curve that, as the eye followed it, seemed to overbalance, like a toppling volcano. It was Black Ritter.

Close behind us stood the seven-pinnacled ridge, and to the right, knife-like edges of granite gleamed hard and clear against a darker sky. On every side there was nothing but rock, water, snow, and sky, nothing but the wild, savage, stern.

A long expanse of soaking bog kept my eyes unwillingly on the ground. It required the greatest care to find safe footing for the animals, especially the pack-mules and burros. Nothing is so demoralizing to a pack-animal as a stretch of boggy country, with its risk of miring down, and a détour, however wide, is apt to be the best of policy. With extraordinary squelchings and snortings we picked our way through half-a-mile of the greenest of turf which turned to blackest ooze at every step. The lovely cassiope, somewhat rare in general, grew here in abundance, but was not yet in flower; nor was the bryanthus, which two thousand feet lower down had been withered for a month past.

Mile after mile the trail climbed over barren granite, sometimes hard and polished, sometimes disintegrated on the surface to a coarse sand as large in grain as peas. At last we stood at the top of the Donohue Pass, at eleven thousand feet altitude. Below and near us lay several small lakes, half frozen over, into which snow-fields plunged steeply; and crossing a wide stretch of softened snow we rounded Mount Lyell in full view of and close under the glacier which lies as in a great shell all along the mountain's northern face. From the foot of the glacier the water ran in a fair-sized creek, which, gathering force from its rapid fall and the accretion of innumerable rills, raced away northward to become the Lyell Fork of the Tuolumne.

Bursts of dazzling sunshine alternated with gloomy shadow as masses of cloud rolled up from the south. The last tree-life was left behind. The arms of the glacier ran up into the cañons and draws of the mountain like surf of the ocean surging into a rocky bay.

I felt a strong temptation to make at least a partial exploration of the glacier; but the threatening weather put it out of the question at the moment, and the complete absence of forage for the animals forbade our making camp in this wild spot. Reluctantly I turned my back upon Lyell for this time, with the hope of revisiting the noble mountain another year and making the ascent.

The trail from the Donohue Pass to the Lyell Cañon offers the hardest piece of work that I know of in this part of the mountains. In two miles it drops two thousand feet, and, being but little used, each traveller finds its passage much the same thing as breaking a trail through new country. The famous Bloody Cañon Pass, by which we had gone over to Mono Lake, is tame in comparison. We tumbled and stumbled our way down somewhat recklessly; but by good fortune and good packing we made the descent without disaster, and by noon came, breathless and perspiring violently, to the head of the remarkably long and level cañon which debouches ten miles to the northwest at the Tuolumne Meadows.

The eastern wall of this cañon is formed by the long, barren ridge of Kuna Crest, under whose other slope we had camped a week before. It here rose in an unbroken rampart from the nine-thousand-foot level of the cañon to twelve thousand feet at the ridge. The west wall is somewhat less high but more broken and timbered. The river was already a handsome stream, winding and looping about in a

manner suggestive of a deputy sheriff earning mile-
age; and the fords were sufficiently wide, deep, and
rapid.

Flowers of a score of kinds blossomed about us,
the castilleias in particular being of giant size and
astonishing brilliance of color. I notice that having
at last brought myself to speak of this plant, I am
beginning to find excellences in it hitherto unknown.
Probably it is often so; half of our antipathies might
be likings if we would, and half of the rest mild ap-
preciations. Still, I do not really care for this flower,
any more than I should care for Carmen; but I cannot refuse my admiration.

Steady travelling for several miles brought us to
the mouth of Ireland Creek, where we proposed to
take a new trail to the southwest over the Tuolumne
Pass; and we went into camp by mid-afternoon. The
stream looked ideally fishable, and Field and I revelled in the experience, new to both of us, and of
which I had felt doubts of the possibility, of catching
trout by twos and threes, for there were candidates
for as many flies as we chose to put on our leaders.
Certainly the Lyell Fork of the Tuolumne is the heaven of the not-too-skilful fisherman; — as such, that
is to say; for I must add that our trout-supper was
embittered by a constant skirmish with the mosquitoes. They rushed upon us in such numbers and
with such diabolical audacity that I found it necessary to force a passage for each morsel as it approached my mouth by gyratory manœuvres with

my left hand, and even then one or two grey imps, I suspect, penetrated my guard and by an unwilling act of justice were miserably incorporated with the food they defiled.

Next morning we were once more climbing to the high levels. Our new trail led up through a forest of unusual density and stateliness, every opening in which was sprinkled with flowers, from the columbine of high degree to the lowly but best-beloved daisy. Giant lupines tumbled in big blue masses across the trail, and bryanthus grew in rounded bosses by every creek-side.

I was in the lead, and rode far ahead. The voices of my companions were wafted to me from time to time by the lazy forest breeze, usually in reprobation of the pack-animals, but otherwise in snatches of song attuned to a pensive minor key. It was one of those blessed mornings of long silences, when the trail is easy to keep and one's thoughts turn inward and revolve upon themselves. One whistles, *sotto voce*, smokes with a deeper peace, notes a million things, infinitely small and precious, and receives freely those little clairvoyances of the past which shake the heart for the moment but leave it calmer. Precipitation takes place rapidly, and the mind is clear and cool like the wind. One praises God, but only occasionally becomes aware of it. The golden silence sings in one's ears, and the inward symphony goes quietly on. P., old fellow, K., old man, I wish you were here; not to talk to, just to commune with at quarter-mile distances. Is that the wind, or the river, booming softly ten thousand miles away? or can it be, in truth, cosmic sound, the very sound of the earth? It might be, it might be.

Two hours had brought us again to timber-line, at between ten and eleven thousand feet. The view opened upon a boulder-strewn plateau rising in terraces to the summit of the divide, where we stood completely encircled by the mountains, with Lyell and McClure to the southeast. The glare of the sun on snow and rock was blinding, and we hastened on to where the low and matted dwarf pines offered some relief to the eyes. I cannot conceive of a more luxurious bed than one of these rugs of *Pinus albicaulis* would make. Beaten and flattened by snow and clipped by the wind as if by a mower, they are so thick and close and springy that they hardly yield to one's weight. The rich, resinous smell of them rises like a spirit. It would be worth while coming to camp at this altitude just to sleep on such a bed.

Crossing the divide, a lakelet lay under a snowy ridge, which we skirted, and continued over a wide stretch of granite pavement. The scene here is wild enough to satisfy the most exacting taste for the savage and desolate ; bare rock, terrified trees, air, and sky, these make up the whole prospect. Another and larger lake lay near the top of the pass, the crisp purple ripples travelling steadily across its surface with that unceasing but soundless motion which is one of the most attractive actions of Nature.

As I rode across a small meadow my attention was caught by what was to me a phenomenon in natural history, — a green butterfly, grass green from head to foot. I know nothing of entomology, to speak of: such insects may be common enough; but I am sure that I never encountered one before. I reined up and pondered. Was I missing the chance of my unentomological life? Was this some hitherto unknown species that should be captured at all hazards, and that would convey me safely down to posterity with a Latin termination? But while I debated he flew down the mountain and was gone, "and," as Bunyan says, "I saw him no more."

The trail here debouched into a broader meadow, scattered with slabs and boulders of granite, and with a circular lake lying close under a precipitous mountain with snow-drifts creeping in its gorges down to the water's edge. To the north rose high peaks, the crests and ridges finely broken and piled in fantastic masses. Westward the view was bounded by timbered ridges fading into the distance, where the Yosemite gorge lay hidden. It was a delightful spot, wild, spacious and lonely; a blue, rippling lake with the purest of snow-water rushing into it in cataracts, snowy themselves, over gleaming rocks; cliffs scored black with shadow, white with snow, a fitting home for eagles; a wind as free and bold as the eagle, too; a meadow flowery and heathery to delight; and to crown all, sky scenery that day which was truly majestic in color, line, and motion.

My mind was exercising itself with conjectures as to the reason for the name of this peak and the lake lying under it, — Vogelsang. I was on the point of giving up the riddle when the strident voice of the Clarke crow, almost the only bird that inhabits these highest solitudes, gave me a clue, and I perceived that a spirit of irony had suggested the name.

Crossing the small creek that carries the water from this lake, we turned southward over a divide among a vast wreckage of débris. Far to the west could be seen the top of a huge split mountain; there was no mistaking that strangest of mountain shapes, the Half-Dome. Another lake lay close on the left, and a deep snow-bank ahead. Skirting these we crossed the head of the Tuolumne Pass at 10,700 feet, among a wild conglomeration of toppling, tottering, staggering rock-shapes piled against a sky across which great clouds were momentarily hurtling.

We were on the main line of watershed of this part of the Sierra. To the north a hundred streams ran toward the deep gorge of the Tuolumne, while southward all drained to the Merced and the San Joaquin. The outlook here again was superb. To the west that fine group of mountains of which Clark is the centre lay under a brooding sky. In the near south and east rose the great barrier which sweeps up to Mounts Florence, Lyell, and McClure. On a shelf of this wall of mountains lay a strangely beautiful lake. Broad snow-fields swept gloriously into it on the south: a fringe of torn pines drew around its northern and western margins. It was my ideal lake, and I then and there marked it for my own, setting it deep in my affections as a lake of lakes, by which some future time I hope to camp for days and nights of pure Sierra delight.

The trail now descended steeply to the McClure Fork of the Merced, which flows through a long flowery cañon. We had not seen much sign of game of late, but here again tracks of deer were plentiful. The cañon narrowed to a gorge, and scattered tamaracks gave place to a fine forest of hemlock. Among these noble and beautiful but mournful trees a heavy stillness reigned. The great plushy fans of foliage, almost black in the gloomy air, but fringed with grey silver, were indescribably rich and sumptuous. The walls closed in, dark and high. Thunder rolled along the northern heights, where twisted junipers clung upon the ledges, and a few drops of rain fell.

The river rushed whitely far below, where the forest swept steep and black to the bottom of the gorge. It grew darker, and still darker. The trees stood listening and longing for the rain, and the meek flowers looked timidly up. Black thunder crackled and roared, and in its pauses the raving of the river as it rushed wildly over boulders and slides of granite rose loud and fearful, like a cry. Still the rain withheld : is it sparing us ? I wish that it would not ; I love not to be made a weakling by my mother : and, Spartanlike, I grudge that I should not be scourged. But so it proved: the thunder continued, the great clouds met and parted, but no rain came.

Again the cañon widened, and a change came over the spirit of the scenery. We were once more in the Yosemite region, surrounded by domes and ice-planed mountains. To the north was a rounded cone of bare granite with a white cascade clasping its base. Every ledge and buttress of every mountain was rounded and polished like a woman's shoulder. Half-Dome was again in view, and again I wondered at him, as I never tire of doing. Far ahead lay a steely sheet of water into which granite slopes plunged steeply: it was Lake Merced.

The miles strung out. Forest alternated with rock and rock with forest. We entered a pretty grove of aspens, mixed with saddle-high lupines and bracken. Then we came to the lake, a lovely piece of water lying at seven thousand feet, fringed with forest, but with slopes and domes rising two thousand feet higher, except where, to the west, the Merced River flowed out in a wide cascade of whirling foam.

We made camp on the edge of the lake, among aspens, with a fir or two for love; and had hardly finished unpacking when the delayed storm broke. Thunder boomed and lightning flashed continuously, and the quiet little lake was struck into sudden panic. Up went our shelter, and we sat on our bedding and watched the pots boiling over the hissing fire just outside, while the rain poured merrily off the canvas and the trees rocked and strained in the gale. It was twelve hours since breakfast, and our meal was extended to the proportions of a banquet. Not even dessert was beyond our resources when Bodie produced from some unsuspected cache of his own a handful of dried apricots.

The storm passed away and the evening was a pastoral of quiet beauty. The last shreds of cloud drifted in films and smirches of gold and rose in a steel-blue sky. A family of wild ducks paddled about in the middle of the lake, quacking happily. Birds chirped and bustled in the wet brush. The earth had been visited and watered, and it was as when one saunters in his garden at home while the scents and the colors sink deeply in, and do their peaceful work.

The next day's travel was to be the last of our trip, for it would bring us to the Little Yosemite. Breaking camp early, we followed the trail along the northern side of the lake, passing over a sheet of polished rock which slopes to the river and rises beyond, forming a narrow trough through which the stream rushes at terrific speed in vertical wheels of white water. These great slopes that slant away steeply from many of the domes are very impressive in their fine simplicity of line. For hundreds of feet they sweep down smooth and unbroken, with something the same suggestion of powerful ease and steadiness that one receives in watching the sailing flight of eagles.

Turning northward the trail followed the west

bank of a pretty, brown stream, and climbed over a high ridge, finely timbered, at nine thousand feet. Little scraps of meadow hung here and there on the steep side of the mountain, and here I first found the Alpine lily (*Lilium parvum*), swinging its campanile of tawny-ruby bells. The mountain pine attains in this region its noblest growth, its sturdy red trunk and powerful arms showing finely against the slender symmetry of the firs.

I was partly glad and partly sorry to find again the ceanothus, manzanita, and chinquapin growing thick and high as we neared the valley, betokening a milder soil and climate than that of the inner Sierra which we were leaving.

At a pretty meadow which keeps alive the memory of some departed worthy of the name of Hopkins, Field and I left Bodie to take the animals on to camp in the Little Yosemite, while we diverged to ascend Clouds' Rest, two or three miles to the west. An easy climb through a forest of fir and mountain pine took us to the summit at 9925 feet, and from this admirable standpoint we were able to review as on a relief map the wanderings of the past month. To the northwest lay the Hetch-Hetchy country and Lake Eleanor, where the long folds of timbered mountain faded into dreamy distance. Straight northward the Matterhorns rose like the peaks of the Enchanted Mountains of our childhood. Farther to the east was Mount Dana, and beyond, the far Mono country with its grey volcanoes and beautiful, deadly lake: I seemed to feel again the shimmering heat, and see the pallid desert sky.

Yonder, where the mountains were clustered most thickly, stood Lyell and his great brethren, the kings of the mid-Sierra. To the west lay the gorge of Yosemite. Sunk in the summer mist, her majestic walls and precipices, washed in pale amethyst, were airy and unsubstantial as a fairy vision: but close beside us stood like a solemn hooded figure the Mysterious Mountain, great Half-Dome. From this point the mountain is in profile, and the splendid line of the southern side rises unbroken in its grandeur and severity ; while from its nearness, the huge bulk of that mass of solid granite overpowers one with an almost nightmare feeling of vastness and oppression.

The top of Clouds' Rest itself is built up of weather-worn slabs of granite laid one on another in steps and ledges. The mountain is heavily forested on its whole southern side, the conifers rising in well-marked belts, ending with a few dwarf pines at the summit. The northern slope is barren, sweeping down in one long, unbroken wall to the Tenaya Cañon, with Tenaya Lake in plain view at its head. There is something of an anomaly in the distribution of timber on this mountain, for it is an almost invariable rule that the northern slopes are forested while the southern, more exposed to the sun, are comparatively barren.

A swift downward march of two hours brought us

to the Little Yosemite, where we found Bodie already
camped, and mighty preparations going forward for
a meal worthy of the occasion. The sinkienon, standing like an obese martyr among the glowing coals,
was almost ready to deliver a fragrant loaf; beans,
the perfect gold of whose hue equalled but could
never surpass in charm the melting smoothness of
their flavor, smoked on a carefully contrived hob, and
even a scratch "mulligan" was in process of con-
coction.

Sitting that evening by our last camp-fire, I passed
in pleasant review the experiences of our expedition: mornings of heavenly freshness on the trail;
cañons on cañons, peaks beyond peaks, ridges beyond ridges; sweet scents of balsam and pine;
stormy sunrises and wistful sunsets; heat and dust;
luxurious turnings-in by firelight, and reluctant turn-
ings-out by moonlight; lakes round, lakes long, lakes
little and big of every shape and no shape, lying
blue in hidden hollows or trembling to sudden silver
as the wind went by; breathless climbs and clattering descents; cheerful pipings of early birds and
sleepy twitterings of late ones; conundrums of trails
mysteriously vanished from the face of the earth;
silent hours of camp-fire meditation; loquacious hours
over errors of the trail; pleasantries of Field and
Bodie; unaccountable aberrations of pack-animals;
exultations at new discoveries; daisies; mosquitoes;
quiet lyings awake by night; solemn glories of sunset

peaks ; communions with friendly trees ; chatterings of brooks, singings of creeks, and roarings of rivers ; dim alleys of forest and aching white rock-highways ; ghostly snow-glimmer by starlight ; peaks in solemn rank against the sky . . .

The next morning we went down to the valley.

UPDATED PLANT LIST
(listed alphabetically)
by Carl Sharsmith

Chase's Usage	Common Name	Today's Botanical Term
TREES		
Cedar	Incense Cedar	*LIBOCEDRUS decurrens*
Coulter Pine	Coulter Pine	*PINUS coulteri*
Digger Pine; Bull Pine	Digger Pine	*PINUS sabiniana*
Douglas Spruce	Douglas Fir	*PSEUDOTSUGA menziesii*
Dwarf Pine	Whitebark Pine	*PINUS albicaulis*
Jeffrey Pine	Jeffrey Pine	*PINUS jeffreyi*
Juniper	Sierra Juniper; Western Juniper	*JUNIPERUS occidentalis*
Knobcone Pine	Knobcone Pine	*PINUS attenuata*
Limber Pine	Limber Pine	*PINUS flexilis*
Mountain Hemlock	Mountain Hemlock	*TSUGA mertensiana*
Mountain Pine	Western White Pine	*PINUS monticola*
Nutmeg Tree	California Nutmeg	*TORREYA californica*
Piñon or Nut Pine	Singleleaf Piñon Pine	*PINUS monophylla*
Red Fir	California Red Fir	*ABIES magnifica*
Sequoia	Giant Sequoia; Sierra Redwood	*SEQUOIADENDRON giganteum*
Tamarack	Lodgepole Pine	*PINUS murrayana*
White Silver Fir	White Fir	*ABIES concolor*
Yellow Pine	Ponderosa Pine	*PINUS ponderosa*
FLOWERS		
Cassiope	Mountain Heather	*Cassiope mertensiana*
Chamaebatia	Fern Bush	*Chamaebatia millefolium*
Cyclamen	Shooting Star	*DODECATHEON sp.*
Heather	Red Heather	*PHYLLODOCE breweri*
Lavender Daisy	Wandering Daisy	*ERIGERON peregrinus*
Manzanita	Manzanita	*ARCTOSTAPHYLOS sp.*
Phlox	Spreading Phlox	*PHLOX diffusa*
Polemonium	Jacob's ladder	*Polemonium sp.*
Willow Herb	Fireweed	*EPILOBIUM augustifolium*

INDEX